Kindergarten Narratives on Froebelian Education

Also available from Bloomsbury:

Early Childhood Studies, Ewan Ingleby
Early Childhood Theories and Contemporary Issues, Mine Conkbayir
and Christine Pascal

Forthcoming:

Friedrich Froebel: A Critical Introduction to Key Themes and Debates, Tina Bruce

Kindergarten Narratives on Froebelian Education

Transnational Investigations

Edited by Helen May,
Kristen Nawrotzki and Larry Prochner

BLOOMSBURY ACADEMIC
LONDON • NEW YORK • OXFORD • NEW DELHI • SYDNEY

BLOOMSBURY ACADEMIC
Bloomsbury Publishing Plc
50 Bedford Square, London, WC1B 3DP, UK

BLOOMSBURY, BLOOMSBURY ACADEMIC and the Diana logo are trademarks of
Bloomsbury Publishing Plc

First published in Great Britain 2017
Paperback edition first published 2018

Bloomsbury Publishing Plc does not have any control over, or responsibility for, any
third-party websites referred to or in this book. All internet addresses given in this
book were correct at the time of going to press. The author and publisher regret any
inconvenience caused if addresses have changed or sites have ceased to exist, but can
accept no responsibility for any such changes.

A catalogue record for this book is available from the British Library.

ISBN: HB: 978-1-4742-5445-8
PB: 978-1-3500-6993-0
ePDF: 978-1-4742-5442-7
ePub: 978-1-4742-5443-4

Library of Congress Cataloging-in-Publication Data
Names: May, Helen, 1947- editor. | Nawrotzki, Kristen, editor. | Prochner,
Laurence Wayne, 1956- editor.
Title: Kindergarten narratives on Froebelian education: transnational investigations
/ edited by Helen May, Kristen Nawrotzki, and Larry Prochner.
Description: London; New York: Bloomsbury Academic, 2016. | Includes
bibliographical references and index.
Identifiers: LCCN 2016016136| ISBN 9781474254 458 (hardback) |
ISBN 9781474254434 (epub) | ISBN 9781474254427 (epdf)
Subjects: LCSH: Frèobel, Friedrich, 1782-1852–Infl uence. |
Kindergarten–Cross-cultural studies. | Early childhood
education–Philosophy. | BISAC: EDUCATION / General. | EDUCATION /
Research. | EDUCATION / Preschool & Kindergarten. | EDUCATION / History.
Classification: LCC LB1162 .K55 2016 | DDC 372.21–dc23 LC record available at
https://lccn.loc.gov/2016016136

Typeset by Deanta Global Publishing Services, Chennai, India

To find out more about our authors and books visit
www.bloomsbury.com and sign up for our newsletters.

Contents

List of Illustrations

Notes on Contributors

Editors

Helen May is Professor of Education and the former dean of the University of Otago College of Education (2006–11), New Zealand. She has been involved in advocacy and advisory roles covering a range of policy initiatives. She is the author of a number of books on the history, politics and pedagogy of early years education.

Kristen Nawrotzki is Lecturer at the University of Education in Heidelberg, Germany. She has authored numerous publications on the history of early childhood education and related social policy in England and the United States. She recently co-edited with Harry Willekens and Kirsten Scheiwe a volume of essays on early childhood education policy in Europe and North America, published by Palgrave Macmillan in 2015.

Larry Prochner is Professor of Early Childhood Education and the former chair of the Department of Elementary Education at the University of Alberta (2011–15). His studies are concerned with issues in education and childhood studies from a comparative, international and sociohistorical perspective.

Contributors

Fusa Abe is Associate Professor at Shoei (Glory) Junior College and the principal of Shoei (Glory) Kindergarten, in Kobe, Japan. The Glory Kindergarten is historically well known as a Froebelian kindergarten in Japan. She has had extensive experience in teaching at several kindergartens and has trained many kindergarten teachers at Glory College.

Nelleke Bakker is Associate Professor of History of Education at the University of Groningen, the Netherlands. She is the president of the Belgian-Dutch Society for the History of Education (since 2004). Her current research deals with the history of child-rearing ideals and health and (ab)normality in education.

Kerry Bethell is a retired senior lecturer in Early Childhood Education at Massey University, New Zealand. Her research takes as its key focus the origins and early work of the kindergarten movement in colonial New Zealand. Her recent projects have taken a transnational approach to explore the two-way global travels of teachers and ideas.

Rosemary Deem, OBE is the vice principal (education) and the dean of the Doctoral School at the Royal Holloway University of London. Her research interests focus on policy, leadership, governance and management of higher education and her work draws on organizational theory, policy analysis, feminist research, new managerialist theory and comparative social science.

Anna Kirova is Professor of Early Childhood Education in the Department of Elementary Education, University of Alberta, Canada. Her research focuses mainly on the need for understanding culturally and linguistically diverse families with young children's experiences in school, and the possibility such an understanding offers for culturally responsive pedagogy.

Yukiyo Nishida is Lecturer of Early Childhood Education at the University of New England in Australia. Her field of research is early childhood and primary education, with particular focus on policy, practice and pedagogy. She has also been extensively involved in comparative research projects and has most recently authored the article: 'A Chrysanthemum in the Garden: A Christian Kindergarten in the Empire of Japan.'

Amy Palmer is Senior Lecturer in Early Childhood Studies at the University of Roehampton in London. She previously worked as a teacher in a number of infant and primary schools. She has an MA in children's literature and has recently completed a PhD in the development of early years education policy. Her current research interests draw on both these fields.

Jane Read is Senior Lecturer in the School of Education, University of Roehampton, London. Her research and teaching focus on the dissemination of Froebelian pedagogy across time and space and in diverse educational settings. Her most recent work has linked sociohistorical perspectives to current policy and practice to illuminate historical (dis)continuities.

Johannes Westberg is Associate Professor (docent) in History and senior lecturer at the Department of Education, Uppsala University, Sweden. Since completing his PhD in 2008 on the educational changes in Swedish early childhood programmes 1835–1945, he has published several articles on the history of Swedish infant schools, crèches and kindergartens.

Figure 0.1 Kevin Brehony at the Fourth International Froebel Society Conference, Jena, Germany 10 April 2010 outside the Froebel Museum in Bad Blankenburg. Photo by Ralph Nawrotzki.

Kevin J. Brehony 1948–2013[1]

Rosemary Deem

My husband, Kevin Brehony, Froebel Professor of Early Childhood Studies at Roehampton University, died of cancer at age sixty-five. Kevin was a lifelong enthusiast for child-centred education and a historian of ideas about early childhood, including those of Friedrich Froebel. He published many academic papers, worked tirelessly for several learned societies and discussed Froebel's work in many countries, inspiring students, practitioners and academics alike.

Kevin was born in Stafford, of an Irish father, Eddie-Joseph Brehony, a factory worker, and an English mother, Ruth Slater. The family began farming in Shropshire in 1951, moving to mid-Wales in 1959. After Ludlow grammar and Lampeter bilateral school, Kevin went to Birmingham University to study geography, but left without a degree. He trained as a teacher at City of Birmingham College of Education and then taught in various West Midlands primary schools.

In 1976, he was awarded a first-class honours degree from the Open University and in 1979 began to study for a PhD on The Froebel Movement and State Schooling, 1880–1914: A Study in Educational Ideology, at the Open University, supervised by Roger Dale. Kevin and I met at the Open University in 1980, at a reading group run by his supervisor. From 1982 until 1984, Kevin was a lecturer at Edge Hill College, Ormskirk. We married in March 1985 and both stood as Labour candidates for Buckinghamshire county council, though Kevin was not elected. He was a supply teacher from 1985 until 1987, then joined Bulmershe College of Education, which merged with Reading University in 1989.

Kevin loved all kinds of music, but particularly Irish traditional music, especially when played in bars. He was an optimistic Wolverhampton Wanderers supporter, even when they played badly. He took up cycle touring in the 1980s with Milton Keynes Cycling Club, embarked on cycle-camping holidays in Europe and also went hill walking. Kevin was a talented cook, though his passion for chillies did not please everyone: friends loved his dinners, filled with music, wine and conversation.

Kevin remained at Reading until 2003, when he was appointed to the Froebel Chair of Early Childhood Studies at Roehampton. There he led the early-years research group, taught master's students, supervised PhDs and became the institution's ambassador for national and international activities focused on Froebel, including serving as president of the International Froebel Society (IFS). Despite his illness, Kevin continued to work until the summer of 2013.

Preface[2]

Helen May and Kristen Nawrotzki

The last word of my theory I shall carry to my grave, the time is not yet ripe for it. If three hundred years after my system of education is completely and according to its real principle carried through Europe, I shall rejoice in heaven. If only the seed be cast abroad, its springing up will not fail nor the fruit be wanting.
— Friedrich Froebel (1782–1852)[3]

Froebel's words were chosen by the Froebelian scholar Kevin Brehony (1948–2013) to preface the guiding principles of the IFS. Kevin was a founder and later president of the society, established in 2002 to provide a twenty-first-century forum for promoting the principles of theory and practice associated with the child-centred philosophy of Friedrich Froebel, the founder of the kindergarten. The IFS has become an international meeting place linking researchers, professionals and practitioners, mainly from countries with a kindergarten heritage, to engage in debate on early childhood education, made all the more timely by expanding provision and political interest and investment in many parts of the world. Among those attracted to the IFS were a group of international of scholars who, like Kevin, were engaged in research on Froebelian and kindergarten education history. As a tribute to Kevin, his history colleagues present this collection of investigative essays concerning the 'casting of the kindergarten seed abroad' across almost two centuries, both within and beyond the cultures and continent of Europe to what in Froebel's life time were the New World settings of the Americas, the Far East and the Antipodes.

The Sixth IFS Conference, held in 2014 at Canterbury Christ Church University in England, was the first conference held without Kevin's engaging presence. Kevin had hosted the first IFS conference in London in 2004 at Froebel College, Roehampton University, where he was the Froebel Professor of Early Childhood Studies. Thereafter, the IFS and its biennial conference, variously held in Britain, Ireland, Germany and the United States, became a meeting place for scholars and practitioners of child-centred education. In 2010 Kevin became president of the IFS, a forum he tirelessly used to promote research, debate, advocacy and practice inspired by the philosophy, ideas and legacies of Friedrich Froebel. At the 2014 Canterbury conference, amidst a range of presentations and workshops concerning the plays, politics and pedagogies of early years education, there was also the presence of 'Kevin's' history scholars variously engaged in investigations concerning the people, places and practices of Froebelian education locally, nationally and internationally. Kevin was also an active participant in the International Standing Conference for the History of Education (ISCHE), as were many of the IFS history scholars. Due in part to his influence, the history of early years education became significantly more visible at recent ISCHE annual conferences. In 2014, at the IFS conference in June and the ISCHE conference held in London a few weeks later in July, participants paid tribute to Kevin's endeavours across the spectrum of education, with an IFS memorial lecture and a memorial symposium at ISCHE. Kevin's friends, colleagues and students from both conferences have contributed to this memorial tribute: an acknowledgement of Kevin's scholarship and recognition of his efforts and energy in linking together this collaborative bevy of historical scholarship.

In the introduction to the papers from the first IFS conference, published in 2006 as a special issue of journal *History of Education*, Kevin lamented the 'relative neglect' of the history of early childhood education at the same time there was a heightened global social and political interest in educating the young child.[4] While inroads have been made in the intervening decade to address this paucity of research, we contend – as would Kevin – that the neglect of history persists in much of the contemporary debates about early educational policy, provision and practice. The authors of this volume respond to his contention that historical perspectives can offer a valuable framework for interrogating current debates and suggest that historical narratives might usefully inform policies and practices in twenty-first-century early childhood settings and contexts. For this reason, we have included in this volume Kevin's unpublished professorial Inaugural Address, 'Working at Play or Playing at Work? A Froebelian Paradox Re-examined' delivered at Froebel College, Roehampton on 16 February 2004.

Kevin's own journey as a history of education scholar began with his PhD thesis from the Open University, 'The Froebel Movement and State Schooling, 1880–1914: A Study in Educational Ideology' (1987). Kevin broke the mould of early childhood history to that point by analysing Froebelian education in England not merely as a well-meaning effort towards educational reform and human progress, but also as an ideological bundle in which the material interests of those involved in the Froebel movement played a significant role. Likewise, where previous accounts of English Froebelianism had cheered the recognition of Froebel methods by influential educationalists and policy makers as an unalloyed victory, Kevin's thesis – and his work ever since – highlighted the ways in which the regulation of schooling, too, was driven not (only) by lofty philosophical or political goals but also by the interests and purposes of individuals and groups within the state apparatus itself.

Kevin had contracts for a book version of his PhD thesis over the years, but he never managed to get it published for, as he put it, 'I always seemed to have articles to write instead.' And write he did.[5] Kevin eventually published over sixty articles in leading education, history and sociology journals, as well as a number of influential essays that appeared in edited volumes.[6] Although in conversations about his work he made much of serendipity and spoke of having miraculously found pieces of intellectual puzzles in the most surprising of places, his success in finding answers – and in connecting the dots between different puzzles – was the result of extremely deft and dogged archival and digital research. Kevin gleefully discovered a image of the first British kindergarten established in 1851 at Tavistock Place London by Berthe Ronge in the *The Lady's Newspaper* (13 October 1855). This is the earliest known image of a kindergarten in action and Kevin sent it to IFS colleagues and friends for his 2012

Christmas card. We have cited this on the facing page of Kevin's Chapter 2. Like many historians, Kevin enjoyed hunting for the arcane and the recondite. But like too few historians of education – especially in early childhood education – he applied complex social theories in a nuanced way to explain what those findings might actually mean for our understanding of lives, institutions and societies past and present.

Much of Kevin's later work remained true to his initial interest, as expressed on page 1 of his thesis, in examining 'the relation between all forms of progressive or child-centred education and state schooling from the 1880's up until the outbreak of the Second World War'. This included articles and papers on topics including the New Education Fellowship and its key contributors, Child Study, theories of childhood, Froebelian metaphysics, the reception of John Dewey in England, the impact of Maria Montessori's ideas in classroom practice, and Lady Astor's 1930s campaign for English nursery schools. But that was not all; in addition to being internationally recognized for his research in the history of education and on Friedrich Froebel in particular, Kevin was often cited for his work in the fields of historical sociology, qualitative methods and contemporary education policy (much of it in collaboration with his wife Rosemary). In his research as in his life, he wore his values on his sleeve, championing efforts towards social justice and decrying the inequality that inevitably results from free-market capitalism and neoliberal education agendas.

Kevin is remembered by his colleagues not only for his excellent research and for his tireless service to scholarship, including the establishment and leadership of the Early Childhood Research Centre at University of Roehampton, his support of The Froebel Trust, UK, as well as his involvement within various international and British scholarly education societies. Perhaps most important is the legacy Kevin left through his mentoring of students, junior staff and fledgling researchers, many of whom now teach early childhood studies in education departments around the world. The chapters in this book are a token of our appreciation and recognition of the networks Kevin forged.

The editors and authors are grateful for the support given to this book by The Froebel Trust.

Notes

1   *The Guardian*, 9 December 2013. Permission of Guardian News and Media Ltd.

2   Sections about Kevin Brehony's published work are adapted from: Kristen D. Nawrotzki, 'Kevin Brehony (1948-2013)', *History of Education: Journal of the History of Education* 43, no. 3 (2014): 575–8. With permission of Routledge Taylor and Francis Group.

3   Baroness Bertha M. von Marenholtz-Bülow, *Reminiscences of Froebel*, trans. M. Mann (Boston: Lee and Shepherd Publishers, 1877) 17.

4   Kevin J. Brehony, 'Early Years Education: Some Froebelian Contributions', *History of Education* 35, no. 2 (2006): 167.

5   Kevin's *Thoughts and Writing Blog* has been archived through the British Library. See http://www.webarchive.org.uk (accessed 10 February 2016).

6   A compilation of Kevin Brehony's publications and presentations (1981–2015) can be found with the following web link: http://bloomsbury.com/kindergarten-narratives-on-froebelian-education-9781474254458/ (accessed 23 May 2016).

1

Tracking Kindergarten as a Travelling Idea

Larry Prochner

Kindergarten Narratives presents new work by historians aiming to document and explain kindergarten's international reach. Much earlier writing on the history of kindergarten education described the idea's travels from its epicentre in Germany to diverse global contexts. The chapters in this collection expand the scope to include kindergarten's connection to issues of educational policy, pedagogy, curriculum and teacher education. The book is timely: young children's well-being is a top priority for governments around the world, established in Education for All goals, in the European Council's Barcelona Agreement and by the Organization for Economic Co-operation and Development's Network on Early Childhood Education and Care, initiatives which together have had a major impact on the discourses and practices of early years education in countries around the world.[1] And there is a call for more child-centred pedagogies, a principle included in the United Nations Convention on the Rights of the Child.[2] A countervailing influence is the impact of PISA – OECD's Programme for International Student Assessment – and the trend towards academic preschools with a government or 'staff-initiated curriculum with cognitive aims for school preparation'.[3] Preschools in the three countries at the top of PISA's ranking in 2012[4] – China, Singapore and Korea – tend to be academically oriented with teacher-directed pedagogies,[5] contributing to pressure to emulate more teacher-directed approaches elsewhere.[6] As Kevin Brehony described,

> The place of play in early years education is under threat in many societies as the neo-liberal emphasis on work and preschool, conceived solely as preparation for school, in the belief that schooling is the key to economic success in conditions of globalization, bids to become hegemonic.[7]

Kindergarten Narratives contributes to the debate on the purpose of preschool by explaining what happens to child-centred forms of early education in diverse contexts.

Friedrich Froebel's (1782–1852) idea of education, in which children engage in developmental, child-centred learning activities under the direction of a specially trained teacher, has become commonplace in many parts of the world, in principle if not in practice. The system originated in schools directed by Froebel over a period of several decades. In 1816 Froebel led a school for older children at Keilhau in Saxony where he

Erziehung / Bildung

developed his theory of education, described in his book *Die Menschenerziehung* (*The Education of Man*) published in 1826; in 1833 he directed an orphanage in Switzerland where he deepened his understanding of the importance of early education to later development and worked out some of his teaching materials; and in 1839 he organized a small school called *Spiel- und Beschäftigungsanstalt* (Play and Activity Institute) in Bad Blankenburg in Prussia, giving it the new name of *Kindergarten* in 1840. The German term was subsequently adopted as a loanword in many English-speaking countries[8] or translated literally, as in the Swedish *barnträdgårdar* (described by Johannes Westberg in this volume).

Froebel's theory drew upon his religious beliefs, his studies in mathematics, physics, crystallography, forestry and architecture, and his observations at Johann Pestalozzi's school, where he lived for two years.[9] Like Jean-Jacques Rousseau, he believed in the innocence of childhood, though for Froebel its nature required ordering. Like Pestalozzi, he understood the importance of connecting learning to real-life experiences, but Froebel used materials with a more symbolic and spiritual purpose. The guiding idea in Froebel's theory was a religious belief in the divine unity of all things, echoing German scientific thinking that 'saw all living things interrelated by a great chain of being raising from lower to higher forms of life'.[10] The kindergarten activities were planned to enable children to make these essential connections. The credo of the kindergarten movement, 'come let us live for our children',[11] did not mean that children took the lead in their own education, but that teachers should show the way on the basis of Froebel's idealistic understanding of the nature of childhood. Froebel believed that children's minds were fully formed at birth and capable of reason but were unfocused. The guidance of a specially trained female teacher – presumed to have qualities of a sensitive mother – could bring children's reason to full flower by providing materials known as play-gifts (*Spielgaben*) and by engaging children in activities called occupations (*Beschäftigungsmittel*). The materials were designed to mediate abstract ideas, bringing children to an integrated understanding of their relation to the world and facilitating their natural development or unfoldment. As Froebel described, in a child's play with the first gift, the ball, 'the life of the child makes itself known, and the outer world makes itself known to the child in unity'.[12]

Froebel surrounded himself with gifted and innovative teachers and students, leaving a group of dedicated women (and some men) who identified as his disciples to more fully articulate his ideas after his death. Others, learning about kindergarten through books or lectures, also took up the cause. They included writers and teachers working in different places and at different times to promote his vision and adapt it to new circumstances. The chapters that follow track some of the meanings of kindergarten over its 175-year history as it circulated the globe as a travelling idea of education for young children.

Many of the chapters in the book touch on the nature of play in kindergarten, considering what play is, who should lead it and its purpose. Kevin Brehony's chapter explores ideas of play and work in Froebel's writings and as interpreted by others. Brehony considers play and work as an apparent binary, reviewing debates across the period from the 1850s to the twenty-first century. Brehony's chapter serves as a primer on ideas of play in Froebelian education, and readers may wish to begin with it before delving into the book according to individual interests. The remainder of the book is organized in three parts. Chapters in part one consider the circulation of Froebelian education in different locations – the Netherlands, New Zealand, Sweden and the United States – and at different times, spanning the period from the 1850s to the present. Nelleke Bakker focuses on the advancement of Froebelian ideas in the Netherlands in the nineteenth century through her study of the work of 'Froebel's Dutch missionary', Elise van Calcar-Schiotling. Bakker describes themes in van Calcar's work in the Netherlands that we see in other chapters in this volume, including tension between calls for freedom in learning on the one hand and love of order on the other. Such order was considered to be natural – 'God's law' – and supported by the apparent fixity of Froebel's gifts, though he meant them to be used alongside other, natural objects. Bakker brings to light developments unique to Froebelian education in the Netherlands: van Calcar added her own notion of 'the importance of first impressions', reminiscent of the English infant school idea in which children's initial impressions were believed to 'form a kind of main spring to all their actions'.[13] As Bakker describes, van Calcar never conceived of Froebelian education as a social project to improve the lives of working-class children. And in spite of her emphasis on children's happiness and self-activity, by 1900 free play was marginalized in the Dutch Froebel school, where play had to be useful and support bourgeois morality and Calvinist work ethos. Although the Dutch kindergarten no longer exists as a distinct institution, the legacies of these debates are present in current discussions on curriculum and practice.

Kerry Bethell examines the demand for reform of the infant curriculum in New Zealand schools along Froebelian lines during the years 1906 to 1926. Education officials in New Zealand looked to Britain to recruit suitably qualified and experienced teachers to lead change in the colony's infant schools. British teachers Dorothy Fitch and Winifred Maitland, who had trained at the Froebel Educational Institute in London, were recruited to head a new Normal School attached to the teachers' college in Wellington, New Zealand, taking up their appointments in 1905 and 1912 respectively. Their brief was to modernize the curriculum for teacher education as a step towards modernizing teaching in schools. Bethell explores influences on the women's work and ideas and identifies challenges they encountered in implementing the changes in New Zealand schools, from old-style classroom architecture in which children were seated in galleries, to large class sizes. Despite obstacles, their normal school became a leading progressive model of infant schooling that gained the interest of teachers and educators throughout the dominion. Fitch and Maitland's work provides insights into the relevance of Froebel's teachings in education today, not just for young children but, as they argued, for all children.

Johannes Westberg describes the phenomenon of exhibitions for fundraising for kindergarten in Sweden in the first half of the twentieth century. The exhibitions fulfilled several purposes in addition to fundraising, promoting the kindergarten idea and an image of bourgeois childhood – even though the kindergartens served working-class children. The exhibitions celebrated kindergarten through elaborate performances, combining a specific notion of 'idyllic childhood' along with cultural elements. While the daily activities of teachers and children in kindergartens were largely hidden from view, the exhibitions brought their work to public attention, transforming it along the way to reflect Swedish culture in its songs, stories and games, along with elements reflecting citizenship and nationalism. The fundraising events promoted kindergarten as a private charitable enterprise, a funding context that contrasts with the current situation in Sweden, in which there is significant state investment along with interest in shaping the pedagogy and practice of early education and, more broadly, the culture of childhood.

In the final chapter in part one, Kristen Nawrotzki turns our attention to the American kindergarten through a case study of developments in Grand Rapids, Michigan from the 1870s to the early years of the twentieth century. Following kindergartens' initial introduction into the United States by teachers trained in Germany, the system was spread through the work of individuals and voluntary women's organizations mobilizing local campaigns. As described by Nawrotzki, developments in Grand Rapids proceeded rapidly at times and only incrementally at others, as a type of 'kindergarten conversion' took hold in communities, which built a base of support for local organizations' private and charitable programmes. Nawrotzki identifies the conditions leading to the growth of kindergarten in smaller urban centres, including: rapid increase in population, the 'discovery' of social problems including poverty, the presence of skilled local leadership and the availability of teachers. In Grand Rapids as elsewhere, the widespread institutionalization of kindergartens as part of public schools, the efforts of individuals and influence of kindergarten networks, marked the decline and eventually the end of the association and its work.

The four chapters in part two consider curricular and pedagogical change, influenced by Froebelian education, which expands or builds upon 'Froebel's kindergarten'. Larry Prochner and Anna Kirova examine kindergarten at John Dewey's experimental school at the University of Chicago in the period 1898 to 1903. Teachers prepared as kindergartners[14] at local training schools organized the Dewey school's 'sub-primary department' for four- to six-year-olds. They led the children in constructive, freer play on the topics of family, home and community. As one of the teachers wrote, they aimed to 'emancipate the kindergarten' from directed play with Froebel's materials,[15] a shift from the idea that 'emancipation of development' required the correct use of the gifts, as in a child's play with the ball.[16] Other teachers at the experimental school's kindergarten held to a more traditional view, illustrating the complexity of educational change. Dewey's kindergarten, though it existed only a few years, was influential elsewhere in the world and across a long span of time, as described in the chapter by Read in this volume.

Amy Palmer's chapter explores the relationship between Froebelian education and drama education, including issues of improvisation versus direction in the plays. Drama was included in Froebel's *Mutter-, Spiel- und Koselieder*, a set of songs and dramatic plays first published in 1844.[17] The use of action songs and rhymes by Froebelian educators has been recognized as a highly significant early instance of 'dramatic activity' in the British classroom.[18] This aspect of their practice developed into a rich tradition of drama teaching, as evidenced by the hundreds of plays for child performers described in *Child Life*, the organ of the London-based Froebel Society from 1892 to 1939. The discussion of these plays, both inside and outside the journal, touches on key issues relevant to the educators' encouragement of children's creative endeavours. In particular, it highlights the question of the balance between offering guidance and permitting freedom. There was a similar tension in scripted plays, as in teachers' scripted use of Froebel's gifts: Were scripts a necessary step to freedom in children's development, or did they restrict their freedom? Palmer notes that dramatic play was also a feature of the psychoanalytic pedagogy of teacher Susan Isaacs, helping children 'work out inner conflicts', an idea not too distant from Froebel's unfoldment theory.[19] Palmer ends her chapter with a metaphor that points to adaptability and the continued appeal of the kindergarten idea: Froebelian teachers' attraction to the 'modern' drama education showed 'their willingness to graft new methodologies onto their core values'.

Jane Read's contribution investigates the impact of revisionist Froebelian pedagogy on teaching methods and the curriculum in English state junior schools from the 1920s to the 1950s. While Froebel is best known for the kindergarten, this chapter builds on research which has shown how Froebelians sought to establish Froebelian pedagogy more widely across the educational spectrum, starting with state infant schools and, increasingly, in schools for older children. In doing so, their work reflected a key focus in *The Education of Man* on the child at school and the Froebelian principle of a holistic approach to education. Pedagogical innovation by Froebelian teachers was based on active learning through projects based on children's own interests, contributing to the transformation of the classroom. This was a slow endeavour, reflecting at least in part the concerns of teachers as they introduced freer practice in a period when success was still governed by the results of formal exams and favourable inspection reports. In response to warnings that 'progressivism' and 'influence' are slippery concepts, a view also held by Kevin Brehony with regard to claims made for Froebelian pedagogy, Read interrogates what was distinctively 'Froebelian' in these developments.[20] Such issues resonate with current debates concerning the legacies of Froebelian child-centred education.

Chapters in part three describe longer-term perspectives on kindergarten education. Yukiyo Nishida and Fusa Abe give an account of Froebelian theory and practice in Japan from the nineteenth century to today. The Japanese government introduced a secular version of kindergarten in the 1870s as an education reform along with other modernization efforts. Coinciding with the government's initiative, American missionary teachers began kindergartens in Japan as a means of Christianization; one of the first was the Glory Kindergarten established in Kobe in 1889. Turning to the twenty-first century, Nishida and Abe describe the efforts of teachers at the Glory Kindergarten to reinterpret the annual sports day in Japan, called *undōkai*, in the framework of Froebel's idea of a *Spielfest* (play festival). The event is held in preschools countrywide and is normally organized and directed by adults; teachers at the Glory Kindergarten, which continues to look to Froebel's ideas for inspiration, involve children in its planning and direction to make *undōkai* 'child centred'.

Like the Glory Kindergarten in Japan, the Dunedin Kindergarten Association in New Zealand marked its 125th anniversary in 2014. In her chapter on the past and present of kindergarten in New Zealand, Helen May describes how social-minded settlers established the Dunedin programme in the style of free kindergarten associations that had developed for poor children in the United States a decade earlier.

Despite reflecting elements of Māori culture, kindergarten in New Zealand remained a 'settler story' until the 1960s. The national curriculum, which was developed in the 1990s, incorporated Froebelian metaphors in its conceptualization while reflecting the new understanding of the relationship between Māori and non-indigenous New Zealanders. As May explains, kindergartens, once the 'flagship' of preschool education, are now one of many government-funded options available to families. Kindergarten organizations wonder what is the relevance of their kindergarten heritage in the current cultural and pedagogical contexts of early childhood education.

The chapters in this book show early years teachers' continuing engagement with Froebel's ideas over a period of 175 years. They also reveal the varied understanding of his ideas. After his death in 1852, it was left to Froebel's interpreters to direct kindergartens' development. From the 1860s they coupled kindergarten to various causes on the basis of different assemblages of Froebel's ideas. Kevin Brehony's description of the way English Froebelian revisionists incorporated ideas of scientific child study, a history featured by several authors in this volume, is one example.[21]

The openness of Froebel's kindergarten to cultural and other influences fits Thomas Popkewitz's concept of the 'indigenous foreigner', which Froebel shares with John Dewey, Paulo Freire and Lev Vygotsky. The notion refers to thinkers whose 'ideas as modes of living' were 'brought into new contexts in which the "foreignness" of the ideas are seen as indigenous or ahistorical and "natural" to that situation in which they are positioned'.[22] Popkewitz used the concept to highlight the role played by a 'hero discourse', such as the one surrounding Froebel's kindergarten, in bringing global reforms into relation with discourses representing the values of a nation.[23] Indigenization is brought about through a remix of the ideas, building what Popkewitz termed a 'travelling library' in which concepts are added to or rescribed by local teachers and authors. van Calcar's reworking of Froebel's theory in the Netherlands, as described by Bakker in the volume, is one example.

In Froebel's case, interpretations flourished: he wrote little about the kindergarten, and the works he published suffered from his obscure writing style. Indeed, while other 'indigenous foreigners' were celebrated as their ideas crossed national and cultural contexts,[24] critics beleaguered Froebel on his travels, often targeting his writing. His style has sometimes been explained as similar to German philosophical writing of the time.[25] However, even during his time his writing was not well understood and required deciphering by colleagues. As one of his biographers remarked, 'Froebel had an instinctive horror of grammar.'[26] In his textbook for prospective teachers in US normal schools, including those studying to be kindergartners, Gabriel Compayré described Froebel's *The Education of Man* as 'a book little read, and, let it be confessed, partly illegible!'[27] Commentators from the nineteenth century to the present have used similar descriptors, calling it ponderous, repetitious, convoluted, cumbersome, verbose and incoherent.[28] Potential readers were thus warned to avoid consulting Froebel's major text themselves.

The kindergarten concept, left without a definitive text, depended more on Froebel's materials for its meaning. Maria Kraus-Boelté, who trained hundreds of kindergartners at her New York City school between 1873 and 1913, was clear on this point: 'The principles of [Froebelian] education cannot be fully mastered, especially in relation to methods, unless illustrated by their application, and these can be done only where they are practiced.'[29] This understanding had a profound impact on kindergartners' training, in which practice teaching generally came before knowing theory, if theory came at all. As a supplement to training by teaching children, which began almost at the start of their programme, instructors guided adult students in play with the gifts in the same way in which children were guided. As Kraus-Boelté explained, Froebel's materials were understood to reveal their meaning through direct manipulation. In this way they were his most important 'texts', and a component of the Froebel travelling library.[30] Writing in 1909, revisionist Froebelian Maria E. Findlay, a lecturer at the Froebel Educational Institute in London, cautioned teacher educators to 'keep Froebel's book [*The Education of Man*] for reference only and give to our students the later authors' who interpreted Froebel's ideas.[31] The tradition to start with practice and add theory in small doses later continued in Froebelian training in England into the 1950s.[32] As Froebel College lecturer Peter Jackson described, 'only the How of it all – the methodology – remained'.[33]

Findlay's warning did not apply to Froebel's practical book for mothers and teachers, *Mutter-, Spiel- und Koselieder* (*Mother Play and Nursery Songs*), which Denton Snider called 'the chief canonical Book in the Kindergarten Bible'.[34] *Mutter-, Spiel- und Koselieder* was reinterpreted, through its translation, in contexts outside Germany and was required reading in many kindergartner training courses. Nishida and Abe describe its adaptation by teacher and missionary Annie Howe, who commissioned illustrations with local themes when she translated it into Japanese.[35] Because Howe did not read German, historians believe her Japanese version was based on English translations[36]; those available at the time were Elizabeth Peabody's American edition of the translation by Josephine Jarvis, published in 1893, and Susan Blow's translation, published in 1895.[37] As for Blow's version, the illustrations were altered from the ones in *Mutter-, Spiel- und Koselieder*, the poems were freely translated, and only 'a few of the best melodies' were retained.[38] In his preface to Blow's book, William Torrey Harris was evidently correct when he called it 'something more than a translation'. Harris explained: 'The ideas of Froebel are *transplanted* into English and made to express themselves in English as if they had been thought and expressed here for the first time.'[39] In his description, Harris detached Froebel's ideas from history, portraying them as natural to their new context, reflecting the notion of indigenous foreigner and depicting Froebel's system as a method of nature. This was a common theme in writing about the American kindergarten. In her *Kindergarten Guide*, Elizabeth Peabody explained that '*kindergarten* means a garden of children, and Froebel, the inventor of it, or rather, as he would prefer to express it, *the discoverer of the method of nature*, meant to symbolize by the name the spirit and plan of treatment'.[40] And as a method of nature it was beyond analysis. As Ralph Waldo Emerson wrote, making his own point about 'the method of nature', 'That rushing stream will not stop to be observed. We can never surprise nature in a corner; we can never find the end of a thread; never tell where to set the first stone.'[41] Interpretations of Froebel's ideas, insofar as they were infused with Froebel's mystical notion of the divine nature of development, were likewise beyond analysis, but not beyond criticism by scientifically minded educationists!

And what is the place of Froebelian education in current debates over early years education? Chapters in this volume describe Froebel's ideas fitted to new contexts. Froebel valued experiment, believing that his system was not yet completed, as indicated in the quote by Froebel included as an epigraph in the preface of this volume:

> The last word of my theory I shall carry to my grave, the time is not yet ripe for it. If three hundred years after my system of education is completely and according to its real principle carried through Europe, I shall rejoice in heaven. If only the seed be cast abroad, its springing up will not fail nor the fruit be wanting.

Froebel foresaw that kindergarten would continue evolving in line with his 'real principle', namely, that 'the divine essence unfolds according to a prescribed and patterned existence'.[42] The spiritual basis of his idea continues today in calls for eco-education and sustainable pedagogy with a focus on the human–environment relationship. For the earliest followers of Froebel, child gardening was a matter of saving children's souls. In the words of one of his followers, Bertha von Marenholtz-Bülow, prospects for children without the aid of kindergarten were bleak: 'Plants shut up in dark cellars degenerate and die, and human nature, which lacks care and attention, especially in its earliest stages, degenerates and dies also.'[43] While the purely religious aspect of this idea is no longer part of Froebelian education, concerns have been raised from a number of quarters that children lack opportunities for natural play. While 'natural play' may be taken to mean 'nature' play by some – seen in the renewed interest in 'forest kindergartens' and the popularity of Richard Louv's book describing a 'nature-deficit disorder',[44] – chapters in this book have addressed natural play as involving greater child direction. The challenge of doing so in a post-industrialized Japan is described in Nishida's and Abe's description of the reconceptualized *undōkai* in Chapter 10.

Froebel's idea that adults need to look to children's nature for direction, including children's natural 'drive' to play, is reified in the place afforded play – both directed and free – in contemporary early years education. However, whilst it is agreed by almost everyone that play is beneficial to children's development, it is not agreed that children should play in school. Indeed, school methods are mostly at odds with play, despite what children may prefer. Alice M. Christie, who translated a number of works on kindergarten, put it succinctly: children 'have always shown a perverse preference for play rather than lessons'.[45] Froebel recognized this 'fact' in his proposal to use children's proclivity to play to advantage in his directed teaching activities. Here, we return to a theme introduced at the start of this chapter and reflected in several of the histories in this volume: the tug of war between adult- and child-centred early years education.

Finally, reconceptualist scholars have challenged Froebel's philosophy as a discourse of development, raising questions about its relevance in the face of what we know about children and childhoods today. Scholarship over a period of three decades has worked to reconceptualize play- and child-centred methodologies, to 'denaturalize childhood' in the words of Affrica Taylor,[46] drawing on Foucauldian, postcolonial, post-human and post-structural arguments.[47] Froebelian principles concerning universal attributes of child nature run counter to many indigenous perspectives on child development.[48]

Froebel's child was not a natural phenomenon, as he believed, but a particular version of nineteenth-century childhood. Historians tracking Froebelian education of the twenty-first century may find it difficult to find traces of the Froebelian spirit in early years education, in programmes focusing on standards and achievement, and in the growing shift away from developmental approaches to postmodern practices.

Notes

1 UNESCO, *The Dakar Framework for Action* (Paris: UNESCO, 2000); European Commission, *Barcelona Objectives* (Brussels: European Commission, 2013); OECD, *Starting Strong: Early Childhood Education and Care* (Paris: OECD, 2001).
2 Appendix to General Comment No. 1 on Article 29 (1) of the *Convention on the Rights of the Child* (United Nations, 2001), item 2. Available online: http://www.unicef-irc. org/portfolios/general_comments/GC1_en.doc.html (accessed 20 May 2016).
3 OECD, *Starting Strong III: A Quality Toolbox for Early Childhood Education and Care* (Paris: OECD, 2012), 84–5.
4 OECD, *PISA 2012 Results in Focus* (Paris: OECD, 2014). http://www.oecd.org/pisa/ keyfindings/pisa-2012-results-overview.pdf (accessed 20 May 2016).
5 Jaipaul L. Roopnarine and Aysegul Metindogan, 'Early Childhood Education Research in Cross-National Perspective', in *Handbook of Research on the Education of Young Children*, 2nd ed., ed. Bernard Spodek and Olivia N. Saracho (New York: Routledge, 2013), 555–72; Doris Pui-Wah Cheng and Shu-Chen Wu, 'Serious Learners of Serious Player?' in *Varied Perspectives on Play and Learning: Theory and Research on Early Years Education*, ed. Ole Fredrik Lillemyr, Sue Dockett and Bob Perry (Charlotte, NC: Information Age, 2013), 193–212. On preschools in Singapore, see L. Ang, 'Singapore Preschool Teachers' Responses to the Introduction of a Framework for a Kindergarten Curriculum in the Context of Three Preschool Settings,' *Asia-Pacific Journal of Research in Early Childhood Education* 2, no. 1 (2008): 55–81; J. Ng, 'Exploring the Perceptions of Stakeholders in a Singapore Kindergarten during a Period of Curriculum Reform', 2009, http://www.aare.edu. au/publications-database.php/5942/exploring-the-perceptions-of-stakeholders-in- a-singapore-kindergarten-during-a-period-of-curriculum (accessed 1 December 2015); Amita Gupta, *Diverse Early Childhood Education Policies and Practices: Voices and Images from Five Countries in Asia* (New York: Routledge, 2015); Young-Ihm Kwon, 'Western Influences in Korean Preschool Education', *International Education Journal* 3, no. 3 (2002): 153–64.
6 William H. Jeynes, 'Standardized Tests and Froebel's Original Kindergarten Model', *Teachers College Record* 108, no. 10 (2006): 1937–59.
7 Kevin J. Brehony, 'Juego, Trabajo y Educación: Situando un Debate Froebeliano' [Play, Work and Education: Situating a Froebelian Debate], *Bordón: Revista de Pedagogia* 65, no. 1 (2013): 71.
8 Phillip Durkin, *Borrowed Words: A History of Loanwords in English* (Oxford, UK: Oxford University Press, 2014).
9 On Pestalozzi's influence on Froebel, see Clem Adelman, 'Over Two Years, What Did Froebel Say to Pestalozzi?' *History of Education* 29, no. 2 (2000): 103–14; on crystallography see Jane Insley, 'Crystallography and the Kindergarten: A Correction?' *Educate* 15, no. 2 (2015): 6–10.

10 Gerald L. Gutek, *Historical and Philosophical Foundations of Education: A Biographical Introduction*, 3rd ed. (Upper Saddle River, NJ: Merrill Prentice Hall, 2001), 233.

11 Friedrich Froebel, *The Education of Man*, 1826, trans. W. N. Hailmann (New York, NY: D. Appleton, [1826]1887), 89.

12 Friedrich Froebel, *Pedagogics of the Kindergarten*, 1861, trans. Josephine Jarvis (London: Edward Arnold, 1897), 60.

13 Samuel Wilderspin, *Infant Education; or Remarks on the Importance of Educating the Infant Poor* (London: W. Simpkin and R. Marshall, 1825), 12.

14 Anglicized version of the German *kindergärtnerinnen* (kindergarten teachers).

15 Georgia P. Scates, 'The Sub-Primary (Kindergarten) Department', *Elementary School Record 1* (June 1900): 137.

16 Baroness Bertha von Marenholtz-Bülow, *The Child And Child-Nature*, 1894, trans. Alice M. Christie (Syracuse, NY: C. W. Bardeen, 1889), 100.

17 Friedrich Froebel, *Mutter- und Koselieder, Dichtung und Bilder zur edlen Pflege des Kindheitlebens. Ein Familienbuch*, 1844, [*Mother Play and Nursery Songs*] (Boston: Lee Shepherd, 1878).

18 Gavin Bolton, *Acting in Classroom Drama: A Critical Analysis* (Stoke-on-Trent: Trentham Books, 1998), 7.

19 Sol Cohen, 'In the Name of the Prevention of Neurosis: The Search for Psychoanalytic Pedagogy in Europe, 1905-1938', in *Regulated Children, Liberated Children: Education in Psychoanalytical Perspective*, ed. Barbara Finkelstein (New York, NY: Psychohistory Press, 1979).

20 Kevin J. Brehony, *The Froebel Movement and State Schooling 1880–1914: A Study in Educational Ideology*, 2 vols. (PhD thesis, Open University, 1987); J. M. Lynch, 'What is the Activity School?' *Elementary School Journal* 36, no. 5 (1936): 344–8; Quentin Skinner, 'Meaning and Understanding in the History of Ideas', *Visions of Politics*, rev ed., vol. 1 (Cambridge: Cambridge University Press, 2002), 57–89.

21 Kevin J. Brehony, 'Working at Play or Playing at Work? A Froebelian Paradox Re-examined', Inaugural Lecture, 2004, University of Surrey, Roehampton, London, UK reproduced as chapter 2 of this volume. See also Peter W. Jackson, 'Child-Centered Education for Pacific-Rim Cultures?' *Early Child Development and Care* 143 (1998): 47–57; Peter W. Jackson, 'Froebel Education Re-Assessed: British and German Experience, 1850–1940', *Early Childhood Development and Care* 149 (1999): 11–25; and Peter Jackson and Sang-Wook Lee, 'Froebel and the Hitler Jugend: The Britishing of Froebel', *Early Childhood Development and Care* 117 (1996): 45–65.

22 Thomas S. Popkewitz, 'Inventing the Modern Self and John Dewey: Modernities and the Traveling of Pragmatism in Education – An Introduction', in *Inventing the Modern Self and John Dewey*, ed. Thomas S. Popkewitz (New York: Palgrave Macmillan, 2005), 9.

23 Thomas S. Popkewitz, 'Globalization/Regionalism, Knowledge, and the Educational Practices: Some Notes on Comparative Strategies for Educational Research', in *Educational Knowledge: Changing Relationships between the State, Civil Society and the Educational Community*, ed. Thomas S. Popkewitz (Albany, NY: SUNY Press, 2000), 10.

24 Ibid.

25 John Howlett, *Progressive Education: A Critical Introduction* (London: Bloomsbury, 2013), 59.

26 Denton J. Snider, *The Life of Frederick Froebel: Founder of the Kindergarten* (Chicago, IL: Sigma, 1900), 118.

27 Gabriel Compayré, *The History of Pedagogy*, trans. W. H. Payne (Boston: D.C. Heath & Co., 1892), 453.

28 David Elkind, *Giants in the Nursery: A Biographical History of Developmentally Appropriate Practice* (St. Paul, MN: Redleaf Press, 2015), 90; Irene M. Lilley, *Friedrich Froebel: A Selection from his Writings* (London: Sage, 1967), 4; Harry Morgan, *Early Childhood Education: History, Theory and Practice* (Lanham, MD: Rowman & Littlefield, 2011), 21; Elizabeth Day Ross, *The Kindergarten Crusade: The Establishment of Preschool Education in the United States* (Athens, OH: Ohio University Press, 1976), 3; Michael Steven Shapiro, *Child's Garden: The Kindergarten Movement from Froebel to Dewey* (University Park, PA: Pennsylvania State University Press, 1983), 20.

29 Maria Krause-Boelté, 'Characteristics of Froebel's Method: Kindergarten Training', *The Addresses and Journal of Proceedings of the National Educational Association, Session of the year 1876* (Salem, OH: Office of the National Teacher, 1876), 215.

30 Harriet Cuffaro made the same point but with reference to Dewey and not Froebel, explaining that materials were the texts of early childhood education, providing 'openings or pathways by and through which children may enter the ordered knowledge of the adult world'. Harriet Cuffaro, *Experimenting with the World: John Dewey and the Early Childhood Classroom* (New York, NY: Teachers College Press, 1995), 33; see also Harriet Cuffaro, 'A View of Materials as the Texts of the Early Childhood Curriculum', *Yearbook in Early Childhood Education*: Vol. 2. Issues in Early Childhood Curriculum, ed. Bernard Spodek and Olivia Saracho (New York: Teachers College Press, 1991), 64–85.

31 Maria E. Findlay, 'Froebel's Principles and Current Idealism in England', *Child Life* 11, no. 52 (1909): 235, cited in Kristen Dombkowski Nawrotzki, 'The Anglo-American Kindergarten Movements and Early Education in England and the USA, 1850–1965' (PhD. diss., University of Michigan, 2005), 37.

32 Tina Bruce, 'Friedrich Froebel', in *The Routledge International Handbook of Philosophies and Theories of Early Childhood Care and Education*, ed. Tricia David, Kathy Goouch and Sacha Powell (London: Routledge, 2016), 22.

33 Peter W. Jackson, 'Child-Centered Education for Pacific-Rim Cultures?' *Early Child Development and Care* 143 (1998): 55.

34 Denton J. Snider, *The Life of Frederick Froebel: Founder of the Kindergarten* (Chicago: Sigma, 1900), 329.

35 Annie L. Howe, *Haha no yugi oyobi ikuji uta* [Mother-Play and Nursery Song] (Kobe: Glory Teacher Training School Press, 1896). http://kindai.ndl.go.jp/info:ndljp/pid/1057343?itemId=info%3Andljp%2Fpid%2F1057343&__lang=en (accessed 1 December 2015).

36 Hideo Hamada, *Pestarocchi, fureberu, to Nihon no kindai kyoiku* [Pestalozzi, Froebel and modern education in Japan] (Tokyo: Tamagawa University Press, 2009), 103; Yoko Shirakawa, *Fureberu no kindagaruten jittssen ni kansuru kenkyu* [The study of Froebel's kindergarten and its practice] (Tokyo: Kazama Shobo, 2014), 40.

37 Friedrich Froebel, *Mother-Play and Nursery Songs*, trans. Fannie E. Dwight and Josephine Jarvis, ed. Elizabeth P. Peabody (Boston: Lee and Shepard, 1893). Jarvis's translation was available from 1878; Friedrich Froebel, *Mottoes and Commentaries of Friedrich Froebel's Mother Play*, trans. Henrietta R. Eliot and Susan E. Blow (New York: D. Appleton and Co., 1895).

38 Susan E. Blow, *The Songs and Music of Friedrich Froebel's Mother Play* [Mutter und Kose Lieder] (New York: D. Appleton & Co., 1895), vii.

39 William Torrey Harris, editor's preface, *Mottoes and Commentaries of Friedrich Froebel's Mother Play*, trans. Henrietta R. Eliot and Susan E. Blow (New York: D. Appleton and Co., 1895), viii.

40 [Mrs] Horace Mann and Elizabeth P. Peabody, *The Moral Culture of Infancy and Kindergarten Guide* (Boston: Thomas Oliver Hazard Perry Burnam, 1864), 10.

41 Ralph Waldo Emerson, *The Method of Nature* (Boston: Samuel G. Simpkins, 1841), 10.

42 Gerald L. Gutek, *A History of the Western Educational Experience*, 2nd ed. (Long Grove, IL: Waveland Press, 1995), 258; Froebel's interpreters as well as his critics published numerous books on the topic of his principles and laws, notably, Matilda H. Krieg, *The Child, its Nature and Relations; An Elucidation of Froebel's Principles of Education* (New York: E. Steiger, 1872); Emily Shirreff, 'Froebel's Principles of Education', *Journal of Education* 11 (1889): 615–6; James L. Hughes, *Froebel's Education Laws for All Teachers* (New York: D. Appleton, 1910); William Heard Kilpatrick, *Froebel's Kindergarten Principles Critically Examined* (New York: Macmillan, 1916).

43 Bertha von Marenholtz-Bülow, 'Froebel's Educational Views', *The American Journal of Education* 30, no. 5 (1880): 343.

44 David Sobel, Patti Ensel Bailie, Ken Finch, Erin K. Kenny, and Anne Stires, *Nature Preschools and Forest Kindergartens: The Handbook for Outdoor Learning* (St. Paul, MN: Redleaf Press, 2016); Richard Louv, *Last Child in the Woods: Saving our Children from Nature-Deficit Disorder* (New York: Atlantic Books, 2010).

45 Alice M. Christie, preface to *The Child and Child Nature* (London: W. Swan Sonnenschein, 1879), iii.

46 Affrica Taylor, *Reconfiguring the Natures of Childhood* (New York: Routledge, 2013).

47 Jo Ailwood, 'Governing Early Childhood Education through Play', *Contemporary Issues in Early Childhood* 4, no. 3 (2003): 286–99; Bernadette Baker, 'Child-Centered Teaching, Redemption, and Educational Identities: A History of the Present', *Educational Theory* 48, no. 2 (1998): 155–174; Elly Singer, 'Prisoners of The Method: Breaking Open the Child-Centred Pedagogy in Day Care Centres', *Early Years Education* 3, no. 2 (1996): 28–40; Affrica Taylor, Mindy Blaise and Miriam Giugni, ' "Haraway's Bag Lady Story-Telling": Relocating Childhood and Learning within a Post-Human Landscape', *Discourse: Studies in the Cultural Politics of Education* 34, no. 1 (2013): 48–62.

48 Karen J. Brison, 'Producing "Confident" Children: Negotiating Childhood in Fijian Kindergartens', *Anthropology and Education Quarterly* 42, no. 3 (2011): 230–44; Peter W. Jackson, 'Child-Centered Education for Pacific Rim Cultures?' *Early Child Development and Care* 143 (1998): 47–57; Marie Lall, 'Pushing the Child Centered Approach in Myanmar: The Role of Cross National Policy Networks and the Effects on the Classroom', *Critical Studies in Education* 52, no. 3 (2011): 219–33; *Unsettling the Colonial Places and Spaces of Early Childhood Education*, ed. Veronica Pacini-Ketchabaw and Affrica Taylor (New York: Routledge, 2015).

Figure 2.1 Berthe Ronge's Kindergarten, Tavistock Place, London, *The Lady's Newspaper*, 13 October 1855.

2

Working at Play or Playing at Work?
A Froebelian Paradox Re-examined

Kevin J. Brehony

It is only fitting and appropriate that here in this place, this college that is named after Friedrich Froebel and where his ideas and practices were reproduced over many generations, that my lecture today addresses a theme central to his thought and writing: conceptions of the role of play in education. I have spent much of the last twenty-odd years researching the kindergarten movement in an attempt to understand the politics of education and the role of ideologies within that field. I have been less concerned with what Froebel said than with what others thought he said, their interpretations of his work and the meanings they made of it.[1] This is one of the first times that I have approached the truth claims raised by Froebel's methods. But rather than ask the empirical question of whether or not they work, I have chosen to focus on philosophers and social theorists who are loosely connected to the intellectual tradition of which Froebel was part and to ask questions about the nature of play and work in school and in society generally.

Play is notoriously difficult to define, but we all have little difficulty in identifying it in the practice of everyday life. Mark Twain, in his novel *The Adventures of Tom Sawyer,* proposed that 'work consists of whatever a body is *obliged* to do, and that Play consists of whatever a body is not obliged to do'.[2] Many have suggested something similar, but our problems begin when we try to theorize or explain what play is. This is perhaps because it signifies a large number of different activities and, as Sutton-Smith has argued, it is highly ambiguous.[3] Much has been written in education on this theme since Froebel's death in 1852 but play, as many authors conclude, continues to defy precise definition. My task today is not so much to supply definitions but to probe a particular dimension of the debates that originate in German philosophy. So I propose we undertake a journey in the history of ideas, or intellectual history, as it now tends to be called, a journey through time and space that begins with Froebel in the German States in the early nineteenth century and terminates in the present.

But first I would like to make a detour to San Francisco and Woodstock in the late 1960s and early 1970s. 'Let the Children Play' is a song recorded by Carlos Santana. I will readily concede that the link appears tenuous between this and Froebel and his views on play and work. I chose it as it raises questions of translation – an issue with

Froebel's texts – and of meaning and interpretation, matters that have been at the centre of most of my academic work in the sociology and history of education. The song's meaning is to be sought both in the music and in the lyric, which, because of its ambiguity, is able to convey more meaning than a literal reading would suggest. The central ambiguity revolves around the use of the word 'children'. In one reading, the song is a demand that children should be allowed to play and it presupposes that there is something restraining them. As research carried out by the Children's Play Council and the Children's Society found,[4] children's play is often constrained by the opposition of adults who see play as trivial or frivolous but who also fear what Sutton-Smith calls its 'dark side'; that is, play's association with subversion, disorder and transgression.

Returning to the song, when the context in which the song was produced is taken into account in the interpretive process, 'children' might be taken to include the young adults of the 1960s who were either labelled, or defined themselves, as hippies. For many hippies, work was something associated with the Puritan ethic; it was a thing that 'straights' did while they, on the other hand, valorized play in all its many manifestations but particularly in its irrational, disruptive and creative forms. The association of play with creativity is a long-standing one and was made forcefully by the German writer Friedrich von Schiller, who died in 1805.[5] Among the 1960s texts that made the association, Richard Neville's *Play Power* was a prominent programmatic statement of hippy notions of work and play.[6]

Such has been the dominance of the work ethic that the 1960s was one of the few historical conjunctures in which play and work have been in heightened tension and opposition. The significance of this binary is that often our definition of concepts depends on our knowing what they are not, that is, that play is not work. Arguably, whenever a concept of play is present, one of work is not far away. In the liberal social climate of the 1960s, attempts were made in the West to incorporate play into the curriculum of schools for young children. In the furtherance of this aim, Froebel's name was invoked to grant it legitimacy, as, for example, in the 1968 Plowden Report.[7]

The Froebel movement and manual training

Froebel is widely heralded as the apostle of play in education, particularly in texts on early years education. To him is often misattributed the often-cited slogan 'play is the work of the child' or, in another, gendered, version, 'a child's work is his play'. The first of these faintly sinister and Orwellian rhetorical statements, whose illocutionary force is to legitimate play by asserting that it really is work, appears in *Woman's Educational Mission*, a book by Froebel's successor as leader of the kindergarten movement, the Baroness Bertha von Marenholtz-Bülow.[8] In a similar vein, nearly one hundred years later, the child psychologist Susan Isaacs affirmed in 1929 that 'play is indeed the child's work'.[9]

Froebel was not the first to suggest that play should be used in the education of children. For example, John Locke argued that play made work in school more palatable, but Froebel made play more central to his pedagogy than any previous educationalist.[10] Interestingly, however, the writings of prominent figures in the Froebel movement in England, such as Eleonore Heerwart and Friedrich Froebel's nephew, Karl Froebel, emphasize work.[11] One Froebelian text in particular does so with great force. The text, published in 1854 at Dresden, is entitled *A Connected Series of Playthings and Occupation for Early Childhood*. Its author is given as F. W. A. Froebel; however it was almost certainly written by the Marenholtz-Bülow, an indefatigable worker in the Froebelian cause who propagandized for the kindergarten and women's work in many European countries. She later wrote a manual training interpretation of the kindergarten entitled *Handwork and Headwork*, and in the Dresden text, she said of Froebel's kindergarten:

> Fröbel goes farther and teaches in play, consequently without much exertion, and in an entertaining manner, the chief rules and knacks of technical skill, in order to pave the way, in the fullest sense of the word, for a *training for labour*, such as the pressing wants of the age demand, and to fit the labouring classes for earning their bread betimes.[12]

Although Marenholtz-Bülow saw the kindergarten as having several functions, preparation for labour was foremost among them. She wrote:

> Only by means of *right occupation,* the great object of education, *moral improvement,* is to be attained, and by a proper preparation for *labour, a certain means of subsistence* may be opened to every one. Let us then not overlook the importance of *Fröbel's* work, and led (*sic*) us strive, by universal application, to facilitate its *progressive development*.[13]

To some extent, this might be viewed as an opportunist adaptation. This grouping in the English Froebel movement became ascendant in the 1890s and promoted the kindergarten as the first stage of a scheme of manual training in elementary schools. Numbers in the Froebel Society were falling and difficulties in securing the implementation of the kindergarten in public elementary schools were seemingly insurmountable, so it was rational for some Froebelians to attach themselves to the programme of those 'Industrial Trainers' who advocated manual training in schools.[14] This strategy may also have been attractive as some of the leading industrial trainers, such as Philip Magnus, were Germanophiles with Froebelian inclinations. In addition, a number of Froebelians who promoted handwork had become interested in wood Sloyd, a system of woodcarving promoted in Sweden by the Froebelian Otto Salomon. It became so fashionable in educational circles that many English teachers and educationists, including Arthur Acland, the so-called first 'minister' of education, spent their holidays learning Sloyd at Nääs in Sweden.[15]

Froebel on work and play

On the other hand, knowing that support for the promotion of handwork was warranted by Froebel's discussion of work enables a new reading of Froebel's texts on play, seeing them as intimately bound up with his conception of work. This understanding is supported in the writing of Elsie Riach Murray, head of the kindergarten at Maria Grey Training College and a prominent figure among English revisionist Froebelians. The revisionists were Froebelian women who revised Froebelian practice in light of criticisms by G. Stanley Hall, John Dewey and the practice of the Pestalozzi-Froebel House in Berlin.[16] In 1914, Murray wrote, 'It is impossible to make plain how Froebel regarded play, until it is known how he regarded work, work, too, not only for a child but for a human being.'[17] In *The Education of Man*, Froebel presented his views on work before discussing play, although he made clear that play should precede work in the education of the young child. He critiqued existing practices, writing, 'At present the popular notions of work and the pursuits of practical industry are wholly false, superficial, untenable, oppressive, debasing, devoid of all elements of life.'[18] He also attacked what he described as 'the debasing illusion that man works, produces, creates only in order to preserve his body, in order to secure food, clothing, and shelter'.[19] 'Religion without industry, without work', Froebel warned, 'is liable to be lost in empty dreams, worthless visions, idle fancies. Similarly, work or industry without religion degrades man into a beast of burden, a machine.'[20]

For the Romantic Idealist philosophers, many of whom Froebel had read, the starting point when considering work and production was the self-constitution of humans through self-activity, but Froebel chose as his point of departure a God who works creatively and productively. He wrote:

> This is the high meaning, the deep significance, the great purpose of work and industry, of productive and creative activity. We become truly godlike in diligence and industry, in working and doing, which are accompanied by the clear perception or even by the vaguest feeling that thereby we represent the inner in the outer; that we give body to spirit, and form to thought; that we render visible the invisible[.][21]

Many of Froebel's ideas exhibit a marked similarity to those of the members of the Jena Romantic circle and other idealist philosophers such as Friedrich Wilhelm von Schelling. This is observable in his claim that 'primarily and in truth man works only that his spiritual, divine essence may assume outward form, and that thus he may be enabled to recognize his own spiritual, divine nature and the innermost being of God'.[22] From this premise, Froebel concluded: 'The young, growing human being should, therefore, be trained early for outer work, for creative and productive activity.'[23]

Froebel on play

Echoing Michel de Montaigne, the great figure of the French Renaissance, who wrote in 1575 that 'the play of children is not really play, but must be judged of as their most serious actions', Froebel declared that in childhood 'play is the purest, most spiritual activity of man at this stage' and that 'play at this time is not trivial, it is highly serious and of deep significance'.[24] In Froebel's most famous aphorism, 'The plays of childhood are the germinal leaves of all later life,' he invested play and childhood with a significance for later life surpassed by no other theorist until perhaps Freud and staked his claim as the leading theorist of play in education. But even in his discussion of play, Froebel emphasized the role of work, as when he wrote of children imitating the work of their parents. He distinguished work from play both developmentally and in terms of productive capacity. In the phase of boyhood (Froebel only spoke of one gender), he wrote, 'What formerly the child did only *for the sake of the activity,* the boy now does *for the sake of the result* or product of his activity' and that if formerly 'activity brought joy to the child, work now gives delight to the boy'.[25]

Later, in *The Education of Man*, Froebel returned to his theme of the desirability of the inclusion of 'some external pursuit, some externally productive work' – in domestic duties such as errands – to be provided by the family and the school in the phase of boyhood. He condemned the Latin and High schools in which he claimed 'the pupils are wholly debarred from outwardly productive work' and argued, in what for him was a rare appeal to experience, that it showed that 'external, physical, productive activity interspersed in intellectual work strengthens not only the body but in a very marked degree the mind in its various phases of development, so that the mind, after such a refreshing work-bath (I can find no better name), enters upon its intellectual pursuits with new vigor and life'.[26]

Froebel's, then, is a theory of self-realization of unfolding through activity that takes the form of play followed by work. If *The Education of Man* were the only text of Froebel's that we had, we might regard him not as an advocate of play in education but, like many contemporary educationists who followed Rousseau, including Pestalozzi, Basedow, Robert Owen and Fellenberg, as a proponent of work. For Froebel, as for these other educational theorists, work took the form of the imitation of adults, hence his examples of domestic work. But he also thought of it as involving manual dexterity that would be useful for 'the training of poorer children'.[27] Significantly, his view of work excluded what we conventionally call learning or formal instruction. When he opposed play to work, he followed Rousseau's rejection of passive learning and learning from books.[28] Finally, it is noteworthy that Froebel's child is almost always a universal subject; otherwise, he rarely differentiated between boys and girls and only infrequently referred to social class differences among children. On one of the rare occasions he did, he recommended that 'every child, boy, and youth, whatever his condition or position in life, should devote daily at least one or two hours to some serious activity in the production of some definite external piece of work'.[29]

Froebel's plans to produce a scheme for educating older children failed and so his kindergarten writings contain almost nothing on productive work in the sense discussed in *The Education of Man*. His later writing was almost entirely concerned with early childhood and the gifts and occupations, play materials he devised for young children. These, together with the *Mother's Songs, Games and Stories*, constitute the core of Froebel's play pedagogy.[30] They were chosen specifically for the lessons that could be derived from them, and he claimed that their arrangement was logical. He provided comprehensive guides to their use, leaving little scope for children to play with them spontaneously. These he referred to as 'sufficing instructions', which, he claimed, would provide 'a direction sufficient to enable parents and nurses and teachers to use the play'.[31] Moreover, he reportedly once said that 'without rational, conscious guidance, childish activity degenerates into aimless play instead of preparing for those tasks of life for which it is destined'.[32]

The intellectual context of Froebel's thought

It is useful to situate Froebel's thought in its wider intellectual context and consider further some of the elective affinities between Froebel's thinking and that of his German Idealist and Romantic contemporaries. The term 'elective affinities' is associated mainly with the German sociologist Max Weber, but it is also the title of a work by Johann Wolfgang von Goethe, whose interest in alchemy and in the occult was typical of German Romanticism.[33] Traces of the occult were also present in the anti-Newtonian nature philosophy of Goethe and others known to Froebel and whose views he shared. Goethe's notion of 'Nature as source', as Charles Taylor put it in his *Sources of the Self,* slides easily into pantheism, the notion that the universe is God.[34] Pantheism is present also in the work of the English poets Coleridge and Wordsworth who, like the nature philosophers, held that a force immanent in nature was responsible for unfoldment or as Taylor, terms it, 'expressivism'.[35] This was a pre-Darwinian notion of an inner power striving to realize itself externally, which for Froebel took place at the level of the individual child. For the German philosopher Hegel, on the other hand, the power, which he termed the Absolute Spirit, realized itself through history and within institutions through a dialectical process.

Marx, labour and alienation

Famously, Marx claimed to have stood Hegel on his head when he replaced the Absolute Spirit with the proletariat. Surprisingly however, the materialist Marx and the idealist Froebel initially at least were close in their views on work and self-realization. In his *Economic and Philosophic Manuscripts of 1844,* Marx used Hegelian concepts to argued, in a way that in some respects paralleled Froebel, that self-realization came through the objectification of labour by making, in Froebel's terminology, the inner the outer.[36] Marx wrote that 'man produces himself not only intellectually, in his consciousness, but actively and actually, and he can therefore contemplate himself in a world he himself has created'.[37] However, due to the existence of private property and the division between labour and capital, the worker experiences 'objectification as loss of and bondage to the object, and appropriation as estrangement, as *alienation*'.[38] Workers become estranged or alienated from the products of their labour, the labour process itself, fellow human beings and their species being or human nature. Alienation in one form or another was present in the thought of Rousseau, Schiller and Hegel among others,[39] but in Marx, the concept took on a new character for, to compress an extensive discussion, work under conditions of capitalist social relations no longer provides self-realization but alienation. There is then in Marx's views on labour a tension or contradiction between its potential for self-creation and its position under capitalism as the source of alienation. For Marx's collaborator, Engels, this contradiction was expressed in language more empirical than Hegelian:

> Another source of demoralisation among the workers is their being condemned to work. As voluntary, productive activity is the highest enjoyment known to us, so is compulsory toil the most cruel, degrading punishment. Nothing is more terrible than being constrained to do some one thing every day from morning until night against one's will. And the more a man the worker feels himself, the more hateful must his work be to him, because he feels the constraint, the aimlessness of it for himself. Why does he work? For love of work? From a natural impulse? Not at all! He works for money, for a thing which has nothing whatsoever to do with the work itself.[40]

In the *German Ideology*, as they moved further away from Hegelian concepts, Marx and Engels located alienation in the division of labour, of which they took that between material and mental to be the most fundamental. It is against this background that Marxist educational theory stressed polytechnical education. This was meant to combine mental and manual labour in order to produce what Marx referred to as 'the totally developed individual'[41] and was developed later by ruling communist parties into an educational orthodoxy.[42] Schooling containing training for productive activity lends itself to the conditions in societies dominated by necessity and scarcity whatever the philosophical claims made for it. In the early years of the Soviet Union, the Bolshevik economists Bukharin and Preobrazhensky, describing their conception of the unified labour school, wrote in almost Froebelian terms:

> A child's first activities take the form of play; play should gradually pass into work by an imperceptible transition, so that the child learns from the very outset to look upon labour, not as a disagreeable necessity or as a punishment, but as a natural and spontaneous expression of faculty. Labour should be a need, like the desire for food and drink; this need must be instilled, and developed in the communist school.[43]

Makarenko, the leading Soviet educationist of the early years of Stalin's regime, stressed the similarities between play and work and, like Froebel, used 'activity' as a term that synthesized their opposition. 'How does play differ from work?' he asked, and answered, 'Work is the participation of man in social production, in the creation of material, cultural or social values. ... Play has only an indirect relation to social goals'.[44] But in spite of his orientation towards production, Makarenko prescribed free play alongside guided play for children under six.

The French communist elementary school teacher Célestin Freinet, founder of a large movement of teachers, had a different approach, distinguishing between play-work and work-play. *Jeu-travail* or play-work was free play including imitative play which could cross the line and become *jeu-haschich* or play-drug; the dark, addictive threatening kind of play. *Travail-jeu*, on the other hand, was real work done by children. What 'drives life onwards from the earliest age' is 'not play, it's *work!*' he wrote in *L'Éducation du Travail*.[45]

Finally, in this selection of Marxist views on play and work, C. L. R James, an independent revolutionary Marxist and former Trotskyist theoretician, wrote in 1951 that 'Children's play is work – work which constantly challenges the child as an individual and as a social being. It is the new mode of labor – cooperative, creative, planned by the children themselves, developing a natural and spontaneous leadership, and obliterating all division between manual and mental labor.'[46] The opening assertion of the identity of play and work was familiar among Froebelians. James' view of play as a new mode of labour is different but his conclusion signalled utopian yearnings. 'Children express in play' he asserted, 'what the worker is denied in production. Free and spontaneous play makes it possible for the child to organize himself, to associate and work with other children in his own way. The activity of a child shows us not only what he wants but what we all want.'[47]

Froebel revised

Returning to the Froebel movement, towards the end of the nineteenth century, Froebel's educational ideas and the Romantic idealist philosophy they were enmeshed in had fallen out of fashion among those in the United States who were constructing the disciplinary field of the sciences of education, including G. Stanley Hall and John Dewey.[48] Based largely on university-based psychology, the disciplinary field of education began to emerge in the early twentieth century as differentiated from philosophy and the 'commonsense' of the teacher trainers. This necessitated a critical evaluation of Froebel's theories and kindergarten practice which had come to dominate the field of early childhood education in the United States, England and elsewhere, even if not always in the schools. What transpired was a thorough revision of what had become the kindergarten orthodoxy by Hall, Dewey and other men from newly established university departments of education.

Hall was awarded the first PhD in psychology in the United States and was prominent in founding educational psychology. This subject, with its positivist approach, soon came to dominate the discourse of early childhood education. Hall promoted Child Study, which, unlike Froebel's approach, relied on the empirical study of children – though Hall's commitment to Darwinian theory frequently inflected his interpretation of the results. Hall regarded the ideas and practices of Froebel and his mainly women followers as, 'in crying need of being supplemented, amplified, occasionally corrected, and in some definite respects abandoned'.[49] His polemics against the 'conservative' US Froebelians, in particular Susan Blow, a member of the St Louis Hegelian circle, were intense, gendered and vituperative. Regarding the gifts and occupations, Hall opined that 'the scheme as it left [Froebel's] own hands was a very inadequate embodiment of his educational ideas, even for his own time. He thought it a perfect grammar of play and an alphabet of industries; and in this opinion he was utterly mistaken'.[50] The phrase 'alphabet of industries' indicates that Hall was fully aware of the work aspect of the kindergarten, a view further reinforced by his description of the kindergarten as 'the little school factory' in which occupations were produced.[51]

In Hall's assault on the conservative Froebelians and their adherence to the gifts and occupations and 'the knights of the holy ghost' (Kant, Fichte and Hegel),[52] he cited research conducted in kindergartens in Santa Barbara in 1898 that provided evidence for the view that, given a choice, children would not choose the gifts and occupations if other play material was available. The Burks, who conducted the research, noted that children were consulted neither on their choice of play material nor on the use to be made of it.[53] This argument for child-chosen activities and free play drew from Blow the observation that children given choice of play would 'transform themselves into sneaking foxes and writhing rattlesnakes'.[54] As Shapiro observed of Blow's position, 'Free play was only one step from complete disorder in the classroom and moral chaos for the child'.[55] He further pointed out that the Hegelians feared the dark side of play and the consequences of kindergarten anarchy spilling out into other social institutions.

Hall's own treatment of play and work saw play from the perspective of contemporary psychology:

> Play is from within from congenital hereditary impulsion. It is the best of all methods of organizing instincts. Its cathartic or purgative function regulates irritability, which may otherwise be drained or vented in wrong directions, exactly as ... psychic traumata may, if over tense, result in 'hysterical convulsions'. It is also the best form of self-expression; and its advantage is variability, following the impulsion of the idle, perhaps hyperemic, and overnourished centers most ready to act.[56]

He saw work on the other hand as 'menial, cheerless, grinding, regular, and requir[ing] more precision and accuracy and, because attended with less ease and pleasure and economy of movement, [as] more liable to produce erratic habits'.[57] The solution, he thought, was to 'so suffuse work with the play spirit, and vice versa that the present distinction between work and play will vanish', and if this did not work, he added, 'We may at least find the true proportion and system between drudgery and recreation'.[58]

Deweyan pragmatism and play

John Dewey, who exchanged the Hegelianism of his youth for Pragmatism, also criticized Froebel's pedagogy and the use of the gifts and occupations in particular, but his tone was much more measured than Hall's. He objected to Froebel's notion of unfoldment on the grounds that concrete facts of experience gained from the gifts and occupations were held to be symbols of a transcendental idea of 'complete unfoldedness'. Since adults were the formulators of the symbolism, Dewey argued, what occurred was not development but 'as arbitrary and externally imposed a scheme of dictation as the history of instruction has ever seen'.[59] He added that 'kindergarten employments are calculated to give information regarding cubes, spheres, etc., and to form certain habits of manipulation of material (for everything must always be done "just so"), the absence of more vital purposes being supposedly compensated for by the alleged symbolism of the material used'.[60]

Rejecting the symbolism that Froebel, like the nature philosophers, thought pervaded the universe, Dewey wrote, 'There is, then, nothing mysterious or mystical in the discovery made by Plato and remade by Froebel that play is the chief, almost the only, mode of education for the child in the years of later infancy.'[61] For Dewey, the distinction between play and work was not one of ends, as Froebel had asserted, but of time span which influenced 'the directness of the connection of means and ends'.[62] He thought play activities, as they become more complex, 'pass gradually into work'. But crucially for Dewey play and work were both 'equally free and intrinsically motivated'.[63] He recognized, however, that the majority did not experience work like this, although, like Marx, he thought they should. 'If the mass of mankind has usually found in its industrial occupations nothing but evils which had to be endured for the sake of maintaining existence, the fault is not in the occupations, but in the conditions under which they are carried on.'[64] In these conditions, work became what he called drudgery and, he explained that

> activity carried on under conditions of external pressure or coercion ... is not intrinsically satisfying; it is a mere means for avoiding some penalty, or for gaining some reward at its conclusion. What is inherently repulsive is endured for the sake of averting something still more repulsive or of securing a gain hitched on by others. Under unfree economic conditions, this state of affairs is bound to exist. Work or industry offers little to engage the emotions and the imagination; it is a more or less mechanical series of strains. Only the hold which the completion of the work has upon a person will keep him going.[65]

This could be taken as an argument for children's rights and for free play, but if work for Dewey was unsatisfying, play had its negative side, too. It could, he wrote, become 'fooling', 'demoralizing', 'idle excitement' and 'idle amusement'. Dewey's disparagement of play even while he advocated it in school indicates his privileging of work over play, despite his criticism of the Puritan work ethic.[66] The ideological conflict in the Froebel movement engendered by Hall and Dewey was very intense, but the revisionists triumphed, as they did in England, and the content of play in the kindergarten was expanded beyond the gifts and occupations by their leading figures such as Maria Findlay, Grace Owen, Henrietta Brown Smith and Elsie Riach Murray.

Free play and the leisured classes

It is evident that Hall and, to a greater extent, Dewey, stressed the free aspect of play and thought that play in school should not be subject to much guidance. The conception of play as a freely chosen activity was also held by Johan Huizinga who, in his classic text, *Homo Ludens*, asserted that 'all play is a voluntary activity. Play to order is no longer play'.[67] The first and main characteristic of play for him was 'that it is free, is in fact freedom'.[68] To the objection that children must play due to their instincts, he responded that they play because 'they enjoy playing, and therein precisely lies their freedom'.[69] Not only is this a highly restrictive definition of play but also it presupposes conditions in which freedom through play can be realized. Often this view has been adopted by advocates of what might be termed 'an aristocratic' ideology of activity for its own sake, freed from necessity and scarcity. The right-wing philosopher Michael Oakeshott expressed this position well when he argued that

> in these days when the satisfaction of human wants is taken to be the only important activity, those who devise our systems of education are apt to find a place for all that I have called 'play' only if they can regard it as 'work' of another sort. In this situation, generations may be deprived of that acquaintance with the activities of *Homo ludens* that was once thought to be the better part of education.[70]

Etymologically, he observed 'school' comes from 'a Greek word *skole*', which means 'leisure' or 'free time.' A school was understood to be a place where one was introduced to those activities and attitudes towards the world that were *not* concerned with satisfying wants, where one was introduced to those activities of explanation and imagination that were 'free' because they were pursued for their own sake and were emancipated from the limitations and anxieties of 'work'.[71]

Marcuse and the 1960s

Challenges to work had been mounted by utopian writers such as Karl Marx's son-in-law, Paul Lafargue, who wrote *The Right to be Lazy*, in which he opposed not leisure but laziness to work, on the grounds that leisure was merely recuperation prior to work and laziness was a refusal of work.[72] However, as mentioned at the outset, the 1960s was perhaps the first period in history when the work ethic was widely criticized, and many claim these criticisms were greatly influenced by Herbert Marcuse, a member of the Frankfurt School who synthesized the theories of Freud and Marx to produce a critique of industrial capitalism.

Following Freud, Marcuse argued that civilization required a transition from the pleasure principle to the reality principle, which among other things necessitated a shift in values from joy (play) to toil (work).[73] This phylogenesis is mirrored in the development of the individual (ontogenesis), so the individual child has to give up the pleasure principle and accept the reality principle. However, the victory of the reality principle is never completely secured. Marcuse adopted Marx's account of alienation to claim that individuals spend the largest part of their life engaged in labour that was 'painful time', as it was marked by the absence of gratification.[74] Moreover, he also discussed Freud's view that humans were naturally averse to work, that work in civilization is labour, and labour is unpleasantness that has to be enforced. Marcuse accepted that some kinds of work, such as artistic work, were pleasurable, but he saw the bulk of work as imposed by necessity and not selected through a free choice.

While for Freud there was no escape from the constraining effects of civilization, Marcuse speculated about the possibility of a non-repressive civilization. He began with Freud's view that some areas of experience escaped repression: children's fantasy play and art. He also thought that the automation of processes of production could provide the necessary material conditions for 'the free play of human faculties *outside* the realm of alienated labor'.[75] Marx, contradicting his earlier position on alienation, had also glimpsed this possibility when he wrote that 'the realm of freedom actually begins only where labour which is determined by necessity and mundane considerations ceases'; and 'beyond it begins that development of human energy which is an end in itself, the true realm of freedom'.[76] The distinction between necessity and freedom, between labour and play, was caught by Marcuse in his assertion that 'play is *unproductive* and *useless* precisely because it cancels the repressive and exploitative traits of labor and leisure'.[77] For Marcuse, the realm of freedom was one in which, as Schiller had suggested a century previously, people would have the freedom to be what they ought to be, which was freedom itself: the freedom to play.

While the leisure industries have expanded rapidly since the 1960s and in the sphere of play in childhood, its commodification has expanded so that the toy and video games industry alone is worth globally US$69.493 billion. But Marcuse's utopia of freedom and play shows few signs of materializing. While some undoubtedly derive satisfaction from their work (after all Froebel pointed to a connection between research and play),[78] the majority of the world's workers probably do not. In many employment sectors, there appears to exist little scope for self-realization. In England, the move towards supply-side welfare-to-work measures has led to an expansion of the low-wage service sector. This also offers little opportunity for the self-development envisaged by the theorists who have been considered here.

Meanings of play today

In this context, it is hardly surprising that play in education has come in for so much criticism in recent years. The emergence in the United Kingdom of the Foundation Stage, the term given to the schooling of young children, was marked by an ideological conflict of considerable proportions. The first attempt to impose a curriculum on children in their early years was defeated when even the government's advisors rejected it; this was replaced by the Foundation Stage of early learning, which is a new stage of education for children age three to five which many practitioners found more acceptable not least because it reinstated a role for 'well-planned play'. Doubtless play in the early years is once again to be subordinated to other requirements. For Minister of State for Children Margaret Hodge, the 'foundation stage is about developing key learning skills such as listening, speaking, concentration, persistence and learning to work together and cooperate with other children. It is also about developing early communication, literacy and numeracy skills that will prepare young children for key stage 1 of the National Curriculum'.[79] The National Curriculum and its assessment procedures are a very good example of how the lifeworld, as Habermas has it, has been colonized by instrumental rationality.[80] In order to illustrate this process, I shall cite Professor Ted Wragg, who when writing of the foundation stage profile explained:

> The multicoloured booklets have pretty ministry logos on the cover. Teachers affix 117 labels for each five-year-old under 13 headings, including: (1) dispositions and attitudes; (2) social development; (3) emotional development; (4) language for communication and thinking; (5) linking sounds and letters; (6) reading; (7)

writing; (8) numbers as labels and for counting; (9) calculating; (10) shape, space and measures; (11) knowledge and understanding of the world; (12) physical development; and (13) creative development. Each of these 13 scales has nine levels, hence the 117 labels which must be affixed – and this must be done each term. A teacher of 30 reception-class children could tick and cross from 3,510 to over 10,000 boxes in a year.[81]

Unsurprisingly, as the instrumental rationality of the National Curriculum with its technologies of targets and constant assessments seeps down into the early years, researchers report that nurturing valuable play activities in school is not that easy.[82] A report by Tricia David concluded that the research in the area found that 'despite their general commitment to integrating play into the curriculum, teachers find a play-based pedagogy difficult to sustain, because precise learning outcomes can be difficult to achieve or measure, and progression in learning difficult to demonstrate'.[83] Teachers' attitudes towards play in the United States seem to be similar,[84] which suggests that the root of the problem lies not only in the performance indicator regime of the National Curriculum but in dominant views of what constitutes work. The issue of measurement, which, as Cutler and Waine have shown, is central to performance regimes that seek to capture intangible outcomes,[85] is the ground on which debates on play in education are now conducted. Defenders as well as critics of play both seek to quantify its utility, mainly from a cognitive perspective. Where once Froebelians grasped at Piaget's work to legitimate their pedagogy, now supporters of play turn to brain research. But citing this work to legitimate play, whatever its other merits, is to fall into the trap of positivism, of the belief that play's utility can be quantified and that rational debate will decide practice. Study of the history of education tends to suggest that the latter is unlikely. Many, such as Tina Bruce, think with good reason, that 'play cannot be pinned down and turned into a product of measurable learning'.[86]

As we have seen, play and work are opposed to each other even though they share many characteristics. Considerations of children's play rarely escape the views of play and work held by adults in relation to themselves. Moreover, for work to take on the characteristics of play, scarcity and necessity need to be overcome. In these conditions, it is vital that children's right to play in and out of school must be upheld not simply as a means of facilitating development and learning but because the freedom it entails is essential both for the child and for society.

Notes

1 Kevin J. Brehony, 'An "Undeniable" and "Disastrous" Influence? John Dewey and English Education (1895-1939)', *Oxford Review of Education* 23, no. 4 (1997): 427–5; Kevin J. Brehony, ' "Even Far Distant Japan" is "Showing an Interest" ': The English Froebel Movement's Turn to Sloyd.' *History of Education* 27, no. 3 (1998): 279–95; Kevin J. Brehony, 'English Revisionist Froebelians and the Schooling of the Urban Poor,' in *Practical Visionaries: Women, Education and Social Progress 1790-1930*, ed. Mary Hilton and Pam Hirsch (London: Longman, 2000), 183–99; Kevin J. Brehony, 'The Kindergarten in England 1851-1918', in *Kindergartens and*

Cultures: The Global Diffusion of an Idea, ed. Roberta Wollons (New Haven: Yale University Press), 59–86; Kevin J. Brehony, 'A "Socially Civilising Influence"? Play and the Urban "Degenerate"', *Paedagogica Historica* 39, nos. 1/2 (2003): 87–106.

2 Mark Twain, *The Adventures of Tom Sawyer* (Hartford: The American Publishing Company, 1876), 32.

3 Brian Sutton-Smith, *The Ambiguity of Play* (Cambridge, MA: Harvard University Press, 2001).

4 The Children's Society, *Grumpy Grown-Ups Stop Play, Reveals Playday Research*, 2003, http://www.the-childrens society.org.uk/news/news_items/playday_national_final. htm (accessed 5 December 2003).

5 Friedrich von Schiller, *On the Aesthetic Education of Man in a Series of Letters*, trans. Reginald Snell (Bristol: Thoemmes, 1994).

6 Richard Neville, *Play Power* (St. Albans: Paladin, 1970).

7 Department of Education and Science and Baroness Bridget Plowden, *Children and their Primary Schools* (London: HM Stationery Office, 1967).

8 Bertha von Marenholtz-Bülow, 'Woman's Educational Mission: Being an explanation of Friedrich Fröbel's System of Infant Gardens', in *The Origins of Nursery Education: Friedrich Froebel and the English System*, vol. IV, ed. Kevin J. Brehony (London: Routledge, 2001), 275–332.

9 Susan S. Isaacs, *The Nursery Years* (London: Routledge & Kegan Paul, 1929), 9.

10 John Locke, *Some Thoughts Concerning Education* (New York: Bartleby.com, 2001), www.bartleby.com/37/1/ (accessed 3 November 2003).

11 Eleonora Heerwart, 'The Kindergarten in Relation to the Various Industrial Products', in *The Health Exhibition Literature*, vol. XIII, ed. International Health Exhibition (London: William Clowes, 1884), 96–105; Karl Froebel, 'Explanation of the Kindergarten for those who are not Satisfied with the Present Results of Education, and Search for Principles which Promise Social Improvement', in *The Origins of Nursery Education: Friedrich Froebel and the English System*, vol. VI, ed. Kevin J. Brehony (London: Routledge, 2001), 167–249.

12 Bertha von Marenholtz-Bülow, *Hand Work and Head Work: Their Relation to one Another, and the Reform of Education According to the Principles of Froebel*, trans. Alice M. Christie (London: W. Swann Sonnenschein, 1883); F. W. A. Fröbel (Bertha von Marenholtz-Bülow), *A Connected Series of Playthings and Occupations for Early Childhood* (Dresden: J. F. Fischer's Printing Office, 1854), 4.

13 Bertha von Marenholtz-Bülow, *Woman's Educational Mission: Being an Explanation of Friederich Froebel's System of Infant Gardens*, trans. Countess Krockow von Wickerode (London: Dalton, 1855), 62.

14 Raymond Williams, *The Long Revolution* (Harmondsworth: Penguin, 1965).

15 Brehony, 'Even Far Distant Japan'.

16 Brehony, 'English Revisionist Froebelians'.

17 Elsie Riach Murray, *Froebel as a Pioneer in Modern Psychology* (Baltimore: Warwick & York, 1914), 126.

18 Friedrich Froebel, 'The Education of Man', in *The Origins of Nursery Education: Friedrich Froebel and the English System*, vol. I, ed. Kevin J. Brehony (London: Routledge, 2001), 37.

19 Ibid., 32.

20 Ibid., 35.

21 Ibid., 31.

22 Ibid., 32.

23 Ibid., 34.
24 William Hazlitt, *The Complete Works of Michael de Montaigne* (London: Templeman, 1842), 41; Froebel, 'The Education of Man', 55.
25 Ibid., 99, 102.
26 Ibid., 236–7.
27 Friedrich Froebel, 'Friedrich Froebel's Education by Development', in *The Origins of Nursery Education: Friedrich Froebel and the English System*, vol. IV, ed. Kevin J. Brehony (London: Routledge, 2001), 338.
28 Jean-Jacques Rousseau, *Émile* (London: Dent, 1974).
29 Froebel, 'The Education of Man', 20–1.
30 Friedrich Froebel, 'Mother's Songs and Selected Writings', in *The Origins of Nursery Education: Friedrich Froebel and the English System*, vol. III, ed. Kevin J. Brehony (London: Routledge, 2001).
31 Friedrich Froebel, 'Pedagogics of the Kindergarten', in *The Origins of Nursery Education: Friedrich Froebel and the English System*, vol. III, ed. Kevin J. Brehony (London: Routledge, 2001), 34.
32 Bertha von Marenholtz-Bülow, *Reminiscences of Friedrich Froebel* (Boston: Lee and Shepard, 1894).
33 Max Weber and Stephen Kalberg, *The Protestant Ethic and the Spirit of Capitalism* (Oxford: Roxbury Publishing, 2002); Antoine Faivre, *Theosophy, Imagination, Tradition: Studies in Western Esotericism* (Albany: State University of New York Press, 2000).
34 Charles Taylor, *Sources of the Self: The Making of Modern Identity* (Cambridge, MA: Harvard University Press, 1989).
35 Ibid.
36 Paul Ricoeur and George H. Taylor, *Lectures on Ideology and Utopia* (New York: Columbia University Press, 1986).
37 Karl Marx, *Economic and Philosophic Manuscripts of 1844* (Marxists Internet Archive, 2000), http://www.marxists.org/archive/marx/works/1844/manuscripts/labour.htm (accessed 3 September 2003).
38 Ibid.
39 István Mészáros, *Marx's Theory of Alienation* (London: Merlin, 1970).
40 Friedrich Engels, *The Condition of the Working Class in England* (London: Panther, 1969).
41 Karl Marx, *Capital: A Critique of Political Economy. Volume 1*, trans. Ben Fowkes (London: Penguin Books in association with New Left Review, 1990), 618.
42 Stephen Castles and Wiebke Wüstenberg, *The Education of the Future* (London: Pluto, 1979).
43 Nikolai Bukharin and Evgenii Preobrazhensky, *The ABC of Communism* (Marxists Internet Archive, 2001), http://www.marxists.org/archive/bukharin/works/1920/abc/10.htm (accessed 9 August 2003).
44 Anton S. Makarenko, *Lectures to Parents. Lecture 4, 'Play'* (Marxists Internet Archive, 2002), https://www.marxists.org/reference/archive/makarenko/works/lectures/lec04.html (accessed 7 November 2003).
45 Nicholas Beattie, *The Freinet Movements of France, Italy, and Germany, 1920-2000: Versions of Educational Progressivism* (Lewiston: E. Mellen Press, 2002).
46 C. L. R. James, *On the Woman Question: An Orientation* (Marxists Internet Archive 2002), https://www.marxists.org/archive/james-clr/works/1951/09/woman-question.htm (accessed 2 December 2003).

47 Ibid.
48 Marc Depaepe, 'Experimental Research in Education, 1890-1940: Historical Processes Behind the Development of a Discipline in Western Europe and the United States', *Aspects of Education* 47 (1992): 67–93.
49 G. Stanley Hall, *Educational Problems* (New York: D. Appleton, 1911), 2.
50 Ibid., 17.
51 Ibid., 18.
52 Ibid., 31.
53 Barbara Beatty, *Preschool Education in America* (New Haven: Yale University Press, 1995).
54 Susan Blow, *Educational Issues in the Kindergarten* (New York: D. Appleton, 1908), 176.
55 Michael S. Shapiro, *Child's Garden: The Kindergarten Movement from Froebel to Dewey* (University Park: Pennsylvania State University Press, 1983), 124.
56 G. Stanley Hall, *Youth: Its Education, Regimen and Hygiene* (New York: D. Appleton, 1907), 116.
57 Ibid.
58 Ibid.
59 John Dewey, *Democracy and Education* (New York: Macmillan, 1916), 68.
60 Ibid., 233.
61 John Dewey, *How We Think* (London: D.C. Heath & Co., 1910), 162.
62 Dewey, *Democracy and Education*, 238.
63 Ibid., 241.
64 Ibid., 235.
65 Ibid., 240.
66 Ibid., 242.
67 Johan Huizinga, *Homo Ludens: A Study of the Play-Element in Culture* (London: Routledge, 1949), 7.
68 Ibid., 8.
69 Ibid.
70 Michael Oakeshott, 'Work and Play', *First Things* (June 1995), http://www.firstthings.com/article/1995/06/003-work-and-play (accessed 4 January 2004).
71 Ibid.
72 Paul Lafargue, *The Right to be Lazy* (Marxists Internet Archive, 2000), http://www.marxists.org/archive/lafargue/1883/lazy/index.htm (accessed 16 November 2003).
73 Herbert Marcuse, *Eros and Civilization: A Philosophical Inquiry into Freud* (Boston: Beacon Press, 1955).
74 Ibid., 51.
75 Ibid., 45.
76 Karl Marx, *Capital. Volume 3 Chapter XLVIII The Trinity Formula*, http://www.marxists.org/archive/marx/works/1894-c3/ch48.htm (accessed 16 January 2004).
77 Marcuse, *Eros and Civilization*, 195.
78 Froebel, 'Friedrich Froebel's Education by Development'.
79 Department for Education and Employment/Qualifications and Curriculum Authority, *Curriculum Guidance for the Foundation Stage* (London: QCA, 2000), 2.
80 Jürgen Habermas, *The Theory of Communicative Action; Lifeworld and System: A Critique of Functionalist Reason* (Cambridge: Polity Press, 1987).
81 Ted Wragg, 'Are they Children, or Tickboxes?', *The Guardian*. London (4 March 2003).

82 Siân Adams, Elise Alexander, Mary Jane Drummond and Janet Moyles, *Inside the Foundation Stage: Recreating the Reception Year* (London: Association of Teachers and Lecturers, 2004).

83 Diane Hofkins, 'Fair Play is not so Easy', *Times Education Supplement* (14 November 2003).

84 Mac H. Brown and Nancy K. Freeman, ' "We don't Play that way at Preschool": The Moral and Ethical Dimensions of Controlling Children's Play', in *Early Education and Care, and Reconceptualizing Play*, ed. Stuart Reifel and Mac H. Brown (London: Emerald Group, 2001), 259–74.

85 Tony Cutler and Barbara Waine, *Managing the Welfare State: Text and Sourcebook* (Oxford: Berg, 1997).

86 Richard House, 'Psychology and Early Years Learning: Affirming the Wisdom of Waldorf', in *Child Development and Pedagogical Issues*, ed. David Mitchell (Fair Oaks, CA: Association of Waldorf Schools of North America, 2003), 69–83.

Part One

International Movement of Ideas: Froebelian Education in Time and Place

Figure 3.1 Elise van Calcar as a young writer c. 1850 aged c. 27 years. A lithograph by A. J. Ebule, printed in J. H. Sikemeier, *Elise van Calcar-Schiotling. Haar leven en omgeving, haar arbeid, haar geestesrichting* (Haarlem: Tjeenk Willink & Zn, 1921), 112.

3

Happiness, Play and Bourgeois Morality: The Early Years of Froebel Schooling in the Netherlands, 1858–1904

Nelleke Bakker

The introduction of Froebel's kindergarten in the Netherlands was largely the work of Elise van Calcar-Schiotling (1822–1904). She has been called 'the Dutch Baroness von Marenholtz-Bülow' (1810–93) after Froebel's German patron.[1] Both women appointed themselves ambassadors of Froebel's educational principles and by 1900 both were famous across Europe as a result of their writings and their travels. Whereas the Baroness Bertha von Marenholtz-Bülow is recalled in many histories of kindergarten education, Van Calcar is remembered only in the Netherlands. Van Calcar's introduction to Froebel's life, work and ideas, published in 1879, was translated into German in 1883 and Italian in 1900.[2] Her practical guide for teachers, published in 1880, was translated into French in 1882.[3] She was well known among the first generation of Froebelians in Germany and elsewhere and corresponded with them. Van Calcar also had access to Froebel's manuscripts, and accompanied Marenholtz to Brussels and Paris and on visits to model kindergartens.[4] Like many early Froebelians, Van Calcar was also a feminist. At the international feminist conference alongside the 1878 World Exhibition in Paris, she defended the kindergarten against accusations that it made the child work instead of educating her.[5]

Thanks to Kevin Brehony, Ann Taylor Allen and authors of this volume, readers of English literature know about the English, German and American Froebelian pioneers and their revolutionary agendas,[6] whereas the Netherlands is still a *terra incognita*. Unlike the German emigrant Froebelians who travelled to England and the United States, Van Calcar was content with the status quo of bourgeois society, except for the role of women. Therefore, Van Calcar represents a different kind of Froebelianism, one that did not support wide social change but rather a conservative maternalist version of feminism. This chapter outlines the development of the kindergarten in the Netherlands between 1858 and 1904, from the first contact between the two women to Van Calcar's death, and provides insights into the successes and failures of Van Calcar's Froebelian activism. It compares Van Calcar's activities and writings on early childhood education with Marenholtz's work[7] and Froebel's own,[8] and analyses Van Calcar's efforts amidst the development of Froebel schooling in the Netherlands.

The introduction of Froebel's pedagogy by Van Calcar: 1858–62

Elise van Calcar, who had trained as a teacher, was a moderately successful writer of didactic novels and children's stories in her late thirties when she met Bertha von Marenholtz while staying at a countryside vicarage in the Netherlands in 1858.[9] Their host, Ottho Heldring, who was developing a pioneering residential institution for penitent women prostitutes, was a member of the Réveil, a northern European romantic evangelical movement, dominated by the elite that emphasized personal piety as inspiration for social work. Van Calcar's letters and autobiographical writing reveal that she was glad to have been admitted to this orthodox Protestant movement. Having searched for 'true' religion throughout her adolescent life and convinced that women as 'spiritual mothers' had a special task in taking care of the poor,[10] she felt attracted to this pietistic movement, to its positive attitude towards women's active participation in philanthropy, and to its maternalist feminist orientation.[11] Born into a humble family herself, she was, moreover, happy to be in close contact with the Calvinist elite.[12] The hosting vicar and Marenholtz had probably become acquainted while travelling and visiting Christian philanthropic institutions in Germany. In her Froebel biography, Van Calcar suggests that the baroness was invited to the Netherlands by the Dutch royal family.[13]

According to her own account, Van Calcar decided to become Froebel's Dutch missionary after being introduced to Froebel's didactic principles by means of the playthings the baroness had shown to her host and his other guests. In the story of her sudden 'conversion', Van Calcar presents herself as an already well-known person who had been mentioned to the baroness as someone worth meeting.[14] Soon after the meeting, Van Calcar participated in one of the baroness's Froebel courses in Paris. In 1860 Froebel's educational message made her cross a symbolic threshold in public space and step forward as the first Dutch woman public speaker, giving lectures on Froebel's pedagogy. Likewise, it was his message that made her plead for a higher level of education for girls. Like Marenholtz-Bülow,[15] Van Calcar believed that every girl had to be educated in such a way that she could become a Froebelian mother, equipped with knowledge about the child and her sensorial, intellectual and motor development.

Van Calcar's lectures coincided with the publication of a six-volume work on early childhood education, *Onze ontwikkeling of de macht der eerste indrukken* (Our Development or The Power of the First Impressions, 1861–62), based on her interpretation of Froebel's theory. She supported Froebel's call for reform of early education, arguing that its emphasis should be more on play and the pleasure of self-activity and less on passive learning and scholastic subjects. She agreed with Froebel that ages three to six were the 'true' age for kindergarten education. She also supported his assertion that mothers could start stimulating the child's active self-development immediately after birth, but unlike Froebel, she focused exclusively on the mother as caregiver and educator in the child's first three years.

Despite her general adherence to Froebel's teachings, the central concept in Van Calcar's series was an idea of her own: 'the power of the first impressions', which covered both the importance of active, early learning and the enormous influence of the mother on a child's life. It was important that a mother let nature have its way and limit herself to enabling a child's 'natural' self-activation. This restraint was inspired by the conviction that God had put everything in a child's lovely nature, which Van Calcar – like Froebel – assumed to be governed by 'God's law of order, harmony and beauty'. A 'natural' kind of upbringing was one in which 'everything was given its due place, time, rank and rate'. This implied that body and mind, reason and feeling should be in harmony and that it was the mother's job to make this possible.[16]

The pedagogical reserve and the patience with a child's 'natural' pace of development, which Van Calcar advised, was limited to a child's cognitive, sensorial and physical development; in the domain of moral upbringing, on the other hand, she deviated from Froebel's concept of development, presenting an enlightened urgency to interfere mixed with a Calvinist fear of sin and moral contamination. In Van Calcar's view, the moral world was the opposite of the natural world and could not be left alone. Virtue had to be instilled, as 'leaving a child to nature … is leaving it to the blind play of his natural instinct to become an animal'.[17] For Van Calcar, nature was a garden to be worked upon, not paradise. The first impressions would mould the child's character; therefore, moral training by mothers was to start as soon as possible. A child's instinct had to be regulated – not gratified – with the aid of love, patience, order and regularity. Sin could easily develop in a child and it was a mother's fault when this happened. God had made the child as a pure but incomplete human being, 'open to perfection'.[18] Child-rearing was thus a mandate, not a gift.

Van Calcar's series opened with an appeal to bourgeois readers to transform motherhood into a 'science of mothers', based on knowledge of the child and equal to a profession, a theme that cannot be found in Froebel's writing but is present in a preface by Marenholtz to a Flemish introduction to Froebel's method, published in 1860,[19] and in her *Die Arbeit und die Neue Erziehung nach Fröbels Methode* (1866).[20] For Van Calcar, child-rearing was the essence of true womanhood: 'Thou are educators because thou are women.'[21] In this way she linked child-rearing to social work as developed in Réveil circles. Femininity included the qualities of a good mother: love, patience and self-sacrifice. Maidservants, however – like any other 'hired nurses' – were excluded from educational competence; she called them stupid, loveless and uncivilized. Men were ignored. These disqualifications along the lines of class and gender did not have their origin in Froebel's writing or practice, as he always worked with male teachers and country girls in his kindergartens and wrote consistently about 'educators' in general.[22] For Van Calcar, as a maternalist feminist only the mother was capable of ensuring a child's moral improvement.[23] Froebel's plea for active stimulation of young children's development provided her with an argument for the importance of preschool education and of a mother's role in moral-religious upbringing. This was helpful with audiences used to the negative stereotype of women as weak and indulgent mothers, fed by the Calvinist tradition that put religion in the centre of child-rearing and which considered fathers the most important and best qualified educators.[24] With hindsight we can say that Froebel's theory has been instrumental to Van Calcar's promotion of her version of feminism.

Compared to Marenholtz's ideas on women's educational mission, Van Calcar had a stronger belief in feminine intuition and was, consequently, less focused on the need for serious child study by girls wanting to become a Froebel teacher. The most important difference between the two Froebel propagandists is the lack of a social mission of the kindergarten in Van Calcar's project. While Marenholtz referred to it as *Volkskindergarten* and mentioned educating the 'good taste and moral feeling of the lower classes' as an aim,[25] Van Calcar meant Froebel's method to be applied solely by bourgeois mothers and teachers in schools for the upper class. Marenholtz did not exclude maidservants or girls from the lower classes in general from Froebel training, only from becoming head teachers.[26]

In the parts of her series on play Van Calcar stuck to Froebel's spirit and words. Play was a child's 'self-instruction, his examination of the world'.[27] The first kinds of play concerned movement and experimenting with the body. In the final parts of her series she introduced Froebel's first six gifts as instruments necessary to stimulate a child's physical and mental development. She also presented these as a means for helping children attain inner harmony, something for which women had a natural talent. Play, self-activity, industry and productivity embodied a young child's natural way of learning. Passivity, such as listening and watching, was unnatural. Froebel's playthings met children's need for active discovery of the qualities and the symbolic meaning of different materials, forms and colours. Van Calcar, like Froebel, emphasized the importance of pleasure in creating things as essential experiences for a 'child worker'.[28] More than Froebel, she emphasized order as essential in a child's play. For example, for Van Calcar, the prescribed order of the use of the gifts and occupations was essential to make the transition from playing to learning which they were meant to accompany. Van Calcar saw order as one of the goals of Froebel's method: inspiring 'love for order, for work, for the beauty of nature, for his friends and care-takers, and for ... the Creator'.[29]

The early years of Froebel schooling: 1863–4

Van Calcar's lecturing tour and her six-volume introduction to Froebel's work stimulated the establishment in Amsterdam in 1863 of two Froebel 'schools' for 'children from the civilised ranks of society' as opposed to the existing infant schools that accommodated the young children of poor working mothers and which had only very limited educational ambitions. The Froebel schools admitted children from the age of three to eight and provided them with an education aiming at a 'harmonious development of their physical and mental capacities'.[30]

However, after visiting the two schools in the first year of their existence the city's health inspector, Samuel Coronel, reported negatively on them, as on all other infant schools. He complained that 'blind following of the so-called Froebel method without a clear insight into his intentions' produced 'a mechanical drilling or plain training of skills'.[31] In his view the Froebel schools were no better than the elementary schools, which at the time were dominated by collective instruction and passivity of the pupils. The inspector also criticized the admission of children over six years of age, claiming their presence had unduly stimulated the inclusion of scholastic subjects in the curriculum.[32] He criticized other infant schools for applying only parts of Froebel's method, such as individual 'exercises'. Nevertheless, the inspector envisaged that free play and individual activities, guided by Froebel's gifts and occupations, should dominate the infant school curriculum, alongside physical exercise, singing, dancing and the exercise of all the senses and of speech. He insisted that preparation for reading and writing should not be practised before the age of five, and that the Bible was to be kept out of such schools.[33]

In spite of this critical report, collective instruction and the Bible remained a feature of Dutch infant schools, although authorities – including directors of teacher training institutions – embraced Froebel's method as the best way to meet young children's educational needs. The number of Froebel schools grew quickly to over a hundred.[34] Van Calcar provided them with practical guidelines.[35] Play was introduced as a subject in the curriculum of all high-quality infant schools.[36] However, there are no indications of substantial improvement in the poor quality of the majority of infant schools – those accommodating the children of working mothers – at that time.

Froebel's method according to Van Calcar: 1864–80

While Froebel's method was embraced by education and health authorities, Van Calcar continued to write in the spirit of Marenholtz, who fed her maternalist feminism. Inspired by the baroness, she added the glorification of motherhood and the natural feminine talent for child-rearing to Dutch Froebelianism. However, even for Van Calcar, motherly intuition was not enough. In order for motherhood to become a 'science', girls needed training. At least two of her treatises gave a stimulus to debate in the Netherlands on the quality of bourgeois girls' education, which started in the 1860s and was one of the first expressions of awakening feminist consciousness. All of the participants – among whom were educators, enlightened reformers and women activists – attacked the existing taboo on professional labour for unmarried bourgeois women and criticized the low intellectual level of the existing girls' secondary schools. Apart from a few radicals, they declined co-education and preferred a curriculum that prepared girls for household, motherhood and a future profession. A minority, among whom Van Calcar was most prominent, advocated an even narrower curriculum, focusing on domestic duties and preparing girls only for 'feminine' occupations such as maternity nursing, childcare and teaching infants.[37]

Van Calcar's plan for a Froebel training institute for girls, published in 1864,[38] seems to have triggered this debate. It was the fruit of several years spent tutoring girls in her own home and was implemented in her Dutch House of Education (*Nederlandsch Opvoedingshuis*), which was first established in Leyden but soon moved to Wassenaar, a village where her husband had recently been appointed mayor. The House was meant to be a laboratory where 'civilized' girls were trained to become Froebel teachers. Its curriculum was limited to subjects such as childcare and Froebel's method, which was practised in a model kindergarten. Compared to Marenholtz's Froebel teacher training programme,[39] this one was limited, as subjects like physics, physiology dietetics and anthropology were not included. After eight years the House closed down because of financial trouble, struggles among the directors and a declining number of pupils.[40] Van Calcar's recent conversion to Christian spiritualism[41] may have been another reason behind the institution's decline.

In 1873, Van Calcar's prize-winning essay on bourgeois girls' education, *De dubbele roeping der vrouw* (Woman's Double Vocation), provided an answer to the question of how women could 'earn their own bread before marriage' and still 'create blessing and prosperity at home'. Again, the answer was a type of training similar to the one in The House. Only 'a harmonious, many-sided and gradual training of body, mind and feeling' would prepare a girl for her 'double vocation', so that she could have a job and be 'saved' for her future family with all her 'sweetness'.[42] With this essay she pushed the debate on girls' education in another direction. The issue was no longer whether a girl would benefit from a serious secondary education, but how far her intellectual training should reach. Van Calcar, like Marenholtz,[43] warned against 'one-sided' intellectual training, which would ruin the softer 'feminine' character; instead moral qualities were to be decisive.[44] Among evangelical feminists across the West, this and the linking up of Froebelianism with the women's issue were accepted positions. This explains the invitation of Van Calcar to lecture on Froebel at the first international feminist conference accompanying the 1878 World Exhibition in Paris.[45]

Van Calcar's writing was more successful than her practical work. In the years that followed the closing of The House, she published a manual explaining the principles of Froebelianism and a practical guide. Both books were reprinted repeatedly until after her death in 1904. The manual *Frobels Methode* (Froebel's Method, 1875) introduced the theory behind the method, as well as the range of activities that comprised it. The book focused on the value of a well-organized kindergarten. She called it a 'delightful place' for a young child, because there was so much more to learn there than in an ordinary infant school. It was the best place to learn not only morals but also social skills such as friendliness and 'self-restraint by collision with different inclinations'.[46] Play was the central activity. It was the teacher's responsibility to ensure that children could learn everything possible from playing with Froebel's gifts and occupations: thinking, moving, building and speaking; observing and recognizing forms, colours, numbers, differences and similarities, unity and diversity and finally letters and numbers; experiencing rhythm and beauty; and acquiring all kinds of manual dexterity such as folding, braiding, drawing, pinning, cutting and tearing. Together these exercises of the body, the senses and the brain would prepare a child in a natural way for the first steps in reading, writing and arithmetic, but not before the age of five.[47] Compared to Froebel's own writing on play, Van Calcar's put more emphasis on learning to think, on usefulness and on speech exercise, which in her view could enrich play by means of singing songs and recounting verse. To this end she added songs and music to the book.

Van Calcar's practical guide for kindergarten teachers, *Maakt de kinderen gelukkig* (Make the Children Happy, 1880), provided exercises and suggestions for how to use the gifts and occupations. Van Calcar advised bourgeois families to join forces in a house with a big garden 'to establish a delightful place for all children in their neighbourhood' in order to put an end to the suffering of all those 'poor little victims of unknowing nursemaids, being carted around without any physical or sensorial exercise'. A design for buildings and indoor and outdoor space was added to the book. Children aged between two-and-a-half and seven years, divided into two age groups, were welcome. Van Calcar advised families to hire as head teacher 'a civilised woman, with good manners, a loving heart and pure speech',[48] who was acquainted with all the things she was expected to teach, which again amounted to more limited requirements compared to Marenholtz's ideal of a well-educated head teacher.[49] Teaching assistants could be trained on the job and study the theory in the evenings, according to Van Calcar.

As in her six volumes on Froebel's theory, Van Calcar's practical guide emphasized moral education and order. The child had to learn that 'everything had a fixed time, a specific extent, and a place of its own'. A loving woman would teach 'respect, trust, gratefulness, and love', without which a child would grow up as 'a slave of his lower instincts'. The virtues that she mentioned explicitly were love for the truth and equity. The list of vices was longer, ranging from disobedience to laziness, lying, anger and vanity. Punishment or reward would not be of much help, but a positive, encouraging approach would teach a child how to keep busy, to love her work and prevent boredom, the prime source of children's faults.[50] There was no room for toys other than the ones that could be used in Froebel exercises. Play had to be useful and to support bourgeois morality and Calvinist work ethos.

In 1879, Van Calcar published a hagiographic intellectual biography of Froebel on behalf of the Dutch Head Teachers Society; it was widely acclaimed and translated into two other languages.[51] The book was based on a study of personal documents and correspondence, edited volumes of Froebel's collected works and publications by his pupils, including Marenholtz's *Erinnerungen an Fr. Fröbel* (Memories of Froebel, 1875). Van Calcar included translated fragments from his letters and a refutation of certain objections against Froebel education. In addition to the confusion about children at work, which Van Calcar had addressed at the feminist conference alongside the World Exhibition in Paris in 1878 by explaining the difference between child labour and the 'child worker' in the kindergarten, she mentioned some other objections. They concerned a mechanical application of the method, the passivity of children being taught instead of teaching themselves and a supposed lack of order in a kindergarten caused by freedom to choose an occupation. She countered each of these by pointing to a degeneration of Froebel schooling and a lack of understanding of the real meaning and correct application of the method. As she explained, Froebel's freedom was not meant to create a 'wilderness'; rather the kindergarten was designed as a sheltered area in which plants could grow freely but were taken care of and 'cut back' as needed. For Van Calcar, Froebelian freedom meant order, harmony and an equilibrium of loving, respectful and trusting relationships.[52]

Figure 3.2 Elise van Calcar, painted by J. Gerstenhauer to celebrate her 80th birthday, 19 November 1902. Collection Nationaal Onderwijsmuseum, Dordrecht, the Netherlands.

The Leyden Training School: 1882–1900

By the early 1880s Van Calcar had made so many converts that the Dutch kindergarten movement had to find a way to continue training their teachers after her own training institution, the Dutch House of Education, closed in 1872. In 1882 a headmaster took over one of the part-time training courses for kindergarten teachers and turned it into a day school. This Leyden Training School developed into the new centre from which Froebel's ideas were spread and school practice was guided. Under the leadership of Wybrandus Haanstra, the institute promoted a practical version of Froebel's method, taught in a preschool with a curriculum that focused on scholastic skills. The so-called Haanstra Method developed into the leading programme of the Dutch kindergartens. It incorporated Herbartian elements and rational concepts, such as 'learning steps' and empirical mechanisms of 'perception', into Froebel's naturalistic philosophy of learning.[53] What is important for our story about Van Calcar is what this method left out: Froebel's philosophy of the child, his concept of the universe as God-ordained harmony, his ideas about the relationship between God, nature and human existence, his emphasis on the importance of spontaneous activity and play for a child's development, and his followers' trust in women as the naturally competent gardeners young children needed. Haanstra left out everything that mattered to Van Calcar.

A closer look at his method, which earned two gold medals at international exhibitions of teaching methods in Paris in 1889 and 1900, reveals that Haanstra pragmatically selected one concept out of the multiplicity of Froebel's key concepts. For him, learning by contrast was essential. In every lesson contrasting impressions were to stimulate a child's accurate observation and the drawing of logical conclusions. Preparation for reading, writing and arithmetic were key aims. Reading progressed through seven 'developmental steps' for which he developed a picture-writing course on the basis of the principle of confronting a child with only one new difference at a time.[54] Although self-activity and pleasure in work remained important in the Dutch Froebel schools, free play was marginalized because the focus was shifted towards learning and collective activity.

In the meantime, the number of Froebel schools increased considerably. Many of the traditional infant schools for working-class children adopted the name of 'Froebel school'. These schools had a growing number of certified teachers. By the end of the century, a 'Froebel school' was synonymous with a good, well-organized infant school using Haanstra's Method. In 1890, with the support of local communities, nine institutions provided infant teacher training, for which Haanstra's interpretation of Froebel provided the main inspiration. It is indicative of the overall improvement of the quality of infant schooling that in 1900 the first Dutch university teacher of education, Jan Gunning, encouraged bourgeois mothers to have their children attend a Froebel school to learn social skills and mix with children from humble social backgrounds – children who now composed the majority of the pupils of these schools.[55]

Van Calcar's disappointment: 1898–1904

The central role of Haanstra's Method in the Dutch kindergarten largely explains Van Calcar's disappointment at old age with the way kindergarten pedagogy had developed. The number of Froebel schools had grown, the principles were widely known and a good infant school almost certainly was a Froebel school. However, according to Van Calcar, then in her seventies, many of these schools were not worthy of the Froebel name because of a mechanical implementation of prescribed routines. Moreover, as she sadly observed, hardly any had a playground of sufficient size, let alone a garden. That is why, in 1898, she set up another model kindergarten in her own home, now in The Hague. In addition to the kindergarten, she founded a course for nursemaids and future mothers called a School for Mothers, where the 'true' spirit of Froebel would reign.[56] The latter turned out to be another failure, as few women wanted to be educated this way. The model kindergarten, where some eighty children were educated according to Van Calcar's ideal, continued for a few years.[57]

At the National Exhibition of Women's Labour in 1898, however, Van Calcar's School for Mothers received praise and approval from the assembled Dutch feminists. In spite of the exhibition's focus on labouring women, motherhood was adulated. The closing conference was dedicated to mothers and educators, and Van Calcar was one of the plenary speakers. Her audience agreed with her concept of a 'science of mothers', implying that women would have to be educated for motherhood as for any other craft. In the discussion, however, the Froebel school met with opposition from bourgeois women who preferred home education for their own children and feared that the kindergarten would contaminate their offspring with the 'impurity' and 'immorality' of poor children, a kind of opposition Van Calcar herself had unwillingly inspired.[58]

From the late 1870s, Van Calcar spent most of her time on spiritualism, but child-rearing continued to be important for her. It was the subject of her last book, *Het jonge leven* (Young life, 1905), published after her death.[59] In it, Van Calcar shows a romantic disappointment in modernity, especially in the industrializing, more rational and more egalitarian society of the turn of the century. Throughout her last years she kept emphasizing the importance of moral upbringing and of parental authority. Instead of insisting on women's vocation in social welfare, she ended up as a promoter of the romantic ideology of domesticity by suggesting middle-class mothers turn their homes into castles, strong enough to resist the spirit of materialism.[60] By 1900 this anti-materialism was not uncommon and was part of a wide spectrum of alternative movements which reverted to the romanticism of the early nineteenth century as part of their critique of contemporary scientism.[61] Spiritualism was one of these movements.

Canonization of Froebel's method: 1900–4

In the early years of the twentieth century, the majority of the Dutch infant schools used Haanstra's interpretation of Froebel's method. It was standardized and canonized, particularly by Johanna Wierts van Coehoorn-Stout's manual *De kindertuin* (The Kindergarten, 1904).[62] As far as the theory was concerned, this manual was equally indebted to Van Calcar's work. Montessori teaching was introduced on a small scale from 1914, attracting primarily children from the bourgeoisie. During the interwar years, elements of the two kinds of infant teaching mixed and created a new amalgam, which became the rule after the Second World War.[63]

Despite the absence of a legal foundation for infant schooling, progress was made in terms of professionalization. Around 1900 it was, for example, generally accepted that teachers in a Froebel school needed a certificate, the requirements for which had become more substantial than in the days of Van Calcar's House of Education – although being 'civilized' was still important.[64] The concept of a 'science of mothers' was approved of in educational journals. Van Calcar's idea that girls who had trained and worked in a kindergarten would improve the level of mothering in their own future families was shared by feminists and pedagogues alike. Well-trained mothers would contribute to a better and happier society. This perspective fitted in with the reigning pedagogical optimism. Experts agreed that early childhood had become a serious educational domain and that the teaching of three- to six-year-old children needed legislation, quality control and standardization of teaching staff requirements. Nevertheless, none of these were introduced in the new Education Act of 1920. Dutch infant schooling had to wait until 1956 before it was regulated by law and state funding was guaranteed.

In the early-twentieth-century discourse on the use of Froebel schooling, however, Van Calcar's prejudice against working-class girls and mothers was only one voice. Others, such as Gunning and Wierts van Coehoorn-Stout, were keen on a kindergarten where children from all classes would be educated together the way Marenholtz had advocated. Bourgeois children would be freed from ignorant nursemaids, and working-class children would move from the hell of a creche staffed by unqualified and disinterested caretakers to the heaven of a Froebel school's enriching environment. It would educate senses and morals, create a sense of community and remedy egoistic inclinations, Wierts van Coehoorn-Stout claimed.[65] Having the children of the masses attend a Froebel school was 'a national interest', Gunning insisted.[66] In his contributions to educational journals, he criticized bourgeois women for their selfishness in keeping their young children at home when they would learn so much more in a Froebel school: from order and obedience to sharing and playing together. Kindergarten fitted a young child's nature and satisfied her need for activity, play and playmates. A kindergarten would stimulate a child to keep herself busy, Gunning and others claimed. Moreover, he contended that a Froebel school provided for a gradual transition from 'natural' learning at home to 'artificial' learning at the elementary school.[67] Froebel schools were increasingly referred to as 'preparatory schooling'.

Around 1904, we must conclude, Froebel schooling was valued first of all in terms of its use on an individual level from which society would profit indirectly. A popular guide to Froebel education summarized it as promoting 'lust for labour ... seeing, observing, working regularly; getting used to order, cleanliness, politeness'.[68]

Conclusion

Although she played the leading part, Elise van Calcar was not the only person who shaped the introduction and early development of Froebel's kindergarten in the Netherlands. Her reading of Froebel, like Marenholtz's, emphasized women's role in infant education and the importance of educating women to become competent Froebel teachers. Froebel's theory on the importance of preschool education and his method provided the reason to turn motherhood into a 'science'. Van Calcar's educational requirements of girls wanting to become Froebel teachers, however, were considerably lower than those of the German Froebel propagandist. Unlike Marenholtz and Froebelians in the English-speaking world, Van Calcar never conceived of Froebel schooling as a social project, meant to improve the lives of working-class children. She continued to disqualify nursemaids as educators because of what she considered their lack of civilization. She stuck to Froebel education as a maternalist, bourgeois feminist project to promote motherhood as a serious occupation, a tendency that resonated in the Dutch discourse on infant schooling. Nevertheless, despite Van Calcar's class consciousness, the Dutch Froebel school became an institute of popular education before the end of the nineteenth century.

In spite of Van Calcar's respect for children's nature and a sincere emphasis on the happiness of the child throughout her work, one finds in her writings a continuous fear of moral degeneration if a child was not educated properly from her earliest days. The power of the first impressions was a mandate, not a gift, to mothers. In her eyes, Froebel education and the proper use of the gifts and occupations, as well as the harmony and synthesis they would bring about in a child's mind and life, would protect her against the threat of immorality. It must have been painful for Van Calcar that the reading of Froebel's method that came to dominate Dutch Froebel schools at the end of the nineteenth century focused on learning by contrast instead of by synthesis. Although at the turn of the century self-activity and pleasure at work remained important in the Dutch Froebel schools, free play was marginalized because of a focus on the preparation of scholastic competences. Therefore, it was no accident that the institutions were called 'schools' instead of 'gardens'. Nevertheless, towards the end of Van Calcar's life, the guiding emphasis on play as useful and supportive of bourgeois morality and Calvinist work ethos was stamped just as much by her own values and outlook as by the broader Dutch cultural climate.

Notes

1 J. H. Gunning Wzn., 'Voorrede', in *Frederik Fröbel: Hoe hij opvoeder werd en wat de kinderwereld hem openbaarde*, 2nd edn, ed. Elise van Calcar (Amsterdam: Wierts van Coehoorn ([1879] 1910), V–VII.

2 Ibid.

3 Elise van Calcar, *Maakt de kinderen gelukkig: Beknopte handleiding om zich in korten tijd Fröbel's opvoedingsleer eigen te maken*, 6th edn (Maassluis: N.V. Maassluische Boekhandel ([1880] 1912) III–VII.

4 J. H. Sikemeier, *Elise van Calcar Schiotling: Haar leven en omgeving, haar arbeid, haar geestesrichting* (Haarlem: Tjeenk Willink & Zn.,1921), 342–404; Van Calcar, *Frederik Fröbel*, 180.

5 Sikemeier, *Elise van Calcar-Schiotling*, 519–34.

6 Kevin J. Brehony, 'The Kindergarten in England 1851-1918', in *Kindergartens and Cultures: The Global Diffusion of an Idea*, ed. Roberta Lyn Wollons (New Haven: Yale University Press, 2000), 59–86; Ann Taylor Allen, ' "Let Us Live With Our Children": Kindergarten Movements in Germany and the United States, 1840-1914', *History of Education Quarterly* 28, no. 1 (1988): 23–48.

7 Particularly: Bertha von Marenholtz-Bülow, *Die Arbeit und die neue Erziehung nach Fröbels Methode* (Berlin: Verlag Enslin, 1866); Bertha von Marenholtz-Bülow, *Women's Educational Mission: Being an Explanation of Frederick Fröbel's System of Infant Gardens* (London: Darton & Co., 1855).

8 Particularly: Friedrich W. A. Fröbel, *Die Menschenerziehung* (Keilhau: Verlag der allgemeinen deutschen Erziehungsanstalt, 1826). Available online: www.froebelverein-keilhau.de/downloads/diemenschenerziehung.pdf (accessed 12 July 2014); Friedrich W. A. Fröbel, *Entwurf eines Planes zur Begründung und Ausführung eines Kinder-Gartens* (Ilmenau: Trommsdorff, 1840).

9 Nelleke Bakker, 'Cylinders and Séances: Elise van Calcar and the Spirit of Froebel', *History of Education* 42, no. 2 (2013): 147–65.

10 Ibid.
11 Annemieke van Drenth and Francisca de Haan, *The Rise of Caring Power: Elizabeth Fry and Josephine Butler in Britain and the Netherlands* (Amsterdam: Amsterdam University Press, 1999).
12 Bakker, 'Cylinders and Séances'.
13 Van Calcar, *Frederik Fröbel*, 175.
14 Elise van Calcar, *Fröbels methode tot harmonische ontwikkeling van lichaam en geest*, 7th edn (Den Haag: Ykema [1875] 1905), 4.
15 Marenholtz-Bülow, *Die Arbeit*, 80–1.
16 Elise van Calcar, *Onze ontwikkeling of de magt der eerste indrukken* (Amsterdam: van Gelder, 1861–2), 6 vols., I, 23.
17 Ibid., 33.
18 Ibid., 10–7, 42–75, esp. 66.
19 J. F. Jacobs, *Kinderen van 2 tot 8 jaar, al spelende, gemakkelijk en leerzaam bezig te houden volgens de ontwikkelingsmethode van Frederik Fröbel* (Brussel: Claassen, 1860). The author established the first Fröbel school in Belgium in 1857.
20 Marenholtz-Bülow, *Die Arbeit*, 76–106.
21 Van Calcar, *Onze ontwikkeling*, I, 5.
22 In German 'der Erzieher' or 'Lehrer': Fröbel, *Die Menschenerziehung*; Fröbel, *Entwurf.*
23 Van Calcar, *Onze ontwikkeling*, I, 38.
24 Nelleke Bakker, Jan Noordman and Marjoke Rietveld-van Wingerden, *Vijf eeuwen opvoeden in Nederland: idee en praktijk 1500-2000* (Assen: Van Gorcum, 2006), 137–49.
25 Preface by von Marenholtz-Bülow in Jacobs, *Kinderen*, 26.
26 Marenholtz-Bülow, *Die Arbeit*, 80–1.
27 Van Calcar, *Onze ontwikkeling*, III, 7.
28 Ibid., 30.
29 Ibid., VI, 36.
30 W. M. Nijkamp, *Van begijneschool naar kleuterschool* (Groningen: Wolters, 1963), 73.
31 S. Sr. Coronel, *De bewaarschool. Haar verleden, tegenwoordige toestand en hare toekomst* (Amsterdam: Van Kampen, 1864), 135–6.
32 Ibid., 137.
33 Ibid., 285–395.
34 J. M. Telders, *Fröbel* (Groningen: Noordhoff, 1931), 136.
35 Elise van Calcar, *De kleine papierwerkers* (Amsterdam: Schadd, 1863), 4 vols.; Elise van Calcar, *De Fröbel'sche kartonwerkers* (Amsterdam: Schadd, 1864).
36 Nijkamp, *Van begijneschool*, 92–7.
37 W. J. Pouwelse, *Haar verstand dienstbaar aan het hart. Middelbaar onderwijs voor meisjes, debatten, acties en beleid 1860-1917* (Amsterdam: Het Spinhuis, 1993), 15–44.
38 Elise van Calcar, *Wat is noodig? Eene vraag over vrouwelijke opvoeding aan het Nederlandsche volk* (Amsterdam: Schadd, 1864).
39 Marenholtz-Bülow, *Die Arbeit*, 76–106.
40 Sikemeier, *Elise van Calcar-Schiotling*, 394–479.
41 Bakker, 'Cylinders and Séances'.
42 Elise van Calcar, *De dubbele roeping der vrouw. Eene prijsvraag beantwoord door* (Arnhem: Thieme, 1873), 9–10.
43 Marenholtz-Bülow, *Die Arbeit*.

44   Van Calcar, *De dubbele roeping*, 69, 103–24.

45   Sikemeier, *Elise van Calcar-Schiotling*, 519–34.

46   Van Calcar, *Fröbels methode*, 10.

47   Ibid., 250.

48   Van Calcar, *Maakt*, V.

49   Marenholtz-Bülow, *Die Arbeit*, 77.

50   Van Calcar, *Maakt*, 1–42.

51   I.e. German and Italian: van Calcar, *Frederik Fröbel*.

52   Ibid., 204.

53   Nijkamp, *Van begijneschool*, 110–29.

54   Ibid. These principles and applications were developed over time in the journal *Maandblad voor het Onderwijs*, 1884–1906.

55   J. H. Gunning, Wzn., 'De kindertuin', *Maatschappelijk Werk Afdeeling B* 2 (1901): 105–6, 117, 121–5, 129–32.

56   Elise van Calcar, *Kindertuin en Moederschool* ('s-Gravenhage: Vereeniging Kindervrienden, 1898), 20.

57   N. van Hichtum, 'Ter herinnering aan Elise van Calcar', *De Vrouw* 12 (1904): 17–8.

58   *Nationale Tentoonstelling van Vrouwenarbeid. Besprekingen over de taak van moeders en opvoedsters, gehouden 14 en 15 september 1898*, part IX in the series *Verslagen van de congressen tijdens de nationale Tentoonstelling van Vrouwenarbeid* (1898–99), 3–4, 45–72. The class issue was equally present in other countries: Taylor Allen, 'The kindergarten'.

59   Elise van Calcar, *Het jonge leven: Hoe het te kweeken en te beschermen. Een boek voor ouders en opvoeders* (Leiden: Kapteijn, 1905).

60   Ibid., 64, 166.

61   Roy Porter and Mikulas Teich (eds), *Romanticism in National Context* (Cambridge, UK, Cambridge University Press, 1988).

62   Johanna Wierts van Coehoorn-Stout, *De kindertuin*, 2nd edn (Amsterdam: Wierts van Coehoorn, 1907).

63   Nijkamp, *Van begijneschool*, 185 270.

64   Wierts van Coehoorn-Stout, *De kindertuin*, 14–31.

65   Ibid., 20–3.

66   Gunning, 'De kindertuin'.

67   Ibid.; J. H. Gunning Wzn., 'De fröbelschool', *Paedagogisch Tijdschrift* 2 (1910): 270–89, 338–55.

68   C. J. Brouwer and A. Bakker, *Het voorbereidend lager onderwijs* (Groningen: Wolters, 1900), 207.

Figure 4.1 Miss Dorothy Fitch, kindergarten mistress, Wellington Training College and 1st head teacher, Kelburn Normal School, 1906–14 c. 1906. Kelburn Normal School Archives.

Figure 4.2 Miss Winifred Maitland, kindergarten mistress, Wellington Training College and 2nd head teacher, Kelburn Normal School, 1915–25 c. 1915. Kelburn Normal School Archives.

4

Froebelian Teachers Abroad: Implementing a Modern Infant Education System in Colonial Wellington, New Zealand, 1906–25

Kerry Bethell

This case study is illustrative of Froebelian education transported to a colonial setting and transposed into a school setting. The state system of education introduced in New Zealand in 1877 made schooling compulsory from the age of seven. In practice, children were enrolled from the age of five, creating a demand for infant classes amidst a call from the colony's supporters of kindergarten pedagogy for reform of the infant curriculum along Froebelian lines. This created a demand for teachers and teacher trainers with specialization in kindergarten pedagogy. New Zealand's educational officials looked 'Home' to Britain to recruit qualified women teachers to lead change in the colony's infant classes for children from five to seven years of age.

The two subjects of this case study, Miss Dorothy Fitch and Miss Winifred Maitland, were appointed to the role of Kindergarten Mistress for Wellington's Teacher Training College in 1905 and 1912 respectively. Both also held Head Teacher positions within the attached experimental Kelburn Normal School and were given responsibility for the introduction of 'modern teaching methods' into the curriculum. Holders of the higher certificate of the British-based National Froebel Union (NFU) and experienced kindergartners (as kindergarten teachers were then known), Fitch and Maitland, brought to the colony skills, knowledge and experience deemed important to plans for reform of both teacher training provision and infant schooling. In turn, colonial experience offered them professional and political opportunities both in their work as teachers and as global travellers outside of the mainstream of colonial settlers.

The women's work and the beliefs they brought with them to the colony made them local and global actors rooted, as Tamson Pietsch argues, 'in specific social and political communities and also wayfarers on international routes of scholarship'.[1] Fitch and Maitland became part of a tradition of women travellers within the global kindergarten movement that expanded after Froebel's death in 1852. Peter Weston has shown that around the turn of the twentieth century trained teachers from London's Froebel Educational Institute (FEI) were travelling to many parts of the world for work.[2] Historians such as Kevin Brehony, Rebecca Wollons and Helen May have shown how

Froebelian beliefs become an 'acceptable' means by which some women were able to push barriers and boundaries globally. Fitch and Maitland may be understood as part of a larger, long-term phenomenon of travelling teachers who transported, relocated, transformed and adapted Froebelian education and practice.[3]

The focus of this chapter is the work of Fitch and Maitland as pedagogical leaders in kindergarten methods. Attention is given to the networks and relationships they used to establish modern professional identities within a gendered world that offered women new opportunities but left them still bound by traditional ideals. Women's own accounts, both personal and professional, supplemented with official records and newspaper reports, provide the data. Such records reflect the archival remains kept over time and as such contain gaps; analysis of these archival fragments allows for the telling of an illuminating if necessarily incomplete story.

Dorothy Fitch and Winifred Maitland – British childhoods

Dorothy Fitch was born in 1877 and Winifred Maitland six years later in 1883. Both were born into England's upper middle class which included a particular set of gendered and class expectations. Fitch was the sixth of seven children born to Laura and Arthur Fitch, a merchant. The family lived at Barnet, North London. Maitland was the fourth child of six. Her family lived in Crieff, Scotland but later settled near Wolverhampton, where Arthur Maitland became Vicar of the Dudley Church.

What is known of the girls' early education indicates it was typical for girls of their class at that time. Fitch's education occurred at home[4] through a combination of the family's live-in governess, parental teaching and independent learning. Maitland's education largely took place outside the home as a boarder in a girls' school and later at a finishing school in Dresden, Germany.[5] Whether the girls' schooling was centred around traditional 'accomplishments' or along more progressive lines promoting some awareness of infant and child pedagogy is unknown. Circumstantial evidence suggests that both girls received a relatively liberal upbringing based around prevailing modern ideas of professional-class parenting.

Historian Nanette Whitbread argues that by the middle of the nineteenth century, members of the upper middle classes were beginning to seek new ways of educating their children by using governesses in the home and enrolling children in private infant schools.[6] The writings of Jean-Jacques Rousseau and Johann Pestalozzi had earlier influenced child-rearing practices and enhanced the role of women as educators within their domestic role within the family.[7] In turn, Froebel's focus on the younger child and his notion of the mother as the child's first teacher strengthened both the link between school and home and the notion of women as, by their nature, the appropriate teachers of the young.[8] By the late nineteenth century, middle- and upper-class families interested in progressive ideas had turned for guidance on child-rearing to Froebel's teachings.[9] For some, this entailed appointing a Froebel-trained[10] governess or enrolling their children in the expanding private-day schools, whilst for others, it involved personal shifts in child-rearing beliefs and practices. Froebel's new and gentler theory of infant education won increasing support amongst the British progressive middle and upper classes.[11]

Whilst Maitland and Fitch received a more liberal schooling than that afforded to many girls at this time, this did not change gendered differences of role expectations. They received an education compatible with their anticipated futures as middle-class wives and mothers, with no expectation of their engaging in paid employment.

State schooling and the schooling of the young along Froebelian lines

When Maitland and Fitch were in their late teens and early twenties respectively, change occurred that widened young women's employment options. The introduction in 1870 of mass education in Britain required the state to provide both the schools to cater for the increased numbers of children enrolled and the teachers to teach these children. In addition, mass schooling provided impetus to the schooling of young children along Froebelian lines.[12] In 1874, prominent figures in the women's movement and in girls' education, such as Maria Grey and Emily Shirreff, established the London-based Froebel Society, which sought to promote Froebelian philosophy and methods and the training of women for employment as teachers as well as for mothers in the home.[13] By 1879 the FEI was one of three institutions offering kindergarten teacher training in England.[14] The NFU was formed as the joint examining body in 1887.

The growth in provision of state schooling brought British Froebelians to focus on what Brehony called the 'conversion' of state schooling provided for young children.[15] In 1890 Froebelian Julia Salis-Schwabe set out a grander version for England in her aim 'to establish an institution which will make its mark upon elementary education as a whole, and lead to the general adoption of better principles in elementary schools'.[16] In 1892 the FEI was constituted to provide training 'for those who wish to become educators of children in Kindergartens, Schools and Private Families'.[17] Such actions marked the increasing vigour within the British Froebel movement and the impetus for the bringing of the kindergarten system into the mainstream of public education systems.

The demand that emerged for Froebel-trained teachers brought acceptance of kindergarten teaching as a suitable occupation for middle-class girls, whether as preparation for motherhood or as a respectable occupation for single women in Britain in need of, or desirous of, a professional life. Fitch and Maitland completed their schooling at a time when nursery and teaching positions for suitable, trained young women were advertised in educational journals such as the Froebel Society's *Child Life* as well as in the popular press. Work with young children aged five to seven within formal schooling came to be seen, as Rosemary Ashton argues, as 'the area in which teacher training for women would be the most acceptable to society at large'.[18]

Fitch and Maitland both attended state-funded day kindergarten training colleges, were examined through the progressive FEI in London and earned certificates awarded through the NFU. Two basic courses were offered. The first, known as the Preliminary Certificate, was for girls over seventeen years of age in preparation for the Elementary Certificate of the NFU. The second was in preparation for the Higher Certificate of the NFU. Both courses underscored the FEI's differing approach to that of most state providers of teacher education, emphasizing 'at all stages a *philosophy of education* and the *wholeness* of the total educational process based upon the *observation* of individual children'.[19] Fitch and in particular Maitland would have experienced at first hand the new education discourse emerging within such institutions supporting revision of the way in which Froebel teachings were interpreted and taught. The new approach incorporated influences from theorists such as John Dewey (1859–1952) and Sigmund Freud (1856–1939). As Kristen (Dombkowski) Nawrotzki argues, 'These increasingly revisionist Froebelians came to be recognised by the Government and by the rest of the teaching profession as the experts in the emerging field of early childhood education, situated as they were in the very best of the government-inspected colleges'.[20]

Dorothy Fitch and her sister Laura studied through the Home and Colonial Infant School Society, an Anglican-based society founded in 1836 to establish infant schools and to train teachers for them. The society's founders, Charles and Elizabeth Mayo, were much influenced by the work of Johann Pestalozzi, and later by Froebel's teachings. The society's Model Infants' School eventually became Highbury Fields School, Islington, a state secondary school for girls. It was here in 1896 that the sisters enrolled and completed the preliminary certificate of the NFU.

In 1897, the sisters enrolled in the Higher Certificate of the NFU.[21] Laura Fitch completed the certificate, but Dorothy did not, and by 1901, the latter was no longer living at home. The 1901 Ireland Census records reveal a Dorothy Fitch living in Limerick, teaching children at the Orphanage and Industrial School run by the St Vincent Convent. This Dorothy Fitch shares many details linking her to the Dorothy Fitch of the study: the same year of birth, same religion – Church of England, marital status as spinster, born in England and with an interest in teaching.[22] This is enough to surmise that Fitch, having gained her preliminary certificate, took up a teaching position in Ireland. By 1903, Fitch had returned to England and to the Highbury Fields School, where she re-enrolled to study for the Higher Certificate of the NFU.[23] Fitch was appointed as a staff member at Highbury Fields, and it is from there that she applied for a position as Kindergarten Mistress at the Wellington Training College, New Zealand in 1905.

Education services in the colony at that time lacked the infrastructure to meet the demand for teachers and regularly looked 'Home' to Britain for teachers, vesting their interests and trust in British-based selection panels.[24] In 1905, the Wellington Education Board looked to Britain for women teachers with the required qualifications, skill and kindergarten experience to help implement the new reforms. Seeking an 'appointee [with a] wide knowledge of recent developments in kindergarten',[25] the board approved a panel headed by Professor Michael Sadler, head of the Froebel Society, along with a Miss Beard, known for her experience in selecting teachers for colonial service, and Evelyn Lawrence, principal of the FEI. Thirty applications were considered by the panel, twelve from within Britain and eighteen from teachers in

New Zealand and Australia. The position was offered to Dorothy Fitch.[26] In his annual report, the head of the Wellington Education Board, Robert Lee (senior inspector), announced Fitch's appointment, praising the panel's 'selection of a candidate with such extensive experience with infants as well as with students in training. Moreover she comes to us with the latest ideas on infant training, a branch of educational work that has been receiving special attention of late.'[27] In early 1906, Fitch left England for New Zealand.

The same year that Fitch left Britain, Winifred Maitland enrolled to study at the FEI. Maitland is likely to have become aware of the travels abroad undertaken by staff members such as Maria Findlay (1855–1912), who had earlier travelled to America where she visited schools based on Dewey's teachings.[28] Having successfully completed her FEI higher certificate in December 1907, Maitland continued her studies at the progressive Fielden Demonstration School in Manchester, where she was appointed as a junior demonstrator at Manchester University. There she worked with Froebelians Grace Owen (1873–1965) and Maria Findlay's brother Joseph John Findlay (1860–1940), the latter a professor of education, a Deweyan and a key advocate of child-centred educational theory in Britain at that time. Around 1910 Maitland accepted a position at Dudley Training College to teach modern infant methods and to supervise trainee teachers' infant school practice. It was from here in 1915 that she too left England for New Zealand.

Reform of colonial infant classes 1877–1906

Wellington had been a site of educational reform beginning with the introduction of a universal state education system there in 1877. Schooling was compulsory for children from seven to thirteen years, but schools typically enrolled children from five years, thus creating infant classes and the need for an infant curriculum. Inspector Robert Lee was active in the reform of primary school education and teacher training in the province of Wellington.[29] At the core of Lee's plan in 1878 was his brief that the most important and the most difficult work of the school lay in the infant room and that 'the means to achieve this lay with the teachings of Froebel'.[30] Further, he argued, the success of the infant school reforms required a teacher with expertise in kindergarten pedagogy and knowledge of up-to-date methods. By 1878, he had acquired both, and the transformation of public infant schooling was underway.[31]

The turn of the twentieth century saw further innovation. George Hogben, director general of the Department of Education from 1899 to 1915, worked to bring about progressive reforms of the primary sector and to introduce a new curriculum on the basis of the best of modern educational thought, including Froebel, Maria Montessori and Dewey.[32] His aim was a sincere 'attempt to import reality into school work, to bring the teaching into closer contact with the outdoor life of the pupils, to throw overboard merely conventional information in favour of what will be genuinely interesting and serviceable'.[33]

A parliamentary select committee report in 1903 led to a reorganization of teacher training. Teacher training colleges, previously closed, were re-established from 1906.

Normal (demonstration) schools were to be built alongside training colleges and to be established alongside university colleges to allow for joint programmes of study.[34] Teachers were accorded greater recognition and increased expectations. Robert Lee, now chairman of the Wellington Education Board, argued in 1907 that as important as buildings were, 'the real need in modern education was the teacher, without whom fine buildings and elaborate apparatus were of little use'.[35] Kindergarten Mistresses were to be appointed for the colony's four teacher training institutions. These dual reforms in teacher training and infant work brought a feeling of energy, confidence and a sense of that period being a time of possibility and experimental approaches in the education of young children.[36]

Dorothy Fitch and the kindergarten context in Wellington, 1906–14

Dorothy Fitch travelled salon class on the Gothic arriving in Wellington on March 26. In a solicited article on her impressions of the colony published that year, Fitch explained her response to her new environs as one of initial dislocation. That the mid-day sun shone to the north she initially found bewildering, 'almost as a personal affront'.[37] She was similarly thrown by the different changes of seasons. Further, Wellington, the colony's capital city and just sixty-six years young, differed in so many ways to her familiar London, and seemed a place 'hard to take seriously'. To Fitch, a lover of nature, the countryside brought more unfamiliar sights and disconnection. Horrified to see 'blackened stumps and gaunt arms of what had once been trees', her indignant 'why!' was not reassured by the answer, 'Frozen mutton'.[38] The native bush, however, garnered lengthy praise, as she found it 'difficult to imagine anything more beautiful'.[39] Fitch's appreciation of the virtues of Wellington[40] came later with admiration as to what its population had achieved in such a short period.[41]

Wellington offered a strong Froebelian base in the form of a Free Kindergarten Association offering kindergarten provision to the children of the poor and a Froebel Society offering regular talks and opportunities to meet like-minded parties. The founder of both organizations was Mary Richmond, herself having been a student at FEI for three months in 1895. Richmond worked to maintain global links with FEI, supporting New Zealanders to travel to study at the FEI as well as employing British graduates in her school and within the free kindergartens. In 1900 on behalf of the Wellington Froebel Society, she applied for affiliation to the FEI. The future looked positive. In the words of Helen May, 'The slow transformation of the infant curriculum in New Zealand schools by gifted "infant mistresses" such as Catherine Francis [appointed by Robert Lee in 1889] was to continue into the twentieth century.'[42]

Fitch's appointment and arrival were reported in the colonial press.[43] Her credentials were presented in approving tones. She had the desired qualification and experience needed for the reforms underway. She also met the prevailing expectations for a teacher of the young: she was female, respectable and unmarried. But the most frequent and approving comment was that the new Kindergarten Mistress was from 'Home'.

In May 1906, Fitch took up her position as the first Kindergarten Mistress for Wellington's Teachers' Training College, with responsibility for the model infant school and with teaching responsibilities for students within the college. In 1906 there were plans for a new training college and model school in Kelburn, but these had not been built. In the interim, the new institution was temporarily located at Thorndon School in an adapted set of rooms that included a new infant department for five- to seven-year-olds 'built on the most modern plan'.[44] Fitch stood tall in the advocacy and implementation of modern beliefs built around the schooling of young children and the ideas of Froebel. Fitch insisted upon provision of an onsite kindergarten for three- to four-year-olds to allow college trainees to have a full record of a child's educational development from as early an age as possible. This was granted. Such facilities received Fitch's approval and her recognition that 'up to date and modern methods are so indispensable'.[45]

In her first month, Fitch was appointed by the Wellington Education Board to a subcommittee to reform the seating arrangements across the schools. The tiered galleries, where children had been seated in rows in order to focus on the central authoritative figure of the teacher leading them in formal work, were to be removed to allow for the flexible arrangements of desks and – in the infant room – floor space for play, ready access to activities and greater freedom of movement.[46] The coming together of these two elements – a suitably qualified teacher and a specially adapted building – was to mark the beginnings of the transformation of infant schooling through the reform of teacher training.[47]

Fitch's interpretation of Froebel's teachings and practice can be glimpsed through evidence from the courses she taught, in a surviving student workbook and in a 1912 submission Fitch made to the Royal Commission of Education. In her work as Kindergarten Mistress, Fitch was tasked with teaching Froebelian handwork to all second-year teacher training students, both male and female, and to teach a special course on infant-room handwork offered to women students only. The latter reflected the prevailing view that women were the appropriate teachers of the young. In addition, Fitch taught Methods of Teaching, a course dealing with the work of the infant room. As training student numbers grew, Fitch was assisted by Margaret Page, an experienced infant teacher and committed Froebelian, and by female student teachers with an interest in infant teaching.[48] Fitch's teaching of Froebel's gifts and occupations is evident in a collection of student work compiled in 1908 by student teacher, Mary Hitchcock. Titled 'Occupation book', it includes examples of drawing, design, paper folding, paper cutting, sand modelling, sewing and bead threading alongside text outlining the teaching methods to be used and the value of each for children's learning.[49]

Fitch was an advocate for the improvement of education and services for women and became an active member of the city's Women Teachers' Association and a council member for the Free Kindergarten Association. In 1912, the Royal Commission on Education met in Wellington to hear submissions from those interested in education. Fitch was one of a group of women teachers who presented a united front in their submissions so as to ensure that both the voices of women in general and those of the free kindergarten and infant schools were heard.[50] Fitch called for more staff in infant classrooms to permit opportunities for kindergarten work and for the introduction of women inspectors and for properly organized education for children aged three to seven years on the basis of Froebel's emphasis on children's interests, ordered freedom, self-activity and expression. She called for a more rational form of education for children from five to seven, defining the essential characteristics of such work as

1. the formation of right habits, such as cleanliness, obedience, attention, industry, independence and politeness;
2. the development of the social feelings by organised games and concerted action;
3. the training of the senses, since the senses are the gateway to all knowledge;
4. the training of the imagination by stories, ear and voice by music and singing;
5. the awakening of thought for others, and sympathy by giving the child pets to care for and attend to.[51]

Fitch argued that the size of many infant classes prevented infant teachers from implementing the new child-centred reforms. Large class sizes, she argued, did not allow teachers to undertake the informed observation of children necessary to support effective development, learning and teaching.[52] A further defect was the 'undue importance attached to formal school subjects such as reading, spelling, writing and number, rather than the healthy all-round development of the child'.[53] Possibly her strongest message was that 'it was impossible to overestimate the importance of the early stages of education, up to eight years of age'.[54] A year later, in 1913, George Hogben expressed his concern that the formal teaching of reading and writing 'threatened to invade the infant room to such an extent as to crush out of our memories, all recollections that such a man as Froebel ever lived'.[55] Reform, it seemed, was not going to be easy.

In 1914, the first stage of the Kelburn Normal School – the infant school and attached kindergarten – was opened, bringing the plan to physically unite the normal school, the teachers college and the university one step closer. Dorothy Fitch was appointed Head Teacher of Kelburn Normal School, but her tenure there was short.[56] The pleasure of working in a modern infant school and attached kindergarten was perhaps tempered by the problem of catering for the rapid increase in enrolment. In addition, outbreaks of measles and other sicknesses in 1914 interfered with children's attendance and opportunities to learn.[57] In late 1914, after eight years as Kindergarten Mistress and one as head of Kelburn Normal School, Dorothy Fitch announced her pending marriage to George Hunter and presented her resignation two months before her wedding in May 1915.

Despite women's increasing career opportunities, the prevailing social convention of marriage as a full-time occupation for women remained, bringing to an end to the careers of most women teachers.[58] Fitch's departure was, however, unexpectedly short-lived, and within the year she returned to the school on contract as Mrs Hunter, taking up a lesser teaching position. She returned not because society's views had liberalized but rather because of a teacher shortage; the demands of war-time military service had seriously depleted the ranks of male teachers, so married women teachers were sought to assist in the war effort by returning to teaching.

Miss Winifred Maitland – Kindergarten Mistress and School Head Teacher

Fitch's resignation brought the need for a new Kindergarten Mistress. Wellington Education Board again looked to Britain. This time the panel, headed by Professor J. J. Findlay from Manchester University, appointed Winfred Maitland. In mid-1915, Maitland took up the joint position of Kindergarten Mistress at the college and as head of Kelburn Normal School. Along with responsibility for the continued introduction of modern teaching methods into the curriculum, she was to 'take charge of 120–150 students; to lecture to students on Kindergarten Methods and Elementary Handwork; and to supervise the practice of students in Infant Department work.'[59]

In her ten years as Kindergarten Mistress, Maitland supported the implementation of a range of ideas drawn from the strands of developmental psychology popular at the time. The liberty of the child, she argued, 'should underlie all the work in the school'.[60] Maitland understood the school's experimental nature and appreciated the open-mindedness of authorities prepared to give teachers a great measure of latitude. A normal school 'must be one prepared to experiment in order that every advance may be built on the solid ground of actual experience'.[61] Her aim was to 'practise as well as preach'.[62] Maitland sought to create a more pleasant learning experience for children. She banned the use of corporal punishment, and like Fitch, advocated for smaller class sizes. Her method was to capture the interest of the child and to use this motive power

Figure 4.3 'Learning about their community through doing', Kelburn Normal School infant class, c. 1920. Kelburn Normal School Archives.

for learning. She insisted on the teaching of the three 'R's but advocated for formal work not to begin until seven years of age.[63]

Maitland inspired the imagination of many school and college staff members and the school's growing reputation for experimentation attracted staff with liberal outlooks and child-centred beliefs. In 1919, for example, five teachers held qualifications from the FEI in London: Maitland and Fitch, plus New Zealanders Dorothy Hursthouse and Ethel Burnett, who travelled to Britain to gain kindergarten qualifications. In addition, long-term teacher Marion G. Thornton, though holder of an FEI qualification, had travelled to Britain in 1911 to study infant and kindergarten methods.[64]

In 1923, Maitland was awarded twelve months leave to visit America and Europe to study their various methods of education. Few archival records of her travels remain. What is known is that she left for San Francisco on 19 December 1922 and five months later in May 1923 sailed from Boston for England.[65] When in England Maitland attended a dinner in honour of Maria Montessori.[66] Based upon earlier educational travels undertaken by other educationalists such as Mary Richmond and George Hogben in America, she most likely made visits to progressive schools and institutions such as Columbia College, New York and Wheelock College in Boston.[67]

That Maitland's leadership and methods helped shape the future of New Zealand schooling was widely acknowledged in reports and in the number of national and international visitors wanting to visit the school – so many that Maitland in 1919 wrote in her log book 'No lessons to be interrupted by visitors'.[68] In a report to the FEI alumni magazine, *The Link*, Ethel Burnett wrote of Maitland: 'She has done splendid work here, work that has been a revelation and an inspiration to schools all over New Zealand, and it is a great opportunity and a great privilege to be allowed to work under her.'[69] John S. Tennant (by then professor of education at the city's university) also acknowledged Maitland's wider influence in infant schooling in his annual report for 1924: 'In no branch of education has there been greater development in recent years than in infant instruction and management, and the infant mistresses in our large schools deserve special commendation for the whole-hearted and admirable way in which they have adopted the new methods.'[70]

Not everyone was impressed with the school's experimental nature. Letters of opposition from some parents appeared regularly in newspapers concerning the school's expectation of children undertaking domestic chores, on handwriting and in particular calling for the continued teaching of the 'basics'. She was supported in her work by Professor Tennant. In 1916, he replied to parental criticism of the school's involvement of children in domestic chores. Citizenship, he explained, 'implies community life, and the proper training for that life comes through living it not through reading or talking about it'.[71] Maitland worked hard to gain parents' support, encouraging their interest and involvement in school life. Whilst not willing to change her educational ideas because of criticism, she valued parental input and work in the school. In 1924, she supported plans to form a parent-teacher association, one of the first in the country.

As male teachers who had survived the war returned to take up their old positions in the 1920s, married women teachers resigned from Kelburn School. Winifred Maitland joined them in 1926, when she announced her resignation as well as her impending marriage to John S. Tennant, with whom she obviously had much more in common than just a shared feeling about the necessity for modern infant work.

Political change

Growing economic difficulties in 1928 saw the government announce changes in the system for training teachers of young children. The Kindergarten Mistress positions in the four teacher training colleges were discontinued and the normal schools would no longer have attached kindergartens where students could observe children's learning. Such changes brought a shift in pedagogical direction away from kindergarten pedagogy to a less specific focus on infant teaching. In Wellington, the abandoned Kindergarten Mistress position became two new positions: one for a Mistress at the normal school and the other for a lecturer in infant-room methods for the training college, thus providing continued recognition of the different pedagogical needs of the infant classes. What was missing was the status in terms of rank and independence accorded to the previous position. Kelburn Normal School continued to operate as an experimental school, but the extent of its broader influence was weakened by the changes.

Whilst elements of Hogben's early-twentieth-century reforms for a scheme of education that would be 'closer to life' had been integrated into the education system, nevertheless 'many schools remained formal institutions dominated by a drive for measurable results'.[72] The kindergarten movement's call for the integration of Froebelian practice in infant classes was weakened in the face of an examination-driven school system, failure to reduce class size to a manageable level, poor recruitment and retention of qualified teachers, and a generally low level of political or public interest in reform of the infant classes along progressive ideals, particularly in rural areas and small schools. The promise of an infant curriculum based on kindergarten methods that arose in the 1880s with the assurance of political acceptance and accomplishment was significantly crushed by the 1920s as large class sizes continued. Froebel's name had largely disappeared from the education vocabulary and kindergarten had become defined as nearly any sort of education of children aged three and four in community settings.[73]

Conclusion

The late-nineteenth- and early-twentieth-century provision of state education in colonial New Zealand and interest in reform of the expanding infant schools opened up professional roles for women as Froebelian educators in mainstream settings. The demand for teachers of young children and interest in kindergarten pedagogy encouraged English women such as Dorothy Fitch and Winifred Maitland to apply for and accept leadership positions abroad. They became boundary crossers in several ways. First, they uprooted themselves physically from all that was familiar to travel to the unknown. Second, they shifted from the private progressive schools in which they had trained and worked to a large state experimental school attached both to a teacher training college and university. Furthermore, they transported ideas and methods that supported the new reforms of the infant curriculum along modern lines and adapted these and themselves to fit the new cultural and educational context – a role for which they gained recognition and status. Their task proved complex in the face of overcrowded classrooms, a lack of resources and abundant criticism from those who did not appreciate their efforts. They persisted nevertheless, and in their work they were able to contribute to the reform of the colonial infant curriculum in line with the progressive ideas emerging globally and to the larger nineteenth-century movements for Froebelian education and for women's education (and employment) more generally.

Abbreviations

AJHR   *Appendices to the Journals of the House of Representatives.*
ATL   Alexander Turnbull Library.
FEI   Froebel Educational Institute.

Notes

1   Tamson Pietsch, *Empire of Scholars: Universities, Networks and the British Academic World 1850–1939* (Manchester: Manchester University Press, 2013), 3.
2   Peter Weston, *The Froebel Educational Institute and the Origins and History of the College* (London: University of Surrey Roehampton, 2002), 37.
3   See Kevin Brehony, *The Origins of Nursery Education: Friedrich Froebel and the English System* (London: Routledge, 2001); Mary Hilton and Pam Hirsch (eds), *Practical Visionaries: Women, Education and Social Progress 1790-1830* (Harlow: Longman, 2000); Roberta Wollons, *Kindergarten and Cultures: The Global Diffusion of an Idea* (London: New Haven, 2000); Helen May, 'I Am Five and I Go to School': *The Work and Play of Early Education in New Zealand* (Dunedin: University of Otago Press, 2011).
4   The FEI Register, Froebel Archive for Childhood Studies. Roehampton University. See also British Census for 1889, 1891 and 1901.
5   Ibid.
6   Nanette Whitbread, *The Evolution of the Nursery-infant School: A History of Infant and Nursery Education in Britain, 1800-1970* (London: Routledge and K. Paul, 1972), 39.
7   Jean-Jacques Rousseau, *Emile, or On Education*, trans. Allan Bloom (New York: Basic Books, ([1762] 1979); Johann Heinrich Pestalozzi, *Leonard & Gertrude: An Attempt to Help Mothers to Teach Their Own Children* (London: Swan Sonnenschein and Co., ([1781] 1787).
8   See Joachim Liebschner, *Foundations of Progressive Education* (London: The Lutterworth Press, 1991).
9   Whitbread, *The Evolution of the Nursery-infant School*, 39.
10 This term described persons trained in Froebelian philosophy, pedagogy, and methods; they were not necessarily trained by Froebel himself.

11 Ibid., 30.

12 Weston, *The Froebel Educational Institute*.

13 The Elementary Education Act of 1880 made school attendance compulsory from five to ten years of age.

14 Kristen Dombkowski (Nawrotzki), 'Kindergarten Teacher Training in England and the United States 1850–1918', *History of Education* 31, no. 5 (2002): 475–89.

15 Kevin Brehony, 'English Revisionist Froebelians and the Schooling of the Urban Poor', in *Practical Visionaries Women, Education and Social Progress 1790-1930*, ed. M. Hilton and P. Hirsh (London: Addison, Wesley, Longman, 2000), 184.

16 Weston, *The Froebel Educational Institute*, 13.

17 Ibid., 14.

18 Rosemary Ashton, *Victorian Bloomsbury* (New Haven: Yale University Press, 2012), 273.

19 Weston, *The Froebel Educational Institute*, 27. (Emphasis in the original).

20 Dombkowski (Nawrotzki), 'Kindergarten teacher training'.

21 NFU Register, Froebel Archive for Childhood Studies. Roehampton University.

22 ancestry.com. *Web: Ireland, Census, 1901* [database on-line]. Provo, UT, USA: ancestry.com Operations, Inc., 2013.

23 NFU Register Froebel Archive for Childhood Studies. Roehampton University.

24 Pietsch, *Empire of Scholars*.

25 Robert Lee, *AJHR*, 1905, II-E.1, 76.

26 'Personal Matters', *Evening Post*, 7 February 1906, 7.

27 Robert Lee, *AJHR*, 1906, E-1b, 26.

28 Weston, *The Froebel Educational Institute*, 31.

29 Kerry Bethell, ' "Not [Just] for a Name that we Plead:" Fashioning the Ideological Origins of Early Kindergarten in Dunedin and Wellington, New Zealand, 1870-1913' (Ph.D thesis, Victoria University of Wellington, 2008).

30 Robert Lee, *AJHR*, 1879, H-2, 81.

31 Helen May, *School Beginning: A 19th Century Colonial Story* (Wellington: NZCER Press., 2005); Bethell, 'Not [Just] for a Name'.

32 George Hogben, *Schools and Other Educational Institutions in Europe and America: Report of the Inspector-General's Visit* (Wellington: Government. Printer, 1908).

33 Alexander E. Campbell, *Educating New Zealand* (Wellington: Department of Internal Affairs, 1941), 96.

34 'Training Colleges', *New Zealand Herald*, 7 September 1903, 6.

35 'Wellington Training College', *Evening Post*, 11 December 1907, 2.

36 Ian Cumming and Alan Cumming, *History of State Education in New Zealand 1840-1975* (Wellington: Pitman Publishing New Zealand Ltd, 1978), 180.

37 Dorothy Fitch, First Impressions, *The Cooee*, Wellington Training College, Vol. 1, no. 1 (December 1907): 7–8.

38 In 1882, the first refrigerated meat left New Zealand for London, providing the opportunity for the colony to develop an extensive export economy. The demand for sheep saw the clearance of the native forest to sow grass for pastures.

39 Fitch, 'First Impressions', 7–8.

40 See Bethell, 'Not [Just] for a Name'.

41 Chris Maclean. 'Wellington Region – Boom and Bust: 1900–1940', *Te Ara – the Encyclopedia of New Zealand*, updated 13 July 2012. Available online: http://www.TeAra.govt.nz/en/wellington-region/page-9 (accessed 18 August 2015).

42 May, 'School Beginnings', 214.

43 For example, *Evening Post*, 15 December, 1905, 7; *Evening Post*, 7 February 1906, 7, *Auckland Star*, 27 March 1906, 2.

44 'Teaching the young idea', *Wanganui Herald*, 18 July 1906, 6.
45 Ibid.
46 May, '*I Am Five and I Go to School*'.
47 Arthur Butchers, *The Education System: A Concise History of the New Zealand Education System* (Auckland: The National Printing Co, 1932), 84.
48 Bethell, 'Not [Just] for a Name'.
49 Mary L Hitchcock, 'Occupation book', 1908 ATL MSX-8895.
50 Bethell, 'Not [Just] for a Name', 291.
51 Fitch, submission to The Education Commission (Cohen) *AJHR*, 1912, 543.
52 Ibid.
53 Ibid.
54 Ibid.
55 'Address by Mr Hogben', *Dominion*, 13 February 1913, 6.
56 *AJHR*, 1915, E-2, vi.
57 Janet McCallum and Ginny Sullivan, *Kelburn Normal School 75th Jubilee, 1914-1989* (Wellington: Kelburn Normal School, 1990).
58 Kay Morris Matthews, *In Their Own Right: Women and Higher Education in New Zealand Before 1945* (Wellington: NZCER Press, 2005).
59 'Advertisements', *Evening Post*, 13 January 1915, 2.
60 'New Methods', *Evening Post*, 30 September 1919, 6.
61 McCallum and Sullivan, *Kelburn Normal School 75th Jubilee, 1914-1989*.
62 Ibid.
63 Ibid. The three 'R's refer to the subjects of reading, writing and arithmetic.
64 'Personal Notes from London', *Evening Post*, 7 November 1911, 2.
65 Shipping records, Ancestry.com.
66 'New Zealand teachers at Home', EP 11 May 1923, 8.
67 Kerry Bethell, 'To Venture With Purpose: Miss Mary Richmond's 1907 Educational Travels Abroad', in *Fröbelpädagogik im Kontext der Moderne. Bildung, Erziehung und soziales Handeln*, ed. K. Neumann, U. Sauerbrey and M. Wrinkler (Jena: IKS, Garamond, 2010), 113–26. See also, George Hogben, *Schools and Other Educational Institutions in Europe and America: Report of the Inspector-General's Visit* (Wellington: Government. Printer, 1908).
68 'Portrait of a school', *National Education*, 1 April 1964, 116.
69 'A school in Wellington', *The Link* (1923), 24.
70 Tennant, *AJHR*, 1924, E-02, P.XV111.
71 'The Aims of Education', *Evening Post*, 7 November 1916, 5.
72 Ibid.
73 Bethell, 'Not [Just] for a Name', 239.

Figure 5.1 Sleeping Beauty at the kindergarten festivities, 20–21 May, 1927. Image no. 112, K1:2, Fröbelföreningen i Norrköping, Norrköpings Stadsarkiv.

5

In the Name of Froebel: Fundraising for Kindergartens in Sweden, 1900–45

Johannes Westberg

In Sweden, kindergartens were established during the first half of the twentieth century. They came to be known as *barnträdgårdar*, which is a translation of kinder (*barn*) garten (*trädgård*). Unlike the expansion of the Swedish preschool sector in the post-war period, which was mainly organized and substantively funded by the local government, these kindergartens were initially funded through private monies. They were run either by private individuals, targeting children of the wealthy classes, or by philanthropic associations, targeting children of the broader strata of society.[1]

Like their counterparts offering other types of fledgling social services, the philanthropic organizers of Swedish charitable kindergartens arranged fundraising events to cover their costs. During this period of initial institutionalization, however, these events did not raise significant amounts of money, which raises questions regarding the reasons behind the continued fundraising practice. In this chapter, I will analyse both the social, economic and cultural context of these fundraisers and how the Swedish kindergarten's fundraising events put the kindergarten movement on display from 1900 to 1945. I will illustrate how these events met objectives that went beyond mere matters of finance. Instead, they were events that produced and reproduced a favourable image of kindergarten and its inventor, the German pedagogue Friedrich Froebel. Most importantly, these festivities raised the profile of kindergartens, promoting them as a significant and genuinely Swedish charitable enterprise. These fundraising events provide an example of the malleability of the kindergarten and its capacity to adapt not only to national culture and politics, but also to specific settings, such as fundraising events.[2]

The theoretical starting point of this chapter is the discourse on fundraising and its functions in the historiography of philanthropy. Empirically, it draws on a case study of the fundraisers organized by Norrköping's Froebel Society (*Fröbelföreningen i Norrköping*), which was the most influential Froebel Society in Sweden; it focuses especially on the society's renowned kindergarten spring parties. The source material consists primarily of newspaper articles and the Froebel Society's meeting minutes, annual reports and account books.

The Swedish kindergarten movement

Unlike in places such as New Zealand, where the kindergarten as a form of early education was introduced via third-country sources, the kindergarten was brought to Sweden by so-called primary acquisition, directly from Germany.[3] This was accomplished through visits to German kindergartens, training at the Pestalozzi-Fröbel-Haus in Berlin and the purchase of books such as *Die Pädagogik des Kindergartens* (1847) and German magazines such as *Kindergarten* (1906–). Sweden's primary acquisition of the kindergarten pedagogy is not surprising; German science, technology, education and culture held such a strong position that Sweden was described as a German cultural province following the unification of Germany in 1871 to the First World War.[4]

The Swedish kindergarten movement first emerged as an informal network of private kindergartens, established mainly by women of the middle and upper classes who used their networks and resources to further the cause of kindergarten education. Like the kindergartens in Netherlands, described by Nelleke Bakker in this volume, the introduction of kindergartens to Sweden was an inherently bourgeois project. The first of these kindergartens, offering Froebelian education to children aged four to seven, were private institutions intended for privileged children, set up in the 1890s. These were followed by the first free kindergartens for working-class children that were established in the early 1900s, which soon became the most common form of kindergarten; eighty-two free kindergartens were established by 1937.[5]

In 1918, the network of kindergartens was organized into the Swedish Froebel Association (*Svenska Fröbelförbundet*), with Anna Warburg as president. Warburg, who was the strongest force behind the association's formation, illustrates the strong ties that the Swedish kindergarten movement had with its German counterpart. Born in Stockholm of German descent, she travelled between the countries and was chairwoman of the Hamburg-Froebel-Seminar before taking office as president of the Swedish Froebel Association.[6]

The purpose of the Swedish Froebel Association was 'to promote a sound development of Froebelian kindergartens' and to 'arouse interest and understanding of the Froebelian educational principles'.[7] During the period under study, this meant that an ongoing discussion was carried out in the association's journal, and elsewhere, on the true nature of these principles and how they should incorporate new currents in psychology and pedagogy. Swedish kindergartens have been described as an educational testing ground, where the educational methods of Maria Montessori, Emile Jaques-Dalcroze and Swedish sloyd were incorporated in the kindergarten.[8] In practice, this meant that the kindergartens employed a wide range of activities. Froebelian gifts featured side by side with plaiting, rhythmic play, Montessori activities and nursery rhymes. Sloyd, children's gymnastics and children's orchestras were also part of the schedule.[9]

The Swedish kindergarten movement's centre was its teacher training institutions. The first was opened in Stockholm in 1897 by Anna Eklund, who had been trained at the Pestalozzi-Fröbel-Haus in Berlin. The other three teacher training institutions were set up in Örebro in 1902 by Maria Kjellmark, in Norrköping in 1909 by the sisters Ellen and Maria Moberg and in Uppsala in 1911 by Professor I. A. Lundell.[10] Norrköping, where Ellen and Maria Moberg founded the Norrköping Froebel Society in 1909, became the main hub of the Swedish kindergarten movement. After teaching at Eklund's kindergarten in Stockholm, the Moberg sisters opened a private kindergarten in their home in 1899. Following their studies at the Pestalozzi-Fröbel-Haus in Berlin in 1900 and a visit to Froebel Educational Institute in London in 1904, the Moberg sisters opened the first free kindergarten (*Volkskindergarten,* or *folkbarnträdgård* in Swedish) in Sweden in 1904. It was named the Froebel House (*Fröbelstugan*), with the intention to instil healthy habits, belief in God, patriotism and a love of nature in working-class children. In 1909, the Moberg sisters inaugurated the kindergarten teacher training institute named the Froebel Institute (*Fröbelinstitutet*). The Froebel Institute would come to shape kindergarten education substantially in the decades to come, with some 500 teachers graduating from the institute by 1940.[11]

Not solely about the money

The Swedish kindergartens' fundraising events were part of a broader philanthropic tradition in the Western world and its colonies, in which fundraising for charity included events such as bazaars, gala dinners and charity anniversaries, but also the more recent fashion shows, sponsored walks and television spectaculars.[12] Kindergarten associations soon began to take advantage of such events. In the United States, for example, fundraisers for kindergartens included New Year's Eve Kindergarten Balls, May Festival Fairs, Thanksgiving bazaars and a wide variety of exhibitions.[13] While varying in size as well as content and social and economic functions, these fundraisers had at least two things in common: they raised money and drew attention to a charitable cause.[14]

The Swedish kindergarten fundraisers were–like, for example, fundraising fairs in the United States–generally organized by women.[15] More specifically, they were run by the female philanthropists from the middle and upper middle classes who were in charge of the kindergarten societies. Ellen (1874–1955) and Maria (1877–1948) Moberg, the leading figures of the Swedish kindergarten movement, are representative examples of such bourgeois women. Their father was a medical doctor with a PhD from Uppsala University and their mother was the daughter of a distinguished business executive. They both had an education suitable for women of their social standing, with studies in England, Germany and Switzerland.[16] This gave them both the required resources and the knowledge necessary to establish kindergartens.

The fundraising activities for Swedish kindergartens during the investigated period included Christmas parties, festivities for the feast day of Saint Lucia, lotteries, soirees, spring parties, fairs, theatre performances and ballroom spectacles. Some of these events were organized to mark a holiday, while others celebrated a kindergarten's twentieth anniversary, a kindergarten pioneer's birthday, Friedrich Froebel's birthday, or the opening of a new kindergarten or a kindergarten teacher training seminar.[17] Soirees, which were evening performances, could include readings, singing and theatre plays. At the recurrent fairs, the kindergarten societies sold both goods donated to the kindergarten for sale and items that the children had created themselves.[18] There were also public displays of kindergartens, where, for an entrance fee, members of the public were invited to visit kindergartens, to experience kindergarten activities and to buy handicrafts produced by the children at the kindergarten.[19]

When analysing the financial circumstances of kindergartens, it becomes evident that the fundraising events did not play a particularly important role. There were, of course, occasions when fundraisers were held primarily for monetary reasons. In 1927, the annual report of the Society for Children's Workshop and Free Kindergarten in Helsingborg noted, for example, that fairs had been held to improve the society's difficult financial position.[20] In Norrköping, a fundraiser was held to cover deficits in the Froebel Society's budget in 1927 and to fund additional expenditure on the kindergartens' premises in 1933.[21] But in general, the kindergartens were funded by private donations and, increasingly, by subsidies from municipalities and parishes. It was only in Norrköping, where grander charity events were arranged, that their revenue could amount to at most 3 per cent of total funding during the first half of the twentieth century.[22]

The limited economic significance of fundraisers may be understood in a wider social and economic context. In Sweden, there were a number of factors that spoke against the financing of welfare through private charity. At the turn of the century, Sweden had a small, albeit wealthy, upper class and a remarkably small middle class. In 1910, 70 per cent of the population lived in rural areas where a majority was either farmers or farm workers. In this poor but relatively egalitarian society, there was consequently not much room for the 'business of benevolence', compared to the United States, for example, which had 4,000 millionaires in the 1890s.[23]

The limited role of fundraisers is not unexpected. Previous studies on the history of philanthropy have shown that while fundraising events may have been one of the least effective methods for generating revenue, they were organized for other reasons. Apart from presenting bourgeois women with an opportunity to participate in public life or distracting middle-class women from the hardships of housework, fundraising events captured public attention, making it possible to expand the number of prospective donors.[24] Fundraisers may be understood as 'rituals of benevolence' that put the generosity of donors on public display.[25] Fundraising events also served as a means for generating internal solidarity among the members of philanthropic society and as occasions that enabled individuals or organizations to secure social status.[26]

As will be shown, the Norrköping Froebel Society's fundraisers had traces of such functions. The fundraisers garnered the general public's attention, which likely increased the kindergartens' potential for receiving subsidies from municipalities and donations from companies and wealthy individuals. The fundraisers were carefully designed to create a favourable image of kindergartens and their Froebelian pedagogy. These events portrayed the kindergarten as a Swedish institution, adapted to children's nature. Thus, they also contributed to the reproduction and dissemination of Swedish nationalist ideology and of bourgeois perceptions of childhood.

Spectacular evening shows

Norrköping Froebel Society's most significant fundraising events were the shows that they arranged each April or May. These so-called spring parties, Froebel feasts

Figure 5.2 The circus building prepared for the kindergarten party of 1924. The city's newspaper reported that the circus was embellished with pink and green ribbons tied together in a large flower wreath under the circus dome. 'Barnträdgårdsfesterna i cirkus' *Norrköpings tidningar*, 7 April 1924. Image no. 91, K1:2, Fröbelföreningen i Norrköping, Norrköpings Stadsarkiv.

or kindergarten parties, with equivalents arranged by kindergarten societies in other cities, were usually held during one or two evenings in one of Norrköping's larger halls.[27] The purpose of these premises, built for amusement and entertainment, reveals the character of these events. A number of shows were arranged in Norrköping's circus building (see Figure 5.2). Built in 1904, with room for 1,900 spectators, it was usually the host of circus companies such as Circus Frankoni and Circus Hoffman. Owing to its size, it was also the site for fundraisers that included the kindergarten party of 1924 and the Froebel feast of 1927. Froebel Society fundraisers were also held at Norrköping's Auditorium, with room for 1,200 spectators, the Norrköping Theatre, which was built in 1908 to accommodate 800 spectators, and the Workers' Association's theatre.[28]

These fundraisers were grandiose events, especially considering that they were organized by a society that, in 1936, ran only three kindergartens with 160 children in total.[29] Norrköping Theatre, once the largest and most modern theatre building outside the Swedish capital of Stockholm, was described as 'packed from floor to ceiling' during the kindergarten spring party of 1935. The kindergarten party in 1924 was sold out, and for the theatre performance at Norrköping Auditorium in 1942, 1,230 tickets were sold.[30] The Froebel Society's fundraisers thus certainly attracted considerable attention to the kindergartens and their cause.

Available source materials do not allow a detailed analysis of the spectators of these events. Since they charged admission fees, and I have not found any indications that poor spectators were exempt from paying, these events were presumably not intended for the poor. The size of the events also indicates that they did not target only the philanthropically minded elite, but instead suggests that they were arranged for a broad stratum of the middle class and the (sufficiently) well-off working class. These evening shows all had a similar setup. They often began with a few musical pieces and then continued with short theatre plays, dances, displays of children playing, tableaux vivants and vocal pieces. Usually the programme consisted of five to nine short pieces, and all performances featured either kindergarten children or student-teachers from the Froebel Institute.

The Froebel Society did not have the same concerns about 'educational stunts', performed only to strengthen the standing of a school, that Amy Palmer has found in the writings of British Froebelians.[31] Instead, it was precisely the stunt quality of these performances that was appealing for audiences and organizers. The events featured ambitious performances which were well suited to the venues chosen by the Froebel Society. One striking example of this is the staging of *Sleeping Beauty* in 1927 (see Figure 5.1). This play, consisting of three acts, had twenty-one named roles, and in addition included some thirty kindergarten children playing the roles of court ladies, pageboys and others.[32] The staging of *The Princess Who Never Smiled* (1939), originally a Russian fairy tale, had a similar setup. Consisting of one act and two tableaux vivants, it had a total of twenty-nine roles. Apart from the eleven main roles, which included the King, the Queen and the Princess, the play had eighteen unnamed roles, including a first and a second butterfly, two trolls and five bridesmaids.[33]

The main focus of the fundraisers was not the donors, whose generosity was often highlighted at such events, but rather the good cause of the kindergartens.[34] Similar to the promotional literature of the US free kindergartens, these events were about raising the public profile of the kindergarten.[35] Naturally, this meant that some light fell on Friedrich Froebel, the kindergarten originator. Froebel was recalled not only in the names of Norrköping's Froebel Society and of the national kindergarten association (*Svenska Fröbelförbundet*), but also at the events themselves, where a bust of him was often placed at the back of the stage.[36] The kindergarten pedagogy was also visualized, typically using rhythmic plays, theatrical performances and songs. Under the heading 'The Childhood Paradise', at the kindergarten party of 1924, the society sought to illustrate how the kindergarten aspired to arouse the children's sense of nature and beauty. Children would perform some of the activities that would constitute a typical day at the kindergarten. In 1927, the children demonstrated seven games, and in 1932, a children's orchestra performed on stage, which was followed by the display of a rhythmic play ('Travelling to Holland').[37]

Occasionally, the kindergarten's merits were also described. At the kindergarten party of 1924, the audience was told about the accomplishments of the kindergartens. In a recital, an orator explained why mothers should leave their children at the kindergarten. The orator told the audience that children receive the best care in kindergartens and compared kindergartens with gardens where plants are watered and nurtured. In the kindergarten, children not only received protection from their urban environment but had their minds challenged and trained as well. In addition, the kindergarten taught them about play and the nature of joy.[38] Apart from such recitals, the fundraisers also featured reports on the history of the Froebel Society and the presentation of slides portraying the society and its kindergartens.[39]

The fundraisers succeeded in attracting public appreciation, not only among the numerous spectators of these events, but also in Norrköping's newspaper. The newspaper articles reporting on these events regularly commented on how the fundraisers were held in festively decorated venues, with sweet little children revealing the good work of kindergartens. The spring party of 1935, for example, was described as extraordinarily successful. A newspaper report noted that the freshness and charm of the young actors made it difficult for the audience not to interrupt the performance with applause and loud approvals. In addition, the report even compared the quality of the pantomimes with acts included in professional variety shows.[40] In 1939, an article noted that the crowded audience of Norrköping Theatre was 'unanimously delighted' by all the beauty that the children and the so-called Froebel ladies created on stage. Apart from the magnificent decorations, the journalist appreciated the natural charm of the kindergarten.[41] Although these evening shows did not result in significant revenue, such gushing reviews helped to generate the attention needed for the Froebel Society to attract private donations and public subsidies.

Bourgeois fundraisers for a bourgeois childhood

Although the Norrköping Froebel Society's fundraisers put Froebel and his pedagogy on display, these events were not comprehensive demonstrations of the complex pedagogy and educational philosophy of the Swedish kindergartens. These events are an excellent example of how Froebelian education was adapted not only to the national context, but also to local and more specific settings. The fundraising events did not present a representative selection of kindergarten activities or illustrate the complexities of a Swedish kindergarten ideology affected by contemporary currents in educational philosophy and psychology. Instead, these events reduced the Swedish kindergartens to a simple, entertaining and attractive image of a bourgeois institution, providing working-class children with a bourgeois childhood.

In this respect, these fundraisers were not cross-class spectacles, which emphasized existing social hierarchies between the rich and the poor.[42] Rather, these events presented a homogenous bourgeois children's culture to the audience while ignoring social and cultural differences. This culture was marked by an ideology of childhood that, in mid-nineteenth-century Europe, had established itself in the middle classes. This ideology, with roots in the Enlightenment as well as in Romanticism, distinguished childhood from adult life, emphasizing the significance of childhood both for the life course of individuals and for the society at large. Childhood thus came to be seen as 'the greatest asset of any civilization', to use the phrase of the Swedish author Ellen Key in her international bestseller *The Century of the Child* (1900).[43]

In line with this children's culture, the Swedish kindergarten movement advocated an idyllic understanding of childhood which emphasized the demarcation between childhood and adulthood.[44] The childhood that was reproduced by the fundraising performances was consequently separated from adult life, a distinction that the Moberg sisters themselves consciously endorsed. They argued, for example, that traditional Swedish songs such as 'High Mountains and Deep Valleys', with lyrics describing all-night dancing, and 'Seven Beautiful Girls in a Ring' were inappropriate for children because of their erotic undertones.[45] This meant that much that was associated with the adult world during the economically and politically turbulent first half of the twentieth century was excluded from the fundraising events. There were exceptions, such as when the vicar Samuel Thysell reminded the audience at a Christmas play in 1942 that children in many other countries would not have a happy Christmas that year.[46] Nevertheless, modern society and its social and political conflicts, such as the bread riot of 1917 in Norrköping, were usually excluded from the world that was portrayed at the fundraising events.[47]

Instead, the audience was treated with performances focusing on issues that were considered as belonging to the world of children, mirroring Froebel's belief in the innocence of children, and his pastoral and romantic visions of childhood. In this respect, the events rested heavily upon a European bourgeois culture. In addition to tales such as *Sleeping Beauty* (*Törnrosa*), *Snow White* (*Snövit*) and *Sandman* (*John Blund*), the events also drew upon a European musical heritage. Among the pieces performed were *Der Maimond*, written by the German-born Danish composer Friedrich Kuhlau, *Sourire D'Avril* written by the French composer Maurice Depret, and Johannes Brahms's *Wiegenlied* (most widely known as *Brahms's Lullaby*).[48]

The topics covered by the events were the same as those deemed suitable for children's songs and children's books in Sweden as the programme of the events focused on nature and the everyday life of rural or small-town society. Consequently, the programme entailed songs about baker boys, sailors and flour mills, and children also performed plays on topics such as sheep shearing and gardening. Attention was devoted to nature's animals and plants, which were common themes in Swedish children's songs at the turn of the century.[49] The fundraisers' programme included songs and plays with titles that mentioned bluebells, dandelions, butterflies and bees and birds such as the great tit, sparrows and bullfinches.[50]

The seasons of the year were also a recurring theme at the Froebel Society's fundraisers, reflecting the distinct seasonal changes in Sweden.[51] At the kindergarten spring party of 1935, the seasons were enacted through tableaux vivants. Autumn was presented in a scene with the children of the forest (*Tomtebobarnen*), inspired by Elsa Beskow's well-known book about a forest family, while winter featured in a scene in which children portrayed snowflakes and winter birds. Spring was depicted by children acting as raindrops and flowers, and summer was represented by flowers, bumblebees and a traditional dance around the maypole.[52] In the Froebel Society's spring parties, spring was naturally the season dominating the programmes. Nonetheless, as in the children's songs of the period, the typical moral message conveyed was that each season was equally important. The song *Olle's Ski Trip*, for example, told the story about how happy the children are when King Winter finally arrives, how delighted they are when Aunt Thaw comes to visit and the joy that Princess Spring brings with her.[53]

A truly Swedish kindergarten

Although the fundraising events were based upon a shared European cultural heritage, the Swedish kindergarten movement emphasized that its kindergartens were genuinely Swedish. Gerda Meyerson, for example, claimed that the Swedish kindergarten was Swedish through and through, for although Froebel's educational teachings were followed, the kindergartens used songs, games and children's tales of Swedish origins.[54] Even though this stance may seem peculiar, not least in light of the ties that the Swedish kindergarten movement had with its German counterpart, it is not unexpected. Indeed, it was consistent with the nationalistic sentiments rising to what historian Eric Hobsbawm termed the 'apogee of nationalism' after the First World War.[55]

This image of a Swedish kindergarten was conveyed by the Froebel Society's fundraising events, where Swedish culture was put on display. Apart from performing plays based on Swedish tales such as *Pelle Snygg och barnen i Snaskeby* (1896), published in English as *Clean Peter and the Children of Grubbylea*, the fundraising events were to a large extent based on tales by Elsa Beskow and songs by Alice Tegnér. Beskow was Sweden's preeminent children's book artist and Tegnér the creator of several of Sweden's best-known children's songs.[56] The significance of Beskow's and Tegner's work was also commented upon by the Moberg sisters, who argued that the lives of Beskow and Tegnér were 'inextricably linked' with the history of the Swedish kindergartens. According to the sisters, it was Beskow and Tegnér who gave the kindergarten 'a true Swedish character'.[57] In addition to presenting Swedish songs and tales, the fundraisers featured a substantial amount of nationalistic content. These events were celebrations not only of the kindergarten, but of the motherland as well. In the child-friendly bourgeois nationalism that the fundraisers reproduced, the Swedish flag occupied a central position. On numerous occasions, flag poles were raised and flags hoisted, accompanied by songs such as 'We're hoisting our flag' and 'The Flagpole', the latter telling the tale of a father and a son who built a flagpole.[58]

The Swedish natural environment was another recurrent theme of kindergarten fundraising events, not least in ceremonial vocal pieces such as 'Sun over Sweden' (*Sol över Sverige*) and 'Blessed the Land' (*Land du välsignade*). In the style of national romanticism, the latter paid tribute to the Swedish motherland and its midnight sun, midwinter snow, thick forests, open plains and rich harvests. Another example is 'Sweden' (*Sverige*), which was a song that was submitted to the contest for the selection of the Swedish national anthem. The performance of such a piece, solemnly describing the Swedish natural environment and the seasonal changes from the deep snow of Christmas to the bright evenings of June, is yet an example of how these fundraisers portrayed the kindergarten as a truly Swedish institution.[59]

A pyrrhic victory?

The fundraising events considered in this chapter were multifaceted phenomena that served a number of functions. Apart from providing kindergartens with some financial contributions, these events garnered the attention the kindergartens needed in order to receive both private donations and public support from municipalities. Norrköping Froebel Society's spectacular evening shows are an excellent example of this type of effort. They drew large crowds in halls that could accommodate as many as 1,900 spectators and reached even wider audiences through the articles that were subsequently published in the city's newspaper.

These fundraisers demonstrated how the kindergarten idea could be transformed, not only by national culture, but also by specific settings, such as the Norrköping Froebel Society's evening shows. Even though Froebel and kindergarten pedagogy were put on public display, these events were not comprehensive demonstrations of the pedagogy and philosophy of kindergartens. Instead, the complexity of the kindergarten pedagogy was reduced to a rather simple and enjoyable message about the kindergartens as a good cause and a genuinely Swedish institution suitable for children's nature, a message conveyed through vocal pieces, theatre performances and tableaux vivants. Unlike British Froebelians who voiced their concerns over so-called educational stunts, Swedish Froebelians intended these fundraising events to be just that.

While these fundraisers managed to raise the public profile of Swedish kindergartens, one might question whether this was a successful strategy in the long run. By emphasizing the institutions' character as Swedish kindergartens, Froebelians also distanced themselves from state representatives who believed that the concept of kindergarten was problematic and who argued that Swedish preschooling should be built upon the most current educational and psychological research. To Swedish politicians such as Alva Myrdal, who later held important positions in the United Nations, the kindergarten and its heritage appeared outdated and excessively dependent on a German cultural context.[60] In this respect, the kindergarten's high-profile fundraising events may be regarded as a kind of pyrrhic victory: while they contributed to the establishment of kindergartens in Sweden during the early twentieth century, they reduced the ability of the kindergarten movement to participate in the post-war expansion of the preschool sector.

Abbreviations

FNN   Fröbelföreningen i Norrköping.

NSA   Norrköpings stadsarkiv.

Notes

1   The standard work on the *Norrköpings tidningar* Swedish kindergartens is Ann-Katrin Hatje, *Från treklang till triangeldrama. Barnträdgården som ett kvinnligt samhällsprojekt under 1880-1940-talen* (Lund: Historiska Media, 1999).

2   The international diffusion and transformation of the kindergarten are discussed in Roberta Wollons, 'Introduction: On the International Diffusion, Politics, and Transformation of the Kindergarten', in *Kindergartens and Cultures: The Global Diffusion of an Idea*, ed. Roberta Wollons (New Haven: Yale University Press, 2000), 1–15.

3   For more on the kindergarten in New Zealand, see the chapter by Helen May in this volume.

4   Regarding kindergarten and the relationship between Sweden and Germany, see Johannes Westberg, 'Den svenska importen av Fröbel', in *Kulturtransfer och kulturpolitik: Sverige och Tyskland under det tjugonde århundradet*, ed. Andreas Åkerlund (Uppsala: Historiska institutionen, 2011), 17–37; Johan Östling, 'Ett gravtal över tysk kultur: Thomas Mann och valfrändskapens växlingar under tidig efterkrigstid', in *Kulturtransfer och kulturpolitik: Sverige och Tyskland under det tjugonde århundradet*, ed. Andreas Åkerlund (Uppsala: Historiska institutionen, 2011), 41.

5   SOU [Swedish Government Official Report] 1938:20, *Betänkande angående barnkrubbor och sommarkolonier m.m.* (Stockholm, 1938), 26.

6   Hatje, *Från treklang till triangeldrama*, 89, 159–64. To commemorate her life's work, a school in Anna Warburg's name has been established in Hamburg, see http://www.anna-warburg-schule.de/ (accessed 24 August 2015).

7   'Stadgar', *Svenska Fröbel-förbundets tidskrift barnträdgården*, nos. 1–2 (1919): 24.

8   Hatje, *Från treklang till triangeldrama*, 104–6. Regarding the kindergarten movement's relation to sloyd in the case of England, see Kevin Brehony, ' "Even Far Distant Japan" is "Showing an Interest": The English Froebel Movement's Turn to Sloyd', *History of Education* 27, no. 3 (1998): 279–95.

9   Johannes Westberg, *Förskolepedagogikens framväxt: Pedagogisk förändring och dess förutsättningar, ca 1835-1945* (Uppsala: Acta Universitatis Upsaliensis, 2008), 178–81; Ann-Christine Vallberg Roth, *De yngre barnens läroplanshistoria: Från 1800-talets mitt till idag* (Lund: Studentlitteratur, 2002), 64–75.

10 Hatje, *Från treklang till triangeldrama*, 160–1.

11 Ibid., 39–40.

12 For a good introduction to several of these events, and their historiography, see Margaret Tennant, 'Fun and Fundraising: The Selling of Charity in New Zealand's Past', *Social History* 38, no. 1 (2013): 46–65. For studies of bazaars, fundraising fairs and charity anniversaries, see also, for instance, Beverly Gordon, *Bazaars and Fair Ladies: The History of the American Fundraising Fair* (Knoxville, TN: University of Tennessee Press, 1998); Sarah Lloyd, 'Pleasing Spectacles and Elegant Dinners: Conviviality, Benevolence, and Charity Anniversaries in Eighteenth-Century London', *Journal of British Studies* 41, no. 1 (2002): 23–57.

13 Roger W. Boop, *Fulfilling the Charter: The Story of the College of Education at Butler University and More* … (Bloomington, IN: iUniverse, 2008), 6; Rosemary O'Day, 'Women and Education in Nineteenth-Century England', in *Women, Scholarship and Criticism: Gender and Knowledge c. 1790-1900*, ed. Joan Bellamy, Anne Laurence and Gillian Perry (Manchester: Manchester University Press, 2000), 99; Jay Winston Driskell, Jr., *Schooling Jim Crow: The Fight for Atlanta's Booker T. Washington High School and the Roots of Black Protest Politics* (Charlottesville and London: University of Virginia Press, 2014), 117.

14 Cf. the discussion on the characteristics of fundraising events in Daniel Webber, 'Understanding Charity Fundraising Events', *International Journal of Nonprofit and Voluntary Sector Marketing* 9, no. 2 (2003): 123–4.

15 Gordon, *Bazaars and Fair Ladies*, xix.

16 H. G.-M (1987), 'Moberg, släkt', *Svenskt biografiskt lexikon*. Available online: http://sok.riksarkivet.se/sbl/artikel/9371 (accessed 24 August 2015). The public portrayal of the Moberg sisters as kindergarten pioneers is analysed in Johannes Westberg,

'The Making of Froebelian Heroes: Ellen and Maria Moberg in the History of
Swedish Kindergartens', in *Fröbelpädagogik im Kontext der Moderne. Bildung,
Erziehung und soziales Handeln*, ed. Ulf Sauerbrey and Michael Winkler (Jena:
Verlag IKS Garamond, 2010).

17 See for example, 'Vid invigningen ...' *Kindergarten*, Spring: (1916), 7;
    'Barnträdgårdarnas Jubileumsfest' (1927), *Tomte-klockan*: 11; 'Festdagar i
    Barnträdgården' (1937), Tomte-klockan: 10.

18 See for example, annual report 1925, B1:2, Föreningen för arbetsstugor och
    folkkindergarten (FAF), Helsingborgs stadsarkiv (HS); Minutes 27 October 1942,
    A1:3, Nya Husmodersföreningen i Örebro, Örebro stadsarkiv.

19 Minutes 15 February 1933, A1:1, FFN, NSA.

20 Annual report 1925, B1:2, FAF, HS. Children's Workshops (*arbetsstugor*) were
    youth recreation centres with a focus on handicrafts and manual training. See
    Anna Hierta-Retzius, *Manual Training of Children: Children's Workshops in Sweden*
    (Stockholm: Proprius, 1904).

21 Minutes 28 March 1927, 15 February 1933, A1:1, FFN, NSA. Economic motives are
    also apparent in Maria Moberg's description of kindergartens' fundraisers. Letter
    from Maria Moberg, 28 March 1926, Disa Beijer's collection of letters, National
    Library of Sweden (KB).

22 Annual reports 1905–47, F1:2, FFN, NSA. For other examples of fundraisers
    organized by kindergarten societies, see 'Prolog vid soirén den 16 mars 1915',
    Kindergarten, Spring (1915): 5; 'Barnträdgårdarnas Dag' (1928), *Tomte-klockan*: 6;
    Minutes 28 February 1942, A1a:1, Västerås barnstugor (VB), Västerås stadsarkiv
    (VS). A brief overview of the funding of Swedish kindergartens, infant schools
    and crèches is presented in Johannes Westberg, 'The Funding of Early Care and
    Education Programmes in Sweden, 1845-1943', *History of Education* 40, no. 4
    (2011): 465–79.

23 Lena Sommestad, 'Privat eller offentlig välfärd? Ett genusperspektiv på
    välfärdsstaternas historiska formering', *Historisk tidskrift* 114, no. 4 (1994): 620;
    Lena Sommestad, 'Human Reproduction and the Rise of Welfare States: An
    Economic-demographic Approach to Welfare State Formation in the United
    States and Sweden', *Scandinavian Economic History Review* 46, no. 2 (1998):
    107–9.

24 Webber, 'Understanding Charity Fundraising Events', 122–34; Annette Shiell,
    *Fundraising, Flirtation and Fancywork: Charity Bazaars in Nineteenth Century
    Australia* (Newcastle upon Tyne: Cambridge Scholars Press, 2012), 8.

25 Elizabeth Rose, *A Mother's Job: The History of Day Care, 1890-1960* (New York:
    Oxford University Press, 1999), 62.

26 Lloyd, 'Pleasing Spectacles and Elegant Dinners', 28; Tennant, 'Fun and Fundraising', 46.

27 See for example, the spring parties held in Västerås Theatre, described in Minutes 28
    February 1942, A1a:1, VB, VS.

28 'En stad med stolta cirkustraditioner', *Norrköpings tidningar*, 23 May 1998: 12; 'Att
    leende säga sanningen ...', *Norrköpings tidningar*, 15 March 2008; Programme, F2b:1,
    FFN, NSA; Image no. 2437, K1: 17, FFN, NSA.

29 Annual report 1936, F1:2, FFN, NSA.

30 'Barnträdgårdsfesterna i cirkus', *Norrköpings tidningar*, 7 April 1924;
    'Barnträdgårdarnas vårfest', *Norrköpings tidningar*, 31 May 1935; Programme 1942,
    F2b:1, FFN, NSA.

31 See Amy Palmer's chapter in this volume.

32 Programme 1927, F2b:1, FFN, NSA; *Norrköpings tidningar,* 21 May 1927.
33 Programme 1939, F2b:1, FFN, NSA.
34 Regarding fundraising events that highlights donors, see Tennant, 'Fun and Fundraising', 47; Westberg, 'The Funding of Early Care and Education', 477–8.
35 Kristen D. Nawrotzki, ' "Greatly Changed for the Better": Free Kindergartens as Transatlantic Reformance', *History of Education Quarterly* 49, no. 2 (2009): 182–95.
36 See for example, 'Barnträdgårdsfesterna i cirkus', *Norrköpings tidningar,* 7 April 1924. Froebel's name was, however, lost when the association in 1939 changed its name to *Educational Association for the Preschool Age* (Pedagogiska föreningen för förskoleåldern). 'Svenska Fröbelförbundets årsmöte' (1939), *Svenska Fröbelförbundets tidskrift,* no. 3: 41–2.
37 'Barnträdgårdsfesterna i cirkus', *Norrköpings tidningar,* 7 April 1924; Programmes 1924, 1927, 1932, F2b:1, FFN, NSA.
38 Programme 1924, F2b:1, FFN, NSA.
39 Programme 1929, F2b:1, FFN, NSA.
40 'Barnträdgårdarnas vårfest', *Norrköpings tidningar ,* 31 May 1935.
41 'Ungdomligt på teatern', *Norrköpings tidningar,* 5 May 1939.
42 The concept of 'cross-class spectacle fundraising' is applied in the analysis of philanthropy in David Huyssen, *Progressive Inequality: Rich and Poor in New York, 1890-1920* (Cambridge, MA: Harvard University Press, 2014), 142.
43 Hugh Cunningham, *Children and Childhood in Western Society since 1500* (London: Longman, 2005), 41. The quote by Ellen Key is from Ibid., 172.
44 Hatje, *Från treklang till triangeldrama,* 104.
45 'Sånglek och fri lek', *Svenska Fröbel-Förbundets Tidskrift Barnträdgården,* nos. 3–4 (1919): 40.
46 'Julspel för barn i Hörsalen', *Norrköpings tidningar,* 21 December 1942.
47 The bread riot of 1917 is analysed in Björn Horgby, *Egensinne och skötsamhet: arbetarkulturen i Norrköping 1850-1940* (Stockholm: Carlsson, 1993), 333–60.
48 Programme 1924, 1929, 1933, 1935, 1939, F2b:1, FFN, NSA.
49 Finn Zetterholm, *Barnvisan i Sverige: barnvisans blomstring kring sekelskiftet; bakgrund, genrer och motiv* (Stockholm: Proprius, 1969), 67.
50 See for example, Programme 1924, 1927, 1933, F2b:1, FFN, NSA.
51 Zetterholm, *Barnvisan i Sverige,* 72–6.
52 Programme 1935, F2b:1, FFN, NSA.
53 Programme 1924, F2b:1, FFN, NSA.
54 Gerda Meyerson quoted in Moje Lindberg, *90 års barnomsorg 1874-1964. En utvecklingsstudie* (Norrköping: Institutionen för förskollärarutbildning, 1991), 50.
55 Eric J. Hobsbawm, *Nations and Nationalism since 1780: Programme, Myth, Reality* (Cambridge: Cambridge University Press, 1992), ch. 5. Regarding Swedish nationalism, see Patrik Hall, *The Social Construction of Nationalism: Sweden as an Example* (Lund: Lund University Press, 1998).
56 Barbro Klein, 'Cultural Loss and Cultural Rescue: Lilli Zickerman, Ottilia Adelborg, and the Promises of the Swedish Homecraft Movement', in *The Benefit of Broad Horizons: Intellectual and Institutional Preconditions for a Global Social Science,* ed. Hans Joas and Barbro Klein (Leiden: Brill, 2010), 269. Regarding Elsa Beskow and Alice Tegnér, see Lennart Reimers, *Alice Tegnérs barnvisor* (Bromma: Edition Reimers, 1983); Stina Hammar, *Solägget: fantasi och verklighet i Elsa Beskows konst* (Stockholm: Bonnier, 2002).

57 'Elsa Beskow och Alice Tegnér', *Svenska Fröbel-Förbundets Tidskrift*, no. 1 (1934): 1.
58 Programme 1924, F2b:1, FFN, NSA.
59 See for example, Programme 1924, 1929, 1933, F2b:1, FFN, NSA. Regarding this competition, in which Tegnér also participated, see Reimers, *Alice Tegnérs barnvisor*, 175.
60 Westberg, 'Den svenska importen av Fröbel', 33.

6

'Such marvelous training': Grand Rapids, Michigan as a Kindergartening Centre, 1870–1905

Kristen Nawrotzki

As in other places, the introduction of the kindergarten to North America was accomplished almost exclusively by women. In the United States, these included the German émigrée Margarethe Meyer Schurz, who founded the first German-speaking kindergarten in Wisconsin in 1856, and Elizabeth Palmer Peabody and Susan E. Blow, who founded English-speaking kindergartens in Boston and St Louis, respectively. These efforts, influenced by the work of Froebel's protégées in Germany and England, were the beginning of what would become a coordinated, powerful and successful nationwide movement for kindergarten education.

Histories of American kindergarten education have highlighted those first efforts in St Louis and in Boston and Peabody's and Blow's roles in drawing American women to the Froebelian cause – and rightly so.[1] However, with the spread of Froebel clubs and kindergarten associations, and the foundation of training schools, additional centres of influence came to drive the movement in the late nineteenth century. The need for locally engaged branches of the kindergarten movement was especially salient, given that expenditures on public education in the United States were (and are) locally determined, so that the inclusion of kindergarten education into public schools had to be negotiated and effected at state and local levels, not at the national level.

Grand Rapids, Michigan became one such centre for the kindergarten movement. In a short span of time, the city went from being oblivious to Froebelian education to being a centre of the state movement and an influence on national movements for private, charity and, eventually, public school kindergarten education. Thus, the people of Grand Rapids not only experienced a 'conversion' to the kindergarten way, but they also served as missionaries elsewhere. For this reason, the city is a prime target for a case-study investigation of the dynamics of the movement and efforts towards the institutionalization of kindergarten education in US public schools. By piecing together the narrative of Grand Rapids' 'kindergarten conversion', we can discover how the growing national movement played out on the local level, and who and what was crucial to its eventual success. This case study utilizes the archival records of the

Grand Rapids Kindergarten Training School (GRKTS) and the personal papers of individuals associated with the kindergarten movement in that city.

The national context 1870–1910

Elizabeth Peabody's initial kindergartening efforts gained attention in the 1860s, but it was not until the 1870s that American educators began to take interest in Froebelian education. There had been infant schools for young children in parts of the United States in the early nineteenth century, but these were shuttered after educational and medical experts issued warnings against the dangers to mind and body of premature academic training.[2] Thus there was a dearth of early childhood education (ECE) provision, and to some extent Americans were 'once bitten, twice shy' when it came to education of the youngest children. It was in this context that Peabody and Blow, both educated and well-connected women, began to promote the merits of Froebelian education. As politically liberal newspapers in the eastern United States began publishing articles about the kindergarten, increasing numbers of educators and social reformers took notice.

In addition to (and because of) Blow's and Peabody's efforts, private kindergartens began in several cities in the 1870s and 1880s, and were attended by the three- to five-year-old children of affluent families. By the late 1870s, kindergartners began experimenting with 'free' or charity kindergartens as a means of education-based social reform and child-saving in urban slums.[3] Quickly allied with social welfare movements, the kindergartens became fixtures in settlement houses and were supported by local and national women's organizations, both secular and religious. 'Free kindergarten associations' soon formed and their members developed networks of communication through newsletters, lecture tours and conventions. Supporters of free kindergarten sought to have their institutions taken up by the expanding public schools in hopes that this would ensure greater availability of kindergarten education. These efforts were successful, but at a cost; the institutional contexts and exigencies of the public schools, plus the added influence of developmental psychology and child study in the early twentieth century and beyond, meant that public kindergartens shared increasingly little with Froebel's theory and methods, and instead became in many ways a uniquely American public educational institution.[4]

Kindergarten comes to Grand Rapids, 1870–80

How did Grand Rapids become a centre of kindergartening? Grand Rapids was (and is) the largest city in western Michigan. Michigan was granted statehood in 1837 and Grand Rapids itself was organized as a village the next year. Soon thereafter, western Michigan's lumber industry began to expand. Grand Rapids, well situated on a river, was incorporated as a city in 1850. Railroad links contributed to the local economic boom, and the representation of Grand Rapids furniture makers at the 1876 Centennial Exposition in Philadelphia, Pennsylvania led to the city being nicknamed the 'Furniture Capital of the World'.[5] This rapid development brought not only immense wealth to the area but also an array of urban problems: the city doubled its population *twice* within the space of twenty years, from 16,500 residents in 1870 to over 60,000 in 1890.[6]

Local lore held that the city's first contact with Froebelian education was via distinguished local resident Dr Frances A. Rutherford, who stayed at the home of a Professor Monroe while visiting Boston in 1872. Rutherford was fascinated to learn that the four Monroe daughters (ages two to eight) attended the Peabody Kindergarten. Having noted 'the satisfaction with which these parents watched the growth of their quartette' due to 'such marvelous training', Rutherford initiated plans to bring a kindergarten teacher to Grand Rapids to work with the city's own equally 'marvelous children'.[7]

Upon returning to Grand Rapids, Rutherford used a Ladies' Literary Club room for a public meeting attended by prominent citizens, including professors from nearby colleges and clergy members. Enough patrons were secured to begin planning for a private kindergarten immediately. The first kindergarten in Grand Rapids opened in May 1873 on the second floor of a downtown building. The teacher, Miss Hyde, came from the Peabody Kindergarten Training School in Boston to teach ten pupils aged four to six years. Maintaining order in her classroom proved to be a difficult task, as 'visitors were constant, in season and out of season'.[8]

With the curiosity of the city's elites piqued, the second year brought an increase of patronage. By the end of the third year, however, 'the first pupils here had entered the public schools and in our families there were no younger children ready for the kindergarten'.[9] More likely there were many children ages four to six who might have attended the kindergarten, but few parents were willing or able to pay the $60.00 per term, causing the first kindergarten in Grand Rapids to close in 1876. Two years later there was a new kindergarten in the city, this one opened by Maria Baker in conjunction with a private school she ran in her home. Like many others offering 'kindergarten' at that time, Baker had no training in Froebelian methods, but instead incorporated Froebelian gifts and occupations, stories and songs into her classes according to her own interpretation.[10] Baker's kindergarten was soon joined by several other private kindergartens, some short-lived.[11]

As Froebelians opened early kindergartens in Grand Rapids, Froebel's ideas were being discussed in the rest of the country, with proponents setting up Froebel clubs and, eventually, kindergarten associations committed to preserving Froebel's theory and practices. Many were in close contact with other Froebelians, exchanging literature, soliciting advice, reporting on progress and organizing visits to and from a core of experts, largely emanating from Blow's and Peabody's respective orbits. Grand Rapids kindergartners became contributors to these national and even international networks, which facilitated the spread of kindergarten education and training.[12] As a result, similar tactics were applied in attempts to develop kindergartening in different places.

Free kindergartens in focus, 1880–90

Like many US kindergarten proponents in the early 1880s, Grand Rapids Froebelians worked towards two goals: one was to open private kindergartens for the children of the city's growing elite and the other was to provide free or practically free kindergarten education to the urban poor. The local market for private kindergarten education expanded in the early 1880s, as new private kindergartens were opened by, among others, former students of Elizabeth Harrison in Chicago and Louise Pollock in Boston.[13] It did not take long for talk of free kindergartens to appear in Grand Rapids, either; despite the strength of the region's expanding lumber and furniture industries, Grand Rapids suffered from the economic recessions of the 1870s and 1880s. That, combined with the vast increase in population, meant that poverty, crime and the cultural integration of immigrants were concerns for local leaders; free kindergartens were one tool they used to cope with these immense challenges.

In this respect, the city reflected the trend in cities across the country; as early as 1880, there were free kindergartens in cities as far afield as New York and Washington DC, as well as in those closer to Grand Rapids, including Chicago, Detroit and Cincinnati.[14] Hundreds of free kindergarten associations were founded between 1880 and 1900, and Grand Rapids was no different – except, perhaps, that its free kindergarten movement was surprisingly active (and successful) for a city of its size. The city's Free Kindergarten Association was founded in 1884 and had seventy-five members by the end of its first year.[15] The founders and officers of this organization included Superintendent of Schools I. N. Mitchell as president and Emma Field (principal of Grandville Avenue School) as vice president; trained kindergartener Clara M. Wheeler was among the first committee chairpersons. The organization sought to establish, maintain and control 'one or more Free Kindergartens within the City of Grand Rapids', to disseminate 'kindergarten literature and knowledge' and to effect 'the amelioration of the children of the city'.[16] Although affluent individuals were involved in the association's founding, most of the free kindergarten funding came from admission fees of $0.25 per person to various public lectures – for example, those held by the literary critic and educationist Denton J. Snider, a founding member of the Hegelian Idealist St Louis Philosophical Society who had taught for a time at Susan Blow's St Louis training school.

The Free Kindergarten Association's first project was to form a free kindergarten for a trial period of one year to show the city how much a class run by a trained kindergartner could benefit its poorest children. This class began in late 1884 with Boston-trained Lilly Gray in charge of approximately twenty pupils.[17] A June 1885 newspaper article declared that 'parents universally were pleased with the work … and would consider it a great misfortune if the kindergarten should be discontinued'.[18] Discontinuation was a possibility, as the association ended its first year with a deficit of $117.15, but only a remote one, as its furniture manufacturer members (including Charles R. Sligh, who would soon become president of the National Furniture Manufacturing Association), could have been relied upon to contribute additional support.[19] Nonetheless, its external fundraising efforts proceeded apace, with members holding talks and meetings at various churches and societies in order to drum up financial and moral support.[20] Other free kindergartens followed; one example was founded in 1888 by the local Circle of King's Daughters (an inter-denominational Christian service organization), which also founded a day nursery in the poorest part of town. Its executive board was dominated by the wives of the city's industrialists and its kindergarten run by a graduate kindergartner.[21]

Attempts at institutionalization 1880–90

In addition to seeing the free kindergartens as a means of social work, Grand Rapids free kindergarten supporters – like their colleagues elsewhere – also wanted to spur the local school board to adopt kindergartening in public schools, thereby expanding access to kindergarten education. They suggested that public school kindergartens might, in addition to providing welfare-oriented forms of support and training to immigrant and poor children in particular, also support the healthy, all-sided development of the child – every child, no matter his or her family background.[22]

As the influential San Francisco kindergartner and novelist Kate Douglas Wiggin emphasized a few years later, the goal of the public school kindergarten was not to create child geniuses, but 'to train the average, respectable citizen. Not to develop exceptional men, but to raise the level of the average.' Mixing a child-saving discourse with a reminder of the Froebelian pedagogy behind it all, she referred to the kindergarten as a means of saving children 'from incapacity and from the grinding poverty, the mischievous idleness which sow the seeds of criminals'.[23] That powerful combination of discourses – plus an emphasis on the kindergarten as key to public school efforts to integrate and to Americanize the immigrant masses flooding US cities at this time – resonated with late-nineteenth-century elites' desires and fears.[24]

Much of the free kindergarten movement's focus on the rapid, radical improvements to be wrought in (and for) poor children was thus transferred to discussions about public school kindergartens, with the addition of claims made about the universal benefits of kindergarten education, recalling the teachings of Froebel himself. Thus, in Grand Rapids, those with an interest in having kindergarten education in the public schools – such as Emma Field, principal of Grandville Avenue School – extolled the classes' ability to develop in *all* children a number of qualities, including: the habit of attention; the power of observation; the power of self-directed control; the knowledge of objects, nature and life required before acquiring the symbolic representation required for reading; work in numbers, signs, and figures and the good use of hands, arms, and control of body movements for greater health.[25]

In 1886, these efforts bore fruit when, under the new and progressive Superintendent of Schools F. M. Kendall, a kindergarten was established in a new annex to Field's school. Kindergartener Constance D. Rourke, a divorced (!) and widowed young mother who had trained at Cook County Normal School in Chicago and taught in St Louis kindergartens, was installed as kindergarten director.[26] Froebelians had hoped that this kindergarten's success would inspire the school board to add others, but that did not happen, at least not in the short term. Despite parents' and teachers' claims that Rourke's pupils later performed better than others in reading and writing (a claim that might throw Rourke's Froebelian credentials into question in any case), the school board declined to purchase of additional kindergarten material and thus no immediate expansion was possible.[27]

By the decade's end, Grand Rapids had at least one free kindergarten still in operation, several private kindergartens serving the city's elite, and the one public school kindergarten operating under Rourke. To many of those involved, there was a pressing need for a comprehensive kindergarten organization to bridge the gaps between these different institutions and – more importantly – to work towards the provision of kindergarten education in all the city's public primary schools. To this end, the leaders of the various arms of the Grand Rapids kindergarten movement joined together under the auspices of the Grand Rapids Kindergarten Association (GRKA), which was inaugurated on 31 March 1891 with Emma Field as president and Clara Wheeler as secretary. The association outlined its mission as being: 'To advance the cause of kindergartens and to aid in general public sentiment in favor of Kindergartens in Grand Rapids'. In essence, this merely put into words the sentiment that had existed separately among the groups' members – those working in and for private and free kindergartens – for a number of years. An invitation for membership was issued to any interested party who would pay the $0.25 membership fee.[28]

Only a few days later, a petition was circulated by Rourke, Wheeler and others to ask that kindergartens be placed in all of the city's public primary schools. Although they succeeded in securing the signatures of over 200 of the city's most prominent citizens, the petition was turned down by the Grand Rapids Board of Education. In its response, the board said that while it was 'not possible' to establish a kindergarten in all of the schools, preference would be given to trained kindergarten teachers when hiring for primary grade teachers in the future.[29] Needless to say, this response was unsatisfying to the GRKA petitioners. Their request was radical, to be sure, but not without precedent; some US cities had incorporated kindergartens into many, if not all of their public primary schools. These included St Louis, where the public schools adopted kindergartening at Susan Blow's urging, and Boston, where fourteen kindergartens were taken over by the public school system in 1888 and continued under its auspices.[30]

In some US states, however, the law proscribed the use of public funds for the education of children below a certain age (often but not always the compulsory school age of that state); in states where 'school age' was defined as age six or older (e.g. in Alabama, Texas and Virginia), public kindergartens for under-sixes were effectively prohibited by law.[31] Michigan, by contrast, was one of many states that did not prohibit local school districts from opening kindergartens if and when they saw fit. Thus in the case of Grand Rapids, a city in which the kindergarten enjoyed a great deal of popular support, budgetary rather than legal concerns were most likely behind the board's 1891 refusal.

The June 1891 passage of a Kindergarten Bill by the Michigan State Legislature empowered Michigan school districts 'to provide a suitable room or apartment for kindergarten work, and to supply their district respectively with the necessary apparatus and appliances for the instruction of children in what is known as the kindergarten method'.[32] Interestingly, this had no effect in Grand Rapids, which in any case already had one public school kindergarten, nor did it seem to have an impact on kindergartening elsewhere in the state.[33] One reason was surely the cost, given that public school budgets were already strapped by the need to accommodate the growing population.[34] Added to that was the lingering belief, especially amongst (male) teachers in the higher grades, that kindergarten was merely 'a superfluity ... entertaining, diverting even, inviting and ornamental, but not greatly helpful, and may be omitted without noticeable loss'.[35] Kindergartners seeking to change people's minds about their work thus struggled against prejudices against the kindergarten, some of which were engendered by the misuse of the gifts and occupations by teachers lacking suitable training in Froebelian theory and methods.

Indeed, the availability of properly trained teachers was essential to the kindergarten movement on an international scale. Moreover, kindergarten teaching was seen in the United States, as in other Anglophone nations, not as a mere job, but rather as a vocation especially suitable for well-educated middle-class women in need of employment.[36] In the 1870s and early 1880s, in order to get someone trained in Froebelian methods, it had been necessary to recruit teachers trained in Boston, St Louis, New York, Washington DC or Los Angeles (by Peabody and Blow, or by German émigrées Maria Kraus-Boelté and Emma Marwedel and protégées, respectively). By 1890 it was possible to find them closer to Grand Rapids, especially in Chicago – the home of several new kindergarten training institutions – which was reachable by rail or steamboat.[37] Now that the Grand Rapids School Board would be looking for primary teachers with kindergarten training, the GRKA decided that such training should be offered locally, both so that the association could be certain of its quality and so that local young women might receive the training. In April 1891, a study group was organized by Constance Rourke with the help of Emma Field, and through a combination of personal invitations and publicity, thirteen women enrolled.[38]

Later that same month, on 21 April 1891, the GRKA held a meeting in honour of Froebel's 109th birthday and to raise awareness of and support for kindergarten education in the city. Held at Park Congregational Church, the proceedings were begun with an address by the Reverend Mila F. Tupper of All Souls Church, 'with favorable words for the Kindergarten cause'.[39] This was followed by readings and lectures on the life and works of Friedrich Froebel, as well as a recapitulation of the kindergarten movement in the city. It was reported that, as of that date, three private kindergartens, two free kindergartens and one public kindergarten were currently in operation, numbers which suggest that only some of the kindergartens founded in the heady years of the mid- to late 1880s survived.[40]

Treat and the training school 1891–5

When in June 1891 it was announced that Constance Rourke could not continue the new training classes, Clara Wheeler sent a request for help to the Chicago Kindergarten College, hoping they would send one person in particular.[41] They did: Lucretia Willard Treat, a fifty-year-old widow with impeccable credentials. A graduate of the renowned Troy Female Seminary in New York state (which her own grandmother had founded), she trained as a kindergartner with Susan Blow in St Louis, taught in a public kindergarten there for six years, then moved to Chicago to work in a private school run by her cousin. Eventually she returned to public kindergarten work as the kindergarten director of a school; she is also credited with helping start the training school which by 1891 had become the Chicago Kindergarten College. Unlike Rourke,

Figure 6.1 Lucretia Willard Treat, principal of the Grand Rapids Kindergarten Training School 1891–1904. Clara M. Wheeler Papers, Box 1, Bentley Historical Library, University of Michigan.

who was described by colleagues as 'a tyrant' (albeit an effective one), Treat was hailed as a mentor 'full of generous good will' and 'an inspiration'.[42]

Treat arrived in Grand Rapids on 1 July 1891. The city's kindergarten efforts were infused with energy upon Treat's arrival; on that same day she is said to have conducted a free kindergarten class for fifty children *and* held classes for teachers, which continued throughout the summer. Whereas Rourke's classes had been held only a few hours each week, Treat's ran several hours a day, running on a strict schedule and to exacting standards.[43] Within a few weeks, Treat had added a new mothers' class for poor and immigrant mothers, and, true to her own St Louis training, Treat encouraged all GRKA members – especially those who were not trained kindergartners, including the men – to discuss the life and works of Froebel and to improve their understanding of kindergarten theory.[44] If they were to be effective missionaries they had better be well versed in Father Froebel's teachings.

By August, the GRKA had amassed a list of twenty-four students set to enrol in a course of kindergarten training classes to be offered by Treat in Grand Rapids under the auspices of the Chicago Kindergarten Training School. However, the GRKA was unhappy with limitations placed on the classes and so its executive committee invited

Treat to sever with Chicago and to start a new training school in Grand Rapids. She accepted and was officially welcomed as principal of the new GRKA Kindergarten Training School in late September 1891.

From this point, the city's kindergarten movement expanded rapidly. In its first term, the training school ran a private kindergarten with eighteen children, enrolled twenty-four women in training classes and conducted classes for twenty-three mothers as well.[45] It offered the Grand Rapids Board of Education a weekly class for non-kindergarten teachers and Treat supervised additional courses of kindergarten study in Muskegon, Kalamazoo, Battle Creek and Detroit, Michigan. Treat, already known from her work in St Louis and Chicago, spent increasing amounts of time outside of the state, lecturing on the works of Froebel in places as far-flung as Albany, New York; Duluth, Minnesota and Salem, Oregon.[46] Her hand-selected Chicago-trained assistants continued Grand Rapids classes in her absence as the training school expanded to a regular enrolment of fifty students in 1892.[47]

Meanwhile, the GRKA itself grew and became increasingly formalized and effective. It was legally incorporated under state law, which allowed it to enter into contracts, such as those to open the new Waterloo Street Free Kindergarten. It also began to offer certificates of completion to those who completed a junior course of study and agreed to supervise the Kindergarten and Primary Departments of the city's Western Michigan College.[48] Thanks to a skilful public relations campaign wrought by GRKA Secretary Clara Wheeler, the work of the GRKA and the training school received almost daily coverage in the Grand Rapids press, with events listed in 'Community Happenings' columns, editorials about the importance of mother's classes, features on 'hometown girls' working in far-off kindergartens and social columns detailing the extravagant teas hosted by GRKA members after lectures by Froebelian notables such as Amalie Hofer of Chicago and W. N. Hailmann, then of La Porte, Indiana.[49] The kindergarten had become an inseparable part of Grand Rapids culture.

In addition to local attention, the GRKA Kindergarten Training School began to receive national attention through kindergarten-related periodicals published in other parts of the country. One publication was the Buffalo [New York] Free Kindergarten Association's *The Kindergarten News*, to which Wheeler sent a stream of content intended to highlight Treat's, the GRKA's and the training school's achievements. Like the dozens of other kindergarten periodicals published at this time, the *News* devoted considerable space to reports of goings-on in other places (in its case, in a column titled 'Progress of the Movement'). Efforts in Grand Rapids were mentioned in almost every issue of the *News*. This drew new students from around the country to Grand Rapids, many of whom later took up teaching positions elsewhere, thereby further expanding Treat's and the GRKA's circle of influence.[50] Wheeler succeeded in growing a well-coordinated Grand Rapids alumnae network, connecting kindergartners for purposes of edification, employment and sisterhood. In addition, GRKA members and training school alumnae were active contributors to wider state and (inter-)national kindergarten movements through participation in bodies such as the International Kindergarten Union (founded in 1893) and the Michigan Kindergarten Association (founded 1895), of which Wheeler was an early vice president.

The movement matures 1895–1905

The expansion of kindergartening in Grand Rapids and the influence of Grand Rapids kindergartners on education elsewhere continued through the 1890s. Where the GRKA's 1891 petition for kindergartens in all primary schools had failed, a piecemeal approach towards kindergarten institutionalization ultimately succeeded. At the turn of the century, Grandville Avenue School's kindergarten was no longer unique; by 1900, the Grand Rapids Board of Education employed thirty-two kindergartners teaching in public primary school kindergartens.[51] At that time around 10 per cent of Michigan cities and towns had public school kindergartens, with more than two-thirds of them in western Michigan, and most of those near Grand Rapids.[52] An exception to this – Michigan's largest city, Detroit, in the southeast – was significantly influenced by the GRKA, including frequent lectures by Treat and Wheeler. It added a public Kindergarten Department with kindergartens in two primary schools in 1895, and by 1904, kindergartens were in operation in forty-six of the sixty-nine primary schools in the city.[53]

Treat remained in charge of the GRKTS until her death of heart disease at age sixty-two in 1904. Her loss was felt keenly by staff, students and alumnae; one obituary recalled her as 'a spiritual mother, a motherly friend; an educator of heart and mind'.[54]

Figure 6.2 Clara M. Wheeler, principal of the Grand Rapids Kindergarten Training School 1904–19, Undated photo by Hamilton, Artifact 1982.121.8, Collections of the Grand Rapids Public Museum.

The training school was then placed under the leadership of Clara Wheeler, who had been the backbone of the city's kindergarten movement for decades. Although perhaps less in-demand than Treat, Wheeler, too, needed to balance in-house responsibilities with the need to travel extensively in the service of the GRKA and of the kindergarten cause in general. By 1905, the GRKA Training School had graduated 269 kindergarten teachers, 'found in nearly all states'.[55]

Just five years later, there were signs of significant change within the local movement, which required reorientation. In 1910, the GRKA, an organization which had once focused on many different aspects of kindergarten work and Froebelian education, was reorganized to become (only, officially) the Grand Rapids Kindergarten Training School. By that time, kindergartens had been institutionalized in the Grand Rapids public school system, and there was little need for an organization mobilizing in favour of public kindergartens at the local level. Free kindergartens, too, were on the wane, such that the training school became the focus of the movement's energies, continuing to train kindergartners, offering summer schools and mothers' classes, and bringing in much-needed funds via tuition fees.

The training school's offerings had been expanded and formalized to comprise three years of studies: a certificate course in the first year, a diploma course in the second and a postgraduate 'normal' course (for teaching in public schools) in the third.[56] By the late 1910s, however, the school was on the wane. In the 1917–18 school year, it employed seven regular instructors (five in the summer) yet enrolled only twenty-one students (eleven in summer courses) – fewer than in its first year and down from fifty or more in Treat's heyday.[57] In 1919, the GRKTS was disbanded. As kindergarten teaching became work increasingly based in the public schools, prospective kindergarten teachers seeking training looked to the institutions where (other) primary teachers were trained, namely the normal schools and colleges and, later, at fledgling university Schools of Education.[58]

Clara Wheeler, age fifty-eight at the closing of the GRKTS, did not retire from educational life in 1919; instead, she spent the next five years running a private kindergarten. From 1921, she also dedicated time and energy to what in 1925 become the National Congress of Parents and Teachers (later the Parent-Teacher Association). She held several positions in the Michigan state organization and remained active in it and other education-related organizations until her death in 1946.[59]

Conclusion

Rather than marking a failure, the training school's 1919 closure may instead be seen as marking the culmination of the kindergarten movement's strength. The thing that ultimately made the GRKTS obsolete – widespread adoption of public school kindergartening – was the result of the kindergarten movement's success.

The narrative arc of the Grand Rapids kindergarten movement, with emphases shifting from private kindergartens to free kindergartens to public kindergartens, mirrors the experience of kindergarten development in other US cities, many of which

* Cp Montessori —
this wasn't the case?
different dynamic?

were dealing with similar conditions in the sense of being booming new cities with extremes of wealth and poverty and young education systems struggling to manage the numbers of children – many of them immigrants. Whether out of enlightenment or out of desperation, they became open to the idea of kindergarten education as a means of alleviating these challenges and building education systems for the new twentieth century.

The success of this 'marvelous training' in Grand Rapids, as elsewhere, was undoubtedly the result of many different influences. What becomes clear from this chapter (and some others in this volume) is the importance of individuals and the power of networks in effecting change on a local level. In terms of individuals, Grand Rapids seems to have had a hero in Lucretia Willard Treat, and indeed her contributions to the kindergarten movement in Grand Rapids and elsewhere would be difficult to overstate.[60] But other names emerge from this history as important as well: Clara Wheeler, for example. Born in Grand Rapids in 1861, Wheeler would have been a child of eleven when Frances Rutherford first brought word of the kindergarten to Grand Rapids. She was a central figure in the movement from at least 1884 onwards – first as a founding member of the Grand Rapids Free Kindergarten Society, then as the person who brought Treat to Grand Rapids and most likely the driving force behind getting her to stay. Wheeler was vital to the founding and operation of the GRKA, too, and as secretary, she was crucial in shaping public opinion about kindergarten education. By the time she took over the training school in 1904, she had been active in local kindergartening for twenty years; by the time of the training school's closure, she had been a constant in the city's kindergarten movement for thirty-five years.

Whereas Treat and Wheeler contributed immeasurably to strengthening support in Grand Rapids for kindergarten education in general, thereby encouraging the development of public school kindergartens, several others played important roles in the actual institutionalization of kindergartens in Grand Rapids schools. Two worth mentioning in particular are Grandville Avenue School's Principal Emma Field, who, along with Wheeler, was a founder of the Free Kindergarten Association in 1884 and served as first president of the GRKA in 1891 and Constance Rourke, who led Field's school's pioneering public kindergarten. Having started teaching in Grand Rapids schools in 1865, Field was a respected, experienced educator. Having come to Froebelian education in mid-career, she was a dedicated attendee of kindergarten summer schools and study groups offered in Grand Rapids. From her position of power as a school principal, she had the teachers in her school suffuse their lessons with Froebelian elements. She assisted in making classes about kindergarten education available to all the teachers in the district and worked together with Superintendent Mitchell – himself known as something of an educational radical – to initiate the kindergarten and hire Constance Rourke.[61] Like Treat, Rourke had worked under Susan Blow in St Louis, and gathered experience in Chicago's burgeoning kindergarten landscape, too. Like Wheeler, Rourke was present – and a presence – in Grand Rapids for many years, successfully demonstrating the possibilities of high-quality public school kindergartening on a daily basis.

Finally, even Treat's and Rourke's presence in Grand Rapids would not have been possible without the existence and effectiveness of networks amongst Froebelians in the United States at this time. These networks were based on extensive and intensive communication between individuals, groups and – increasingly – institutions, whether by individual correspondence, periodical publications or travel. In the absence of teaching certificates or even of standardized teacher training, these networks enabled the identification and recruitment of kindergarten teachers across great distances, starting with the arrival of Miss Hyde from Boston in 1873, and continuing through to Rourke, and Treat. And then there is the way in which the networks thus established broadcast the work of Grand Rapids kindergartners and their supporters such that others might learn from their example, if not from them personally. Not only Treat's and Wheeler's travels but also the streams of visiting lecturers and Froebelian guests to Grand Rapids appear to have been vital to the rise of Grand Rapids as a centre of American kindergartening and to the spread and success of the kindergarten in the United States in general. The intricacies of this culture of travel and exchange and the experience of these women's educational intinerance have yet to be explored but might indeed illuminate more about the workings of these movements and the lives of the women who inhabited them.

Abbreviations

GRKA   Grand Rapids Kindergarten Association.
GRKTS   Grand Rapids Kindergarten Training School.

Notes

1 Elizabeth Dale Ross, *The Kindergarten Crusade: The Establishment of Preschool Education in the United States* (Athens: Ohio University Press, 1976); Michael Steven Shapiro, *Child's Garden: The Kindergarten Movement from Froebel to Dewey* (University Park: Pennsylvania State University Press, 1983); Barbara Beatty, *Preschool Education in America* (New Haven: Yale University Press, 1995).
2 Caroline Winterer, 'Avoiding a "Hothouse System of Education": Nineteenth Century Early Childhood Education from the Infant Schools to the Kindergartens', *History of Education Quarterly* 32, no 3. (1992): 289–314.
3 Beatty, *Preschool Education*.
4 See, for example, ibid.; Larry Prochner, 'The History of Kindergarten as New Education: Examples from the United States and Canada, 1880-1890', in *The Development of Early Childhood Education in Europe and North America: Historical and Comparative Perspectives*, ed. Harry Willekens, Kirsten Scheiwe and Kristen Nawrotzki (Basingstoke: Palgrave Macmillan, 2015), 289–308.
5 Christian G. Carron, *Grand Rapids Furniture: The Story of America's Furniture City*. Public Museum of Grand Rapids, 1998.
6 U.S. Bureau of the Census, *Population of the 100 Largest Urban Places: 1870*. https://www.census.gov/population/www/documentation/twps0027/tab10.txt [Retrieved on 28 January 2016]; U.S. Bureau of the Census, *Population of the 100 Largest Urban*

Places: 1890. https://www.census.gov/population/www/documentation/twps0027/tab12.txt [Retrieved on 28 January 2016].

7   GRKTS Records 1891–1919, Box 1, Book 1, Bentley Historical Library, University of Michigan.

8   Ibid.

9   Ibid.

10 Beatty, *Preschool Education*.

11 Newsclipping, *Grand Rapids Herald*, undated, Box 2, Clara M. Wheeler Papers, Bentley Historical Library, University of Michigan.

12 Beatty, *Preschool Education*; Kristen Nawrotzki, 'The Anglo-American Kindergarten Movements and Early Education in England and the USA, 1850-1965' (diss. University of Michigan, 2005).

13 GRKTS Records, Box 1, Book 1.

14 'Notes on Charity and Parochial Kindergartens', in Barnard, *Papers on Froebel's Kindergarten*, 734–5.

15 'Free Kindergarten Association', *Grand Rapids Morning Telegram*, 17 June 1885.

16 GRKTS Records, Box 1, Book 1.

17 *Grand Rapids Morning Telegram*, 25 November 1884, 4.

18 Untitled clipping, *Grand Rapids Daily Democrat*, 17 June 1885, C. M. Wheeler Papers, Box 2.

19 Sligh Family Papers, 1842–2012. Finding Aid. Michigan Historical Collections, Bentley Historical Library, University of Michigan.

20 'Free Kindergarten Association', *Grand Rapids Morning Telegram*, 17 June 1885, 1.

21 GRKTS Records, Box 1, Book 1.

22 Ibid.

23 Kate Douglas Wiggin, *The Kindergarten* (New York: Harper & Bros., 1893), 55.

24 Vandewalker, *The Kindergarten*.

25 Unnamed, undated document. C. M. Wheeler Papers, Box 5, Kindergarten Programs (1); also GRKTS Records 1891–1919, Box 1, Book 1.

26 Joan Shelley Rubin, *Constance Rourke and American Culture* (Chapel Hill. UNC Books, 1980).

27 GRKTS Records, Box 1, Book 1.

28 Ibid.

29 Ibid.

30 Untitled clipping, undated, C. M. Wheeler Papers, Box 2; also Vandewalker, *The Kindergarten*, 190, and Beatty, *Preschool Education*.

31 Vandewalker, *The Kindergarten*, 188–9.

32 State of Michigan. Act 119. An Act authorizing the introduction of the Kindergarten Method in the public schools of this State. 1891. (160) 4792, section 1.

33 Richard G. Boone, 'To the Michigan Kindergartners', *The Kindergarten Magazine* vol. IX (1896–97): 363.

34 Untitled clipping, undated, C. M. Wheeler Papers, Box 2.

35 Boone, 'To the Michigan Kindergartners', 362.

36 Kristen Dombkowski (Nawrotzki), 'Kindergarten Teacher Training in England and the United States 1850-1918', *History of Education* 31, no. 5 (2002): 475–89.

37 These included Cook County Normal School under arch-Progressive Col. Francis W. Parker, which opened a kindergarten training department in 1883, and Elizabeth Harrison's Training School (later National Kindergarten College) founded in 1886. Shapiro, *Child's Garden*, 149; Vandewalker, *The Kindergarten*, 192. On Chicago, see also Chapter 7 by Prochner and Kirova in this volume.

38 GRKTS Records, Box 1, Book 1.

39 Ibid.

40 Ibid.

41 Meeting Minutes 18 June 1891. GRKTS Records, Box 1.

42 Rubin, *Constance Rourke*, 5; C. M. Wheeler, 'Lucretia Willard Treat, 1838-1904,' in International Kindergarten Union, Committee of Nineteen, *Pioneers of the Kindergarten in America* (New York: Century, 1924), 235.

43 GRKTS Records, Box 1, Book 1.

44 Ibid.

45 Ibid.

46 See, for example, 'Field Notes', *Kindergarten Magazine* V, September (1892): 85–86.

47 Dwight Goss, *History of Grand Rapids and its Industries*, vol. 2 (Grand Rapids: C. F. Cooper, 1906), 408.

48 Ibid.; Clipping, *The Kalamazoo Daily*, 14 April 1893, C. M. Wheeler Papers, Box 2.

49 GRKTS Records, Box 1, Clippings; L. W. Treat Papers, Box 1.

50 C. M. Wheeler Papers, Box 2.

51 Michigan Department of Public Instruction, *Report of the Superintendent of Public Instruction of Michigan, 1900* (Lansing: The Superintendent, 1900). By this time, Rourke had moved up to become principal of Widdicomb Street School. Goss, *History of Grand Rapids*, 339.

52 Michigan Department of Public Instruction, *Report of the Superintendent of Public Instruction of Michigan* (Lansing: State Printers, 1904).

53 Detroit (Michigan) Public Schools, *Annual Report of the Board of Education of the City of Detroit* 1904–1905 (Detroit: Detroit Public Schools, 1894), 15.

54 'Grand Rapids Kindergarten Training School', *Kindergarten Journal* (Chicago: Kindergarten College Alumnae Association) 1, no. 3 (1910): 115.

55 Goss, *History of Grand Rapids*, 409.

56 'Grand Rapids Kindergarten Training School', 115.

57 L. E. Blauch and H. R. Bonner, *Statistics of Normal Schools 1917-18*, Bureau of Education Bulletin, 1919, no. 81 (Washington DC: Government Printing Office, 1920), 113.

58 Dombkowski (Nawrotzki), 'Kindergarten teacher training in England and Wales and the United States', 475–89.

59 C. M. Wheeler Papers, Box 6.

60 Wheeler, 'Lucretia Willard Treat', 234–9.

61 Ernest B. Fisher (ed.), *Grand Rapids and Kent County, Michigan: Historical Account of their Progress from First Settlement to the Present Time* (Chicago: Robert O. Law Co.: 1918), 408; also Goss, *History of Grand Rapids*, 26.

Part Two

Curricular and Pedagogical Change: Froebelians beyond the Kindergarten

7

Kindergarten at the Dewey School, University of Chicago, 1898–1903

Larry Prochner and Anna Kirova

Some were angels and some were devils. This was educator and literary critic Denton Snider's categorization of the varieties of kindergarten teachers in his book *The Psychology of Froebel's Play-Gifts*, published in 1900.[1] Not only were there extremes when it came to views of kindergarten teachers, but also when it came to views of kindergarten curricula. While kindergarten's worth as an anti-poverty programme for poor children in the United States was generally acknowledged at this time, as it was introduced into more and more public schools, the place of Froebel's gifts and occupations as the institution's core activities was hotly debated by leaders in the kindergarten movement. Snider's portrayal of the three prevailing views of kindergarten education demonstrates the debate's passion.[2] The stationary view was a literal interpretation of Froebel in which those who departed from the 'transmitted text' were destined for the 'kindergarten Inferno'. Using religious imagery to reinforce the orthodoxy of Froebelians, the most conservative followers of the founder of the kindergarten, was common. Psychologist G. Stanley Hall wrote of Froebelian Susan Blow: she 'dominates, with her thought and powerful personality, the entire intellectual field of the American kindergarten, like a pope intimidates every dissenter, and her nearer disciples seek to suppress, by condemnation and even social ostracism, all those that seek to breathe a freer and larger air', that is, those depicted by Snider as evolutionists and revolutionists.[3] Snider saw the evolutionary view as a middle ground, 'unfolding with the progress of time', which he identified as his own position. In the revolutionary view, the Froebelian philosophy and materials were cast away. Snider likened teachers with a revolutionary bent to 'those children of God who conspired to dethrone God' – they were 'followers of the Destroyer, veritably the Satanic element of the kindergarten'.[4]

The field of kindergarten education in the United States was in ferment in the period 1890 to 1920, coinciding with the Progressive Era and developments in scientific child study and educational psychology that were part of Progressive Era reforms.[5] As historian Barbara Beatty described, 'A new generation of American kindergartners began modifying Froebelian pedagogy along scientific lines. But some kindergartners continued to adhere to orthodox Froebelianism, and deep divisions opened up in the kindergarten movement.'[6] This adherence was shown in their reluctance to release their hold on the kindergarten gifts, which were considered the essence of the kindergarten philosophy. Thus those who resisted the introduction of new materials, or a reinterpretation of old materials, along with changes to philosophy and teacher preparation, were criticized for delaying the revolution – that is, educational change.

How the debate played out in individual schools has not been well researched. In this chapter we describe the situation in one school: the kindergarten at Dewey's laboratory school at the University of Chicago in the years 1898 to 1904.[7] The Dewey School has been called 'the most important experimental venture in the whole history of American education'.[8] We ask, what was the nature of the experiment with regard to kindergarten education? Did it reflect a 'revolutionary' view? To answer these questions, this chapter traces the particular contributions made by two influential educational leaders, Anna Bryan and Elizabeth Harrison, and their staff, on kindergarten practice at the Dewey School.[9] While Dewey's reliance on trained kindergarten teachers shaped the experiment at his school along more traditional lines, it also revealed the ways by which conservative teaching practice adapted to a more progressive approach.

The gifts as a gauge

The Dewey School's kindergarten teachers' stance on Froebel's gifts, as described in their weekly work reports and suggested by their training, is used in this chapter to gauge their alignment with Snider's three interpretations of kindergarten education, with a less-directed approach indicating a more revolutionary view. The gifts were a collection of five children's toys with a specialized educational purpose. In Froebel's plan, gifts were to be used sequentially, with one preparing the way for the next. They were numbered, and Froebel's original five were added to in the various guides written by others at a later date, with an eventual total of twenty gifts. The first gift was a set of six brightly coloured knitted balls, each attached to a string. Gifts two through nine were manipulative materials. The second through sixth gifts were sets of small blocks; each set contained in a wooden box with a sliding cover so that the child could gain an 'impression of the whole, of the self-contained'.[10] The seventh gift was a collection of paper or wooden shapes; gift eight consisted of sticks and gift nine of rings. These were for 'laying figures' on a flat surface. Gift ten was drawing materials, and eleven to twenty were constructive or occupational materials used mainly for crafts such as weaving or folding paper, sewing or modelling with clay. Using them in a prescribed way was called 'dictation'. Using the materials more freely was termed 'constructive work'.

In the most conservative, stationary view, using the gifts was controlled by what came to be seen as Froebel's 'rules'. As Susan Blow described, 'In each exercise the child shall recognize and respect the relationship of whole and parts ... [and] he shall develop each new form from its predecessor'.[11] Regimented practices developed from this idea, including the manner by which the gifts were presented to children, removed from their box and arranged on a special table, which was scribed with a one-inch grid. Evolutionists kept the symbolism and developmental presentation of the gifts. In *The Kindergarten Building Gifts*, first published in 1903, Elizabeth Harrison and Belle Woodson, who were teachers at the Chicago Kindergarten College, describe the unpacking of the third gift: 'Care must be taken that the blocks always come out from the box as a whole. This is most easily done … by turning the box upside down, then drawing out the cover, and carefully lifting the box off, when the eight little cubes will stand before the child as one whole.'[12] A colleague of Harrison's set out the procedure for packing up the blocks, which was in the reverse: 'Pile the blocks up in an orderly manner on the cover, all together [children simultaneously] lifting the boxes and placing them over the blocks; then draw them towards you off the table and slide in the cover.'[13] Taking the middle ground, evolutionists stressed that free play with the blocks was important, but only after a period of 'imitation, dictation or suggestion'.[14] For revolutionaries, free play was essential for education. Critics of the gifts, such as the American psychologist G. Stanley Hall, charged that they were not only unscientific, but actually harmful to children, causing eye strain and anxiety, and if they were to be used, it should be for creative play in conjunction with other, larger sets of blocks.[15]

Snider based his 'evolutionary' view on a Hegelian understanding of the person as 'essentially self-unfolding'.[16] His colleagues Elizabeth Harrison and Belle Woodson explained the practical side of the gifts in their 'companion volume' to Snider's book.[17] In their view, teaching strategies for using the gifts must 'correspond to the child's unfolding power', which progressed according to a preset order.[18] When children first encountered a material, they were unconscious of its possibilities. In this 'unconscious stage', they used their senses to explore the material in an experimental, undirected and unfocused way. In the second or 'conscious stage', children required play directed by a more knowledgeable partner – a teacher or experienced peer – to lead them to higher-order thinking (i.e. classification).[19] This stage was followed by the 'creative stage', in which play is self-directed and involves combinations and transformations. Harrison and Woodson noted that the stages can be passed through 'in almost instantaneous succession' and that there is more play at the 'creative stage' with the higher-numbered building gifts.[20] However, critics of the evolutionary view believed that the preponderance of play in kindergarten was highly regimented and directed.

John Dewey used child development research as the basis for the 'revolutionary' view in an article published in 1899. He claimed that play in infancy was based in motor and intellectual development and the increased coordination and discrimination that was purposefully aimed at 'gain[ing] new experiences'.[21] A second stage, called the play period, involved exploration of objects and began at about age two and lasted to age six or seven. Dewey described the start of this stage as characterized by a 'growing freedom of activity'; however, a child's repetitive actions and the 'comparative poverty of the idea' placed it for him 'on the borderland of play'.[22] Activities with objects become more purposeful over time and were often taken up through participation in productive activity in the family, for example, by helping with baking, carpentry or gardening. This view ascribed no special significance to Froebel's gifts.

Dewey reasoned that because such productive opportunities were limited for children in cities, kindergartens and other institutions were developed to 'compensate for the limitations'.[23] However, Dewey believed that 'in more favored surroundings the child is often relatively stunted because adults are not willing to take the time and effort required; or have not the intelligence necessary to supply proper conditions'.[24] He felt this on a personal level, as shown in his letter to Alice Dewey describing his observations of their daughter Evelyn at kindergarten in Michigan: 'Poor

Evelyn ... playing with cubes, to find out about the edges & 'surfaces ... [expression] of 'complete boredom ... inner perplexity as to why they were doing all these unreal things to find out what she [already] knew'.[25] How could Evelyn's activity in the kindergarten be meaningful to her life in and out of school? It was essentially this point that Dewey aimed to address in his experimental kindergarten.

Training for a revolution

There were five kindergarten teacher training programmes in Chicago in the 1890s.[26] Dewey initially ignored all of them in his search for a teacher for his laboratory kindergarten. However, in the end, he recruited graduates from two of the schools: the Chicago Free Kindergarten Association's (CFKA) training school, led by Anna Bryan, and the Chicago Kindergarten College, led by Elizabeth Harrison. Harrison professed an evolutionary middle-of-the-road view on Froebel education: almost twenty years later, she would side with the minority 'conservative-liberal' camp in the International Kindergarten Union's report on theory and practice published in 1913.[27] Anna Bryan was a revolutionary, an 'avant-garde teacher' in the words of historian Evelyn Weber.[28] However, while Bryan's influence on Dewey is recognized in many accounts of the school,[29] the details of her role are vague. In a report published after the kindergarten's first year, Dewey merely acknowledged her in a footnote, recognizing the 'numberless suggestions regarding both materials and objects for constructive work' made by Bryan and her staff.[30] The contribution of Harrison and her teachers to the laboratory kindergarten has never been examined. This chapter traces the particular contributions made by Bryan and Harrison and their staff on kindergarten practice at the Dewey School.

Anna Bryan and the Chicago Free Kindergarten Association

Wealthy patrons with ties to the Women's Christian Temperance Union established the CFKA in 1881 to provide kindergartens for poor children. The free kindergarten association was a charity project managed by a volunteer board employing a professional staff hired to conduct the activities of the organization. Tuition at the Chicago Association's training school was free. Funds to cover the association's expenses, which were mainly salaries for professional staff, were raised through subscription and donation. The individual kindergartens, which were managed by the association, shared resources, with the most important being students who worked as unpaid assistants in the kindergartens as part of their training.

The association's first director was Matilda H. Ross. In her first year in Chicago, she organized nine kindergartens as part of the association,[31] and in 1882, she began a training programme preparing students 'by the careful study of the Froebel system and Bible texts ... and temperance, to reach the masses in their schools'.[32] Anna Bryan, from Louisville, Kentucky, completed her two-year course at the association in 1885, graduating six months after Ross resigned as director.[33] Patty Smith Hill, a kindergarten educator who was a student of Bryan's, was dismissive of Ross. In her biographical sketch of Bryan, Hill noted that Bryan's 'training [under Ross] was poor, even for that day'.[34] However, we have not found evidence to support Hill's view, and her remarks may have been meant as criticism of Ross's Froebelian approach. Bryan's studies with Ross followed the usual schedule of supervised practice teaching in the morning and lectures in the afternoon.[35] Bryan learnt about the kindergarten philosophy through hands-on experience with the gifts, and she was assessed on the basis of her portfolio containing samples of occupation work (e.g. sewing, weaving and drawing) along with written examinations and evaluations of her teaching.

In 1884, CFKA student teachers demonstrated kindergarten activities at the training school's graduation ceremony. Graduates took the role of children in a model kindergarten following a teacher's dictation.[36] The demonstration was similar to the way the students were trained to use the gifts, which resembled strategies for training children. The difference was in the complexity of the work: Ross described how kindergartners were required to 'copy' complex designs, while the children's work was kept 'as simple as possible'.[37]

Bryan taught in an association kindergarten for two years after she graduated. It may have been during this time that she started to experiment with a freer approach. However, the large numbers of children at the kindergarten likely limited the opportunity for constructive play.[38] In 1887, she returned to Louisville to establish a training school at a new free kindergarten association. As in the Chicago training, Bryan's students taught in a kindergarten in the morning and attended classes with Bryan, the only teacher, in the afternoon. A report by a visitor in 1889 indicates that her methods were different from those used by Ross in Chicago. Bryan's students 'had no use for note books, for the young ladies, when they leave the class, cannot remember that Miss Bryan has said anything. She develops the theory from their experiences, and they do most of the talking.'[39] Bryan used the same approach in teaching children, an earlier form of what today might be called 'child centered'. As she described it in plain language to a reporter when she first arrived in Louisville: 'The method of the kindergarten is precisely that of a women who is blessed with a pigheaded husband. The children are not allowed to know that they are being instructed.'[40]

Bryan quickly gained renown for her methods through her publications and lectures and reports by visitors to the Louisville training school. In 1894, she was returned to Chicago as principal of the training school at the CFKA, which had gained a reputation as a leading training school in Chicago in the years Bryan was in Louisville. In 1893, the association moved into rooms at the Armour Institute, a trade and technical school in the packinghouse district founded by industrialist Philip Armour. Students were given access to the institute's library and courses.[41] The kindergarten at the Armour Mission had been part of the CFKA since the kindergarten opened in 1888, and was used as a model kindergarten by the association. All students were required to complete practice teaching at the school.[42]

The directed use of gifts and occupations had already been diminished, if not abandoned, prior to Bryan's arrival. Bryan made further changes to the association's training shortly after she arrived, increasing the admission standards and lengthening the programme from one to two years. As in Louisville, students began their studies by reflecting on their own childhood and experiences with children, which was intended to lead them to a natural understanding of Froebel's teachings. There was a scientific basis to their studies: Amy Eliza Tanner, a graduate student from the University of Chicago under Dewey's supervision, taught child psychology.[43] Students were assigned readings from psychologists William James and John Dewey, including Dewey's *Pedagogic Creed*, along with studies of Froebel's philosophy and the theory of and practice with the gifts.[44] In the latter, Bryan emphasized children's creative play rather than instruction or drill.[45]

Under Bryan's leadership, there was also more attention to the quality of the kindergartens that were affiliated with the association and in which students conducted their practice teaching. Bryan adopted a research approach in which teachers' work in the mornings 'furnished data for director's meetings', and a freer approach was shown through an increase in the amount of constructive work. According to Bryan's colleague at the training school, Eva Whitmore, by 1898 constructive work had 'found its place in the kindergartens, and so we find students discussing the same, and preparing occupations in addition to those planned by Froebel'.[46] Whitmore taught occupations, and despite her training with Froebelian Maria Kraus-Boelté and work with Ross, she observed that her curriculum had 'undergone many changes' and 'much of the work done by the students could not be mounted in books [portfolios] as formerly'.[47] Bryan was at the height of her career at this time, and the assistant superintendent of Chicago schools, Ella Flagg Young, remarked, 'Her ideas of child study are in line with those of Dr. John Dewey. I consider her the foremost kindergartner of the United States'.[48]

Elizabeth Harrison and the Chicago Kindergarten College

Whereas Anna Bryan was notable for her revisionist Froebelian pedagogy, Elizabeth Harrison, who would also become influential in the Dewey School, maintained a conservative Froebelian approach. Elizabeth Harrison trained with many of the 'first generation' of kindergarten experts in the United States, including with Alice Putnam at the Chicago Froebel Association's newly established training school in 1879. She completed her practice teaching in the kindergarten at the Loring School, a private school for girls.[49] She remained there for two years until Putnam recommended further training with Susan Blow in St Louis and Maria Kraus-Boelté in New York. When Harrison returned to Chicago, she led her own training class at the Loring School in 1885, which included lectures by Denton Snider. Harrison's school developed over time to become the Chicago Kindergarten Training School (1887) and later the Chicago Kindergarten College (1891).[50]

By the early 1890s, the college offered both a two-year programme leading to a certificate and a senior diploma for kindergarten trainers and supervisors after a third year. The curriculum was Froebelian, with the first year devoted to 'gifts, games, and occupations of the kindergarten as taught by Froebel'. Froebel's *Mother Play*[51] was studied as the 'foundation of the entire Kindergarten system'.[52] The third year included selections from Froebel's *Education of Man*,[53] additional history and philosophy, and practical work in science. Students had supervised teaching experience in kindergartens each morning and lectures in the afternoon. Until the early 1900s, they prepared elaborate portfolios with samples of occupations along with explanatory notes on theory.[54] The college's faculty included Harrison, who taught Froebelian philosophy, and her niece Grace Fulmer, who was instructor in the theory and practice of gifts and games. Fulmer, who would later teach at Dewey's school, graduated from the college in 1893. Denton Snider taught psychology, 'including a thorough and comprehensive study of the psychological basis of Froebel's gifts and games', and the philosophy of literature, art and history.[55] As a further indication of the school's dedication to a conservative Froebelian approach, in 1900–1, Susan Blow was on staff at the college teaching principles of education.[56]

The kindergarten at the Dewey School

While Harrison and Bryan were leading their training programmes in Chicago, Dewey was building up the institution that would become known worldwide as the Dewey School. Dewey started a school for children at the University of Chicago in 1896 as a site for scientific research on his ideas of curriculum and teaching. The school also served as a laboratory for studies of child development.[57] The Dewey School was not the first of its kind: an example of an earlier laboratory school 'was the kindergarten that started in the Department of Education at Leland Stanford Junior University in 1892.[58] However, the Dewey School aimed to encompass a wider range of grades and ages.[59] Dewey wanted his teachers to work as researchers, 'to exhibit, test, verify and criticize theoretical statements and principles, to add to the sum of facts and principles in its special line'.[60] Their main research question was 'the proper organization of the subject-matter of the curriculum, and the relation of the subjects ... [mathematics, history, etc.] to other means of expression'.[61]

Dewey was initially not concerned with developing teaching methods to be replicated elsewhere. He claimed that, 'while [the school] does not aim to be impractical, it does not aim primarily to be of such a character as to be immediately capable of translation into the public school'.[62] And despite its confusing nomenclature – it was called a 'practice school' in a newspaper report on its opening in 1896 – it was in no way similar to a 'normal school'.[63] A normal school was a teacher training institution with a focus on imparting basic 'normal' standards of teaching. This aim was achieved in part through practice supervised by a 'critic teacher' in an associated model school, called a 'practice school'. As explained by Dewey's graduate student Frederick Eby, the children at Dewey's school were safeguarded from practice teachers. Eby wrote, 'It is not in any sense a school where the students of education are permitted to indulge their theories or even to gain practical experience in the art of teaching'.[64]

The qualifications for teachers at the Dewey School comprised prior teaching experience, expertise in a specialized subject, openness to Dewey's ideas and a scientific bent. The first teacher, Clara Isabel Mitchell, had been a critic teacher at the Cooke County Normal School in nearby Englewood. Col Francis Parker, the principal at the normal school, had recommended Mitchell to Dewey.[65] The school opened under her direction with sixteen students in January 1896. While not much is known about the first few months, it appears there were rough spots. Susan Blow, visiting the school at this time, afterwards wrote to her friend the United States Commissioner of Education

William Torrey Harris, 'They said it was not a fair showing, but the whole principle they were working on seemed wrong.'[66] In their history of the school, former teachers Mayhew and Edwards concluded that the first six months were 'chiefly indicative of what not to do'.[67] This matched Dewey's assessment: he wrote to his graduate student Frank Manny, who assisted Dewey with the school's administration, that 'the instruction is, relatively, scrappy and clearly below the children's real capacity'.[68]

Dewey was on the lookout for new teachers for the next school year who had experience with children, but not necessarily 'any technical philosophic training'.[69] His new recruits, including sisters Katherine Camp and Anna Camp, whom he knew from the University of Michigan, were more aligned with his educational ideas.[70] By 1899, he felt sufficiently confident to declare, 'The period of experimentation [with the curriculum] is practically at an end.'[71] As the Camp sisters observed in their history of the laboratory school, this success was 'the result of the combined experimental efforts of trained specialists'[72] (i.e. college-trained content area experts and, for the most part, not trained teachers).

Dewey had planned a kindergarten for the laboratory school from the start.[73] Financial problems, lack of a suitable building and the ongoing research on curriculum with the older groups meant the kindergarten was delayed. The financial barrier was lifted when philanthropist Harriet Castle of Hawaii, who was an acquaintance of Dewey, gave him funds to train a teacher to lead a charity kindergarten in Honolulu.[74] Castle paid the teacher's salary and for the furnishings and materials for the laboratory school kindergarten, a cost of $1,500.[75] As Dewey described the situation to a potential teacher, Castle's interest in his ideas led her to 'propose that [the laboratory school] should engage their teacher [the teacher that would work at the Castle kindergarten] and have her start the work with us – that is, as a class for younger children from 4½ to 6 in connection with our Elementary School'.[76]

Castle's request came to Dewey in the summer, leaving him little time to recruit a teacher. He was sure he did not want one who had been trained along Froebelian lines. A few years earlier he had observed Elizabeth Harrison teaching a class at the Chicago Kindergarten College, which he derided in a letter to his wife, Alice Dewey.

> Heavens! I wonder if grown people have to become as little children in brains as well as in spirit to enter that particular branch of the kingdom of heaven. Miss Harrison told a kindergarten story to that class of grown people just as if she were telling it to children; and all the oh's and ah's and holy tones in to duly impress them. I don't doubt she does lots of good, but it strikes an outsider as driveling idiocy.[77]

His first choice for a teacher was Flora Juliette Cooke, who had no kindergarten background. Cooke was the first grade critic teacher at the Chicago Normal School.[78] She was well known to Dewey, having taught his own children in grade one, Fred in 1895 and Evelyn in 1896.[79] She was also Castle's first choice and a favourite with Alice Dewey.[80] He wrote to Cooke in August 1898, explaining, 'The intention is not either with us [in Chicago] or over there [in Honolulu] to start an orthodox kindergarten, but simply to do for the little tots whatever seems best for them.'[81] In another letter, he assured her that her lack of 'technical "kindergarten" training is of no importance.'[82]

Alice Dewey followed up, writing that she hoped Cooke would teach her son Gordon at the laboratory school kindergarten 'in order to really test the new education. ... I can't trust him to anybody but you.'[83] Cooke nevertheless declined and recommended Bertha Payne, director of kindergarten training at the Chicago Froebel Association.[84]

However, with the school's opening less than two weeks away, Dewey needed to act quickly, and he hired twenty-five-year-old Florence Elizabeth La Victoire, who, in spite of Dewey's resolve to do otherwise, was noted to be a 'teacher of thorough training and experience in subprimary [kindergarten] methods'.[85] Specifics about La Victoire's training are not presented in available historical sources, other than that she had taught at a Chicago public school in the primary grades for several years. Nothing is known about her kindergarten background.[86]

After moving the school three times in the first two-and-a-half years, Dewey located a house to rent near the university for the school's start in Fall 1898, likely with the kindergarten in mind. The house was grand, with twenty-three rooms, three bathrooms, a stable and 'every other convenience', as described in the realtor's listing.[87] Mayhew and Edwards noted it had the added advantage of being 'sufficiently like the children's own homes to give a sense of familiarity to their first away-from-home experience'.[88] Multiple sets of Froebel's second to fifth gifts were ordered along with two sets of larger blocks for floor play, called Hennessy blocks, and materials for constructive play.[89] Furnishings included scribed kindergarten tables and small-sized chairs. The kindergarten opened with eight children aged four to six gathered in the living room, which was to be their classroom at the Ellis Avenue school.[90] Numbers were small as they were for all classes: Dewey believed this was necessary for laboratory conditions.[91] Although twenty children had enrolled by January, daily attendance was generally half that number. Enrolment was eventually set at twenty-four 'to bring the average attendance to ten or eleven'.[92]

La Victoire was assisted by Georgia Price Scates. Scates graduated from the Chicago Free Kindergarten's training school in 1896, the first class to be taught by Anna Bryan.[93] In 1898 Scates passed the Chicago Board of Education examination permitting her to teach kindergarten in a public school. She was offered a teaching post at a public school, but turned it down to work at the Dewey School.[94] When La Victoire left for Honolulu the following year, Scates took the role of lead teacher, which was likely part of an overall plan. In terms of research, the task Dewey set for the teachers was to undertake work 'along the general lines followed in the [laboratory] school'[95] 'with such modifications as are necessary to adapt them to younger children'.[96] La Victoire's efforts were documented in her monthly work reports over the school year 1898 to 1899. Dewey's rushed arrangements for the kindergarten, including hiring his lead teacher at the last minute, left little time for staff to deliberate on curriculum considerations that might reflect a 'revolutionary' view. La Victoire was likely guided by Scates in establishing the work.

Mayhew and Edwards referred to the kindergarten class's schedule as flexible. However, La Victoire's reports suggest it was followed quite closely on most days. The day began at 9.00 am with constructive work (thirty min.), followed by songs and stories (sixty min.), marching and games (thirty min.), toilet (ten min.), dinner (thirty-five min.) and ending with dramatic play and rhythms (thirty min.).[97] Most time was spent in the classroom apart from play outdoors in the yard and garden; the work reports note only a few neighbourhood excursions over the year.

Dewey described the kindergarten's focus in *The School and Society*, published at the end of the programme's first year, as simple: 'The younger children begin with the home and occupations of the home.'[98] In a later edition, he wrote that the curriculum was purposefully 'unambitious' in comparison with the 'over-symbolic' approach of conservative kindergartens and the amount of children's directed work with gifts and occupations.[99] The first topic La Victoire introduced was 'home as shelter', which was the same as for older children, though they focused on the historical aspects of home from the time of 'primitive man'.[100] The topic of 'home' was explored through collaborative and constructive play in which the children furnished a small-scale model of a playhouse that had been built by older students and made individual models to take home. The whole year's work advanced from this starting point.

Children determined the rooms and furniture for the home, its heating and lighting, the roles and activities of mother, father and siblings; and related topics such as transportation, the trades and the cycle of production, from natural resources and their processing to retail and then to the home. The children's study of home heating gives an idea of a typical lesson, starting with the children's response to the teacher's question, constructing models on the theme and undertaking dramatic play.[101] Much of the content would have been familiar to Froebelian teachers studying the 'trades' with their children. However, the method of teaching, involving questioning and constructive work, indicated an evolutionary if not revolutionary view.

At the end of the school year, La Victoire set off for Honolulu to lead the charity kindergarten, and in Fall 1899, Scates took over as lead teacher, assisted by students from the CFKA training school, Grace Dolling, May Foster and Sylvia Ruger. Scates published an account of her year at the kindergarten on the basis of work reports, in the *Elementary School Record*.[102] While she indicated there were twenty four children divided into three groups with an assistant working with each, classes would have been much smaller: the actual daily attendance was ten to twelve.[103] The work under Scates was similar to the programme with La Victoire and was replicated the following year under the direction of Grace Dolling. Indeed, the lessons were closely matched from year to year in both timing and details: the dramatic play about the coal man described above occurred each year.

Most days children spent some time making things for the large-scale play house: they wove mats with one-inch cloth strips, made rugs with quarter-inch candle wicking and did other work in which they were provided with materials, such as stiff paper, and given suggestions (e.g. make a house). In her published account of the year's work in the *University Record*, Scates addressed the question of whether teaching in this way, that is, using creative constructive play, was harder than teaching using directed work with the gifts. She wrote, 'It does require more work than placing a box of gifts before a child and demanding that he shall follow minute directions in order to evolve some sequence play from which he is expected to get wonderful principles. ... It requires thought on teacher's part, a definite knowledge and planning of the work to be done by the children.'[104]

The teachers' work reports support Scates's explanation: there were only two instances of play with gifts in the first two years at the Dewey School's kindergarten. In the first instance, La Victoire described that the children 'played with the "fifth gift," making birdhouses'. She took special care to note, 'This was "free play," i.e. not dictated in any way. They [also] made birdhouses of wood and took them home'.[105] The second instance involved the use of the scribed kindergarten table, not for gift play but to answer a child's question regarding measurement. A boy in Scates's classroom wondered about the scribed marks on the kindergarten table, and he used the larger Hennessey blocks to pursue an experiment to determine the size of the marks.[106]

Scates's successor, Grace Dolling, described more use of the gifts, including in directed play, in her year as lead teacher in 1900 to 1901. Dolling's work was closer to an 'evolutionary' approach, with adaptations. She wrote, 'We had carpenter play with the third gift. It was a directed sequence'.[107] She repeated the experience the following week. The gifts were also used for free construction: the third and fourth gifts were used to build a bookcase for their playhouse, with children adding paper strips for shelves.[108] Children used the second gift to make a lamp post for their streetscape.[109]

The work reports, however, are unlikely to have included all the activities of the kindergarten. Dolling's reports were perfunctory, about half the length of Scates's from the year before. A visitor to Dolling's class in 1901 saw what might have been a more typical session with a gift, and one that was not mentioned in a report:

> When the story was finished, the children went naturally and quietly, without any ceremony, to the tables, where, with the assistance of one active boy, they were given the Fifth Gift. With a simple 'Let's wait till we all have them', the kindergartner secured unity of action; for the boxes were all opened at once but without direction. A toboggan slide and skating ponds were suggested, and some good results were evolved from the busy little brains. One child, who could not accomplish a successful slide, asked for help; so the kindergartner gave him several directions from across the table, which he followed and developed. A careful suggestion was given here and there among the rest of the children, bringing about a happy and successful Gift lesson, with the development of considerable individuality. It is a significant fact that each child *made* something; he was not embarrassed by his material, as so many are with the larger Gifts, but was able to use it and express something definite with it. When the work had been accomplished, the Gift was put back into the boxes; and by piling the blocks in the box (instead of piling them on the lid and then putting the box down over them) the children were able easily to put all the blocks into the boxes without help. When they had finished this, they themselves put the boxes away in neat rows on the proper shelf in the proper cupboard.[110]

This account shows that the children were familiar with the routine of using the gifts. It is probable that the play referred to by La Victoire – making birdhouses with the fifth gift – would have followed a similar process. However, while Dolling's work appeared closer to an 'evolutionary', more traditional approach, it was criticized by Froebelians, who offered a 'deprecatory word' concerning Dolling's 'use of songs and games having unrythmic and unrhymed words', considered harmful for children's developing sense of rhythm.[111] However, they offered no comment on her informal use of the gifts, indicating that it was a practice that was not unique to the Dewey School.

For the kindergarten's first three years, staffing followed a pattern where the assistant in one year became the lead teacher in the next. This pattern changed in 1901 when Dolling left and none of the three student assistants stayed on in the kindergarten. The teacher in 1901–2 was Grace Fulmer, assisted by Virginia Kendall; in 1902–3, the final year of the laboratory school, Faith Brooks assisted Fulmer. All were from the Chicago Kindergarten College, whose teaching methods Dewey had dismissed as drivelling idiocy. Unfortunately, there are no records of the work at the Dewey School kindergarten in its last two years. Teachers' work reports were continued after 1901–2, but they have not surfaced in the archives.[112] The mode of teaching in the kindergarten department starting in 1901–2 is, therefore, surmised from the training and experience of the teaching staff. No evidence has been found to explain the shift to recruit teachers from Chicago Kindergarten College instead of the CFKA. However, the hiring pattern suggests a substantial change in direction for the kindergarten from its experimental, research-based mission.

The period from 1900 to the school's end in 1903 was a time of turmoil for the Dewey School. In 1899, Chicago philanthropist Anita Blaine created a private school of teacher education called the Chicago Institute, headed by Col Francis Parker, whom she had recruited from the Chicago Normal School. The institute included a practice school, and Parker brought along many of his teachers from the normal school. University of Chicago president William Rainey Harper convinced Blaine to bring the institute into the university. From 1901 there were two elementary schools: the Dewey School, which was renamed the Laboratory of the Department of Education, and the Francis W. Parker School at the School of Education, which was the new name of the institute. Dewey resisted pressure to merge his school with Parker's, and with financial support from his school's parents, he was able to convince Harper to continue the laboratory school. In June 1901, Dewey appointed his wife, Alice Dewey, as principal. Following Parker's death in 1902, Harper appointed Dewey as head of the School of Education while continuing as head of the Department of Education, and the next year, Dewey merged the two elementary schools, with Alice Dewey as principal of both schools. Teachers' complaints about Alice Dewey caused Harper to ask her to resign, triggering John Dewey's move to Columbia University in 1904.[113]

The change in kindergarten staffing occurred with Alice Dewey's appointment as principal, and the reasons for the change are likely to have been entangled in the politics of the school. Events outside the school suggest additional motives. Anna Bryan died in February 1901 following a long period of illness. She had been on leave from the CFKA for most of the time from Spring 1898. Bryan's involvement with the Dewey School, though limited by her ill health, may have been the main tie between the association and the laboratory kindergarten.

Grace Fulmer continued teaching the theory and practice of Froebel's gifts at the college while teaching kindergarten at the Dewey School, working as a 'revolutionary' in the morning and an 'evolutionary' in the afternoon. Her course on play gifts at the college included a review of the gifts from the first two years of the programme, 'including all the new psychological gifts with original sequences and games given by each student to class; study of the fourteen crystal forms intended by Froebel for the transition class; architectural forms with 5th and 6th gifts combined for use in primary grade'.[114] With her background in Froebelian education, what can we imagine about Fulmer's teaching in the experimental kindergarten? Could it have been described as revolutionary? The writing of Alice Dewey and Fulmer's own writing and recollections provide us with clues. Alice Dewey, who was then the Dewey School's principal, set out her ideas on the gifts in a talk at the Chicago Kindergarten Club in 1902. Fulmer was teaching at the Dewey School at that time. Alice Dewey wrote:

> The changes made in the scheme of kindergarten work up to the present have been made because some details of the scheme did not relate to the needs of the child. However appealing and inspiring the metaphysics lying behind the gifts and occupations, we have, as a matter of fact, gradually found it desirable to simplify and even to discard many of the exercises which were given to children in the early days of the kindergarten.[115]

Fulmer described her own view of the importance of the gifts in her book *The Use of the Kindergarten Gifts*, published in 1918, showing that she remained close to her mentor Elizabeth Harrison.

> The materials peculiar to the kindergarten were selected because of their value in the organization and control of human experience – because of their universal significance – and not because they happened to be the few things in which the founder of the kindergarten had become interested, or because of their appeal to a few individuals.[116]

In Fulmer's recollection of her time at the Dewey School, as described in Durst, she 'felt that while Dewey didn't always approve of her work, she nonetheless felt free to "work in [her] own way, while his ideals and influence upon [her] educational experiences … increased with the passing years" '.[117] It could be imagined that Fulmer continued gift play in a manner similar to that of Dolling in the year before, but using an even more directed approach. Her teaching was unlikely to have been experimental in the way John Dewey had envisioned, though she may have simplified some of the work, as Alice Dewey noted. Yet, as Fulmer recollected, the importance of her two years at the school become clearer to her over time, for example, in her work at Teachers College, Columbia University, with Patty Smith Hill from 1906 to 1912, where Fulmer was an assistant professor of kindergarten education, and in her later work at her own private training school in Los Angeles.

Fulmer's assistants at the Dewey School were also her students at the college. Virginia Kendall was in the third year of her studies in 1901–2 while she worked in the school to fulfil her practice teaching requirement. She continued as assistant after graduating with her senior diploma the following year. Elizabeth Harrison and Belle Woodson dedicated their book *The Kindergarten Building Gifts* to Kendall and the other members of her graduating class, and it could be expected that it reflected the methods taught at the college.[118] The teaching strategies included 'dictation' for children at the 'conscious stage' of play, involving 'controlling the child's attention long enough to give him, in simple and correct language, some new movement of the blocks'.[119] Again, it could be imagined that Kendall led children in this sort of 'dictation play' with the gifts at the Dewey School in her two years at the kindergarten.

Another of Fulmer's students, Faith Brooks, joined Kendall in 1902–3.[120] Brooks had completed a two-year kindergarten course at Alma College in Minnesota and further studies in Berlin before coming to Chicago Kindergarten College for her senior diploma in 1902. Brooks went on to teach at Indiana Normal School after her graduation from the college. Her biography described her work in Chicago with reference to Dewey's children and not his ideas, nor even the laboratory school: 'It is a notable fact that Miss Brooks, in her work, has had charge of the children of Prof. John Dewey, the distinguished psychologist of the University of Chicago.'[121]

Conclusion

In our conclusion, we return to the questions we posed at the beginning of the chapter, where we asked what was the nature of the experiment with regard to kindergarten education? Did it reflect a version of a 'revolutionary' view? For Dewey, revolutionizing the kindergarten was never the aim. As he wrote in his letter to Cooke, the idea was 'simply to do for the little tots whatever seems best for them'.[122] He advocated an approach to teaching that reflected the middle ground: 'Nothing is more absurd than to suppose that there is no middle term between leaving a child to his own unguided fancies and likes or controlling his activities by a formal succession of dictated directions.'[123] Kindergarten at the Dewey School was a version of the 'middle ground', which likely shifted somewhat to the right of centre under the direction of Fulmer and her students from the Chicago Kindergarten College.

Our understanding educational change as an incremental process supports this view[124]; angels and devils are not so easily distinguished. Experts from England who toured the United States in 1900 to study education, including the kindergarten, illustrated this point. When they were in Chicago, they interviewed Dewey at the University of Chicago, as well as Harrison and Fulmer at the Chicago Kindergarten College. Their report, which referred to Snider's categories of kindergartners, concluded that 'to judge from actual observation there would seem to be a considerable amount of direction even about the free play and free work, and quite sufficient freedom about the directed play and work'.[125] Dewey objected to his daughter Evelyn's kindergarten activities in 1894 – 'playing with cubes, to find out about the edges & 'surfaces' – We are left to wonder about his impressions when, a decade later, five-year-old Lucy Dewey and her six-year-old brother Gordon, as students in the Dewey School kindergarten, were very likely engaged in some amount of directed work with the gifts, led by Fulmer and her students.

Kindergarten pedagogy at Dewey's school was influenced by the ideas of two of the most prominent teachers in the period, Bryan and Harrison, who brought many of Dewey's rather philosophical ideas to life and who trained and supervised the work of the other kindergarten teachers on staff. Bryan's 'revolutionary' view of the use of Froebel's gifts, as seen in the practices of La Victoire and Scates, was perhaps closer to what both Dewey and his wife wanted to see in the school. However, while Harrison's views and those of her student Fulmer were more traditional, they were likely modified in the context of Dewey's kindergarten to allow for freer work. Looking beyond the use of Froebel's gifts at the practices in the Dewey School more broadly, we see them as contributing to a fundamental educational change, at least as seen in the influence of the practices in other contexts. As one example, Scates's report on her year's work in 1899–1900 was studied by Froebelian revisionists in England, reprinted in 1913 and again in 1929, and used to guide project or activity-based teaching (see the chapter by Read in this volume).

However, Bryan's and Harrison's influence on the development of early childhood teacher education (ECTE) goes beyond their views of Froebel's gifts and how they conveyed them to their students. In spite of differences, both Bryan and Harrison adopted Dewey's interest in scientific study of children and included coursework in psychology in their kindergarten teacher training programmes. It is important to note that their views on the need for specialized training for kindergarten teachers, which is still prominent today, were in sharp contrast to Dewey's persistent claim that candidates for kindergarten positions at his school did not need a kindergarten background. Not only did Bryan and Harrison oversee training schools, but they also made changes in their training programmes to improve the overall quality of education. Many of the changes Bryan instituted in Louisville are elements of both the structure and the content of ECTE programmes today. Beginning teachers are still asked to reflect on their own childhood and on experiences with children as a beginning of their understanding of theories taught in ECTE programmes. Most importantly, Bryan experimented with what is now known as 'practice-based theory', that is, developing pedagogical theory based on students' experiences.[126]

An emphasis on teachers' fostering children's creative play with blocks rather than by instruction or drill has become a core belief reflected in the philosophies of many ECTE and early childhood programmes around the world. Bryan also piloted the 'indirect approach to teaching children' that is the essence of what the now-famous Reggio Emilia's 'provocations' represent. This indirect way of inspiring children's curiosity about the world is evident in the reports by the Dewey School's kindergarten teachers of children's exploration of the topic of home: the teachers used questions to stimulate children's interest and ideas and engaged them in developing models and making and testing predictions while using a variety of materials. These activities remain at the core of the project work promoted by progressive approaches to early childhood education.[127]

Abbreviation

CFKA   Chicago Free Kindergarten Association.

Notes

1   Denton J. Snider, *The Psychology of Froebel's Play-Gifts* (St. Louis, MO: Sigma, 1900).
2   Snider, *Psychology of Froebel's Play-Gifts*, vii–viii.

3   G. Stanley Hall, 'Some Defects of the Kindergarten in America', *The Forum* (January 1900): 583.

4   Snider, *Psychology of Froebel's Play-Gifts*, viii.

5   The Progressive Era was marked by reforms aimed at addressing social problems in the context of rapid change. For an overview of the Progressive Era and education, see Lawrence A. Cremin, *The Transformation of the School: Progressivism in American Education 1876–1957* (New York: Vintage Books, 1961).

6   Barbara Beatty, *Preschool Education in America: The Culture of Young Children from the Colonial Era to the Present* (New Haven, CT: Yale University Press, 1995), 72–3.

7   From 1896 to 1901, the school's official name was the University Elementary School, Department of Pedagogy. It was popularly known as 'Dr Dewey's school' ('Adventure in Education', *Chicago Daily Tribune*, 28 May 1899), 14. From 1901 to 1904, it was renamed the Laboratory of the Department of Education, the latter being the new name for the Pedagogical Department. The name change was triggered by the creation of a School of Education in 1901 and the incorporation of the Chicago Institute, which also had a practice school called the University Elementary School. In 1903, the laboratory school and the University Elementary School were merged under principal Alice C. Dewey. For ease of reading, the school will be referred to simply as the laboratory school or the Dewey School.

8   Sidney Hook, *John Dewey: An Intellectual Portrait* (New York: Prometheus Books, [1939] 1995), 15.

9   Sources used include the Dewey School teachers' work reports, course calendars, correspondence, newspapers and Dewey's publications with a focus on the years 1894 to 1903.

10 Friedrich Froebel, *Friedrich Froebel's Pedagogics of the Kindergarten*, trans. Josephine Jarvis (London: Edward Arnold, [1861] 1897), 123.

11 Susan E. Blow, *Letters to a Mother on the Philosophy of Froebel* (New York: D. Appleton and Co., 1899), 147.

12 Elizabeth Harrison and Belle Woodson, *The Kindergarten Building Gifts: With Hints on Program Making*, 2nd edn (St. Louis, MO: Sigma, 1905), 97.

13 'Eighth Talk to Mothers' Classes', *The Kindergarten Magazine* 4, no. 9 (1892): 531. Note: from a lecture by Lucretia Willard Treat. Treat trained with Blow and taught at the Loring School kindergarten in the same period as Harrison (1888–92).

14 Harrison and Woodson, *Kindergarten Building Gifts*, 103.

15 Hall, 'Some Defects of the Kindergarten in America', 586.

16 Denton J. Snider, *Psychology and the Psychosis* (St. Louis, MI: Sigma, 1896), 5.

17 Snider, *Psychology of Froebel's Play-Gifts*; Harrison and Woodson, *Kindergarten Building Gifts*. 'Companion volume', in 'Book Reviews', *The Kindergarten Building Gifts*, book review, *Kindergarten Review* 15, no. 1 (1903): 56.

18 Harrison and Woodson, *Kindergarten Building Gifts*, 29.

19 The highest stage of thinking was classification. See Snider, *Psychology and Psychosis*, 454–59.

20 Harrison and Woodson, *Kindergarten Building Gifts*, 30.

21 John Dewey, 'Principles of Mental Development as Illustrated in Early Infancy', in *The Collected Works of John Dewey, 1882–1953*. Electronic edition, CD-ROM, ed. L. A. Hickman, InteLex, [first published in *Transactions of the Illinois Society for Child Study* 4 (1899): 65–83], 185.

22 Ibid., 196.

23 Ibid., 199.

24 Ibid.

25 John Dewey to Alice Chipman Dewey, 12 June 1896 (01247), in *The Correspondence of John Dewey* [electronic resource] (Carbondale, IL: Southern Illinois University Press, 1999–2004).

26 Nina C. Vandewalker, 'The Kindergarten in the Chicago School System', *Kindergarten Magazine* 9, no. 9 (1897): 679.

27 International Kindergarten Union, *The Kindergarten: Reports of the Committee of Nineteen on the Theory and Practice of the Kindergarten* (Boston: Houghton Mifflin, 1913).

28 Evelyn Weber, *The Kindergarten: Its Encounter with Educational Thought in America* (New York: Teachers College Press, 1969), 47.

29 Barbara Beatty, *Preschool Education in America*; Weber, *The Kindergarten*.

30 John Dewey, 'Froebel's Educational Principles', *Elementary School Record* 1 (June 1900): 149–50.

31 'Teachers Employed in Cook County, 1 January 1881', *Annual Report of the County Superintendent of Schools* (Chicago: J.M.W. Jones, 1880), 64. Report of the Secretary of the Interior, vol. IV, Report of the Commissioner of Education, Kindergarten (Washington, DC: Government Printing Office, 1884), 106; Luelja Zearing Gross, *Kindergarten Magazine* 15, no. 5 (January 1903): 329; 'The Chicago Free Kindergarten Association', *Kindergarten Magazine* 5, no. 19 (1893): 734–8.

32 'Free Kindergarten Training', *The Inter Ocean* (Chicago), 30 September 1888, 6.

33 Bryan completed her certificate in 1884 and diploma in 1885. 'Free Kindergarten', *The Inter Ocean* (Chicago), 26 June 1885, 5.

34 Patty Smith Hill, 'Anna Bryan', in *Pioneers of the Kindergarten in America* (New York: The Century Co., 1924), 225.

35 'Kindergarten Schools', *Chicago Daily Tribune* (Chicago), 2 February 1882, 9.

36 'Kindergarten Graduates', *Chicago Daily Tribune*, 28 June 1884, 6.

37 'Fingers and Brains', *Chicago Daily Tribune*, 10 December 1893, 41.

38 The number of children enrolled at the Marie Chapel Kindergarten where Bryan was director was 95. See the Department of the Interior, Bureau of Education, *Report of the Commissioner of Education for the Year 1885-6*. Appendix IV, Kindergartens (Washington, DC: Government Printing Office, 1887), 338. Daily attendance would likely have been about fifty. See Vandewalker, 'The Kindergarten in the Chicago School System', 681.

39 Cora L. Stockham, 'The Louisville Free Kindergarten', *Kindergarten Magazine* 1 (1889): 282.

40 'A Free Kindergarten', *The Courier Journal* (Louisville, KY), 11 August 1887, 8.

41 Cross, 'The Work of the Chicago Free Kindergarten Association', *Kindergarten Magazine* 10, 8 (1898): 510.

42 'Kindergarten Work', *The Inter Ocean* (Chicago), 7 February 1889, 9.

43 Amy Tanner, *The Child: His Thinking, Feeling, and Doing* (Chicago: Rand McNally, 1904).

44 Cross, 'Work of the Chicago Free Kindergarten Association'; 'Chicago Kindergarten Training Schools, *Kindergarten Magazine* 7, no. 2 (1894): 149.

45 Anna Bryan, 'Are the Kindergarten Gifts Educational?' *Kindergarten Magazine* 7, no. 8 (1895): 606–8.

46 Cross, 'Work of the Chicago Free Kindergarten Association', 512.

47 Ibid., 514.

48 'Educational Notes', *The Inter Ocean* (Chicago), 24 August 1897, 10.

49 'Miss Harrison and the Chicago Kindergarten College', *Kindergarten Magazine* 5, no. 10 (1893): 739–45; Shannon P. Hart, 'Female Leadership and the "Cult of

Domesticity": The Contributions of Elizabeth Harrison and Rumah Crouse to the Chicago Kindergarten Movement, 1879–1920', *American Educational History Journal* 38, no. 1 (2011): 127–44.

50 The college became the National College of Education in 1930 and National Louis University in 1990.

51 Susan E. Blow, *The Songs and Music of Friedrich Froebel's Mother Play* [Mutter und Kose Lieder], (New York: D. Appleton, 1895).

52 Chicago Kindergarten College, *1895-1896 Course Catalogue*, File 01/001, Course Catalogues, 1849-Present, Box 1 [01/001], 9, 12. National Louis University Archives and Special Collections.

53 Friedrich Froebel, *The Education of Man*, trans. W. N. Hailmann (New York, NY: D. Appleton, [1826] 1887).

54 Ibid.

55 Ibid., *1900-1901 Course Catalogue*, File 01/001, Course Catalogues, 1849-Present, Box 1 [01/001], 16.

56 Chicago Kindergarten College, *1900-1901 Course Catalogue*, File 01/001, Course Catalogues, 1849-Present, Box 1 [01/001].

57 'Child Study Congress', *University Record* 1, no. 9 (1896): 166.

58 Michael Knoll, 'John Dewey as Administrator: The Inglorious End of the Laboratory School in Chicago', *Journal of Curriculum Studies* 47, no. 2 (2015): 203–52.

59 Dewey noted the Stanford school in John Dewey, 'Significance of the School of Education', *The Elementary School Teacher* 4, no. 7 (1904): 444. The kindergarten, which was directed by Prof. Earl Barnes, is described in Orrin L. Elliott, *Stanford University: The First Twenty-Five Years* (New York: Stanford University Press, 1937), 111–12.

60 John Dewey, 'The University School', *The University Record* 1, no. 32 (Chicago: University of Chicago, 1896): 417.

61 Ibid., 419.

62 Ibid., 418.

63 'Practice School for Teachers', *The Inter Ocean* (Chicago), 14 January 1896, 8.

64 Proceedings of the Thirty-Seventh Annual Convention of the Ontario Educational Association (Toronto, ON: Rowsell and Hutchison, 1898), 289.

65 'Recommended to Dewey', John Dewey to Clara Mitchell, 6 November 1895 (00268), in *The Correspondence of John Dewey*. Mitchell's background is described in the *Annual Register, July 1906 to July 1907* (Chicago: University of Chicago, 1907), 23.

66 Susan Blow to William Torrey Harris, 12 June 1896 (01247), in *The Correspondence of John Dewey*.

67 Katherine Camp Mayhew and Anna Camp Edwards, *The Dewey School: The Laboratory School of the University of Chicago 1896-1903* (New York: D. Appleton-Century Company, 1936), 8.

68 John Dewey to Frank Manny, 26 May 1896 (00526), in *The Correspondence of John Dewey*.

69 Ibid., 16 March 1896 (00519).

70 Durst, *Women Educators*.

71 John Dewey, 'University Elementary School, Report for Year 1898–9', *The President's Report* (Chicago: University of Chicago, 1899), 197.

72 Mayhew and Edwards, *The Dewey School*, vi.

73 In his report on the school for 1897–8, Dewey stated that the school was originally planned for children from age four (John Dewey, 'The University Elementary School,

Report for the Year 1897–8', *The Presidents Report* (Chicago: University of Chicago, 1898), 232.

74 Teachers in Hawaii were familiar with the work of Parker and his teachers at the Chicago Normal School: Anne Allen had accompanied Parker to Hawaii in 1898 where she gave a course on kindergarten. *The Courier-Journal* (Louisville, KY), 1 July 1898, 4.

75 John Dewey, 'University Elementary School, Report for Year 1898–9', 197.

76 John Dewey to Flora J. Cooke, 16 August 1898 (00633), in *The Correspondence of John Dewey*.

77 John Dewey to Alice Chipman Dewey, Chicago, 2 August 1894 (00168), *The Correspondence of John Dewey*.

78 In 1899, Cooke joined Parker at the new Chicago Institute; had taught under Parker at the Cook County school from 1889.

79 G. L. Kroepel, 'Flora J. Cooke: Progressive Educator'. Unpublished doctoral dissertation (Chicago: Loyola University of Chicago, 2000), 8.

80 Alice Chipman Dewey to John Dewey, August to September 1898 (21826), in *The Correspondence of John Dewey*.

81 John Dewey to Flora J. Cooke, 16 August 1898 (00633), in *The Correspondence of John Dewey*.

82 Ibid., 1 September 1898 (00612), in *The Correspondence of John Dewey*.

83 Alice Chipman Dewey to Flora J. Cooke, 16 September 1898 (00634), in *The Correspondence of John Dewey*.

84 John Dewey to Flora J. Cooke, 20 September 1898 (00635), in *The Correspondence of John Dewey*.

85 University of Chicago, *University Record* 3, no. 28 (1899): 166. Elsewhere she is described as 'an experienced kindergartner'. University of Chicago, *University Record* 3, no. 35 (Chicago: University of Chicago Press, 1899): 176.

86 Dewey noted that she had 'primary work' in the year before coming to the laboratory school: John Dewey, 'Froebel's Educational Principles', *Elementary School Record* 1 (June 1900): 150. La Victoire was teacher at the Madison Avenue School in Chicago in 1894–5, 1895–6, and 1896–7: in Board of Education, City of Chicago. *Proceedings of the Board of Education of the City of Chicago* (Chicago: John F. Higgins, 1895); and in 'Where the Teaches will Recreate', *The Daily Inter Ocean* (Chicago), 23 June 1895, 27. The location of her teaching in 1897–8 is unknown.

87 *Chicago Daily Tribune* (Chicago), 29 April 1898, 10.

88 Mayhew and Edwards, *The Dewey School*, 56.

89 Kindergarten Inventory, Laboratory Work Reports, June 1899, Special Collections Research Centre, University of Chicago Library.

90 John Dewey, 'University Elementary School, Report for the Year 1897–8', 232.

91 John Dewey, *The School and Society* (Chicago: University of Chicago Press, 1899), 128.

92 Mayhew and Edwards, *The Dewey School*, 57.

93 'Kindergartners Get Diplomas', *The Inter Ocean* (Chicago), 18 June 1896, 8.

94 Board of Education, City of Chicago, *Proceedings of the Board of Education of the City of Chicago, 13 July 1898 to 28 June 1899* (Chicago: John F. Higgins, 1899), 29, 362.

95 University of Chicago, *University Record* 3, no. 28 (1899): 166; Ibid.

96 John Dewey, 'University Elementary School, Report for the Year 1897–8', *The Presidents Report* (Chicago: University of Chicago, 1898), 232.

97 Mayhew and Edwards, *The Dewey School*, 57.

98 John Dewey, *The School and Society* (Chicago: University of Chicago Press, 1899), 123.

99   John Dewey, *The School and Society*, rev. edn (Chicago: University of Chicago Press, 1915), 120.

100 John Dewey, 'University School', *University Record* 1, no. 32 (Chicago: University of Chicago, 1896): 421.

101 Laboratory Work Reports, 13 January 1899, Special Collections Research Centre, University of Chicago Library.

102 Georgia P. Scates, 'The Sub-Primary (Kindergarten) Department', *Elementary School Record* 1 (June 1900): 129–42.

103 This level of staffing was similar in some other experimental schools. Three teachers worked with eight children at the Harriet Johnson Nursery School in New York. See Ise Forest, *Preschool Education: A Historical and Critical Study* (New York: Macmillan, 1927).

104 Ibid., 134.

105 Laboratory Work Reports, 8 April 1899, Special Collections Research Centre, University of Chicago Library.

106 Ibid., 11 November 1899.

107 Ibid., 11 January 1901.

108 Ibid., 15 February 1901.

109 Ibid., 16 March 1901.

110 Geneva Mary Clippinger, 'A Visit to the Sub-Primary Class of Dr Dewey's School', *Kindergarten Review* 11, no. 7 (March 1901): 425.

111 The *Kindergarten Review's* editors, Emilie Poulsson and Laura E. Poulsson, added their criticism in a note to Clippinger's report. Clippinger, 'A Visit to the Sub-Primary Class', 426.

112 Mayhew and Edwards, *The Dewey School*, x.

113 Michael Knoll, 'John Dewey as Administrator: The Inglorious End of the Laboratory School in Chicago', *Journal of Curriculum Studies* 47, no. 2 (2015): 203–52.

114 Chicago Kindergarten College, 1902–3 (Calendar) (Chicago: Published by the College, 1902), 11.

115 Alice Dewey, 'The Place of the Kindergarten', *The Elementary School Teacher* 3, no. 5 (1903): 285.

116 Grace Fulmer, *The Use of the Kindergarten Gifts* (Boston: Houghton Mifflin, 1918), 7.

117 Durst, *Women Educators*, 138.

118 Harrison and Woodson, *Kindergarten Building Gifts*, dedication page.

119 Ibid., 82.

120 Brooks taught at Riverside School, Cook County in the same year. Department of Public Instruction, Cook County, Illinois, *Biennial Report of the County Superintendent of School from 1 July 1900 to 30 June 1902* (Chicago: The J.M.W. Jones Stationary and Printing Co., 1902), 139.

121 Five-year-old Lucy Dewey and her six-year-old brother Gordon. 'Miss Faith Brooks, Personal and Educational Department', *The Educator-Journal* 6, no. 3 (1905): 124–5.

122 John Dewey to Flora J. Cooke, 16 August 1898 (00633), in *The Correspondence of John Dewey*.

123 John Dewey, 'Froebel's Educational Principles', 150.

124 Larry Cuban, *How Teachers Taught: Constancy and Change in American Classrooms, 1890-1990* (New York: Teachers College Press, 1993).

125 H. Thiselton Mark, 'Moral Education in American Schools', in *Special Reports on Educational Subjects*, vol. 10. Education in the United States part I (1902), 191. House of Commons Parliamentary Papers Online.

126 Deborah Loewenberg Ball and David K. Cohen, 'Toward a Practice-Based Theory of Professional Education', in *Teaching as the Learning Profession: Handbook of Policy and Practice*, ed. Gary Sykes and Linda Darling-Hammond (San Francisco: Jossey-Bass, 1999), 30–2.
127 Lilian G. Katz and Sylvia C. Chard, 'The Project Approach: An Overview', in *Approaches to Early Childhood Education*, ed. Jaipual Roopnarine and James E. Johnson, 6th edn (Boston: Pearson, 2013).

Figure 8.1 Colet Gardens Demonstration School, c. 1904, 'A dramatic game'. FA/PH/6.1. Froebel Archive for Childhood Studies, University of Roehampton, London.

Figure 8.2 Colet Gardens Demonstration School, July 1908, Form II, *Alice in Wonderland*. FA/PH/6.1. Froebel Archive for Childhood Studies, University of Roehampton, London.

8

Guiding Creativity: British Froebelian Educators and Plays for Children, 1891–1939

Amy Palmer

The teaching of drama, both as a subject in its own right and as an approach to learning across the curriculum, is by its nature associated with a child-centred, active approach to education where children are freed from desk-bound, formal instruction. Notable early British enthusiast Henry Caldwell Cook associated drama with play: 'the natural means of study in youth' and with learning through one's own experiences.[1] It is not surprising, therefore, that drama has had a long association with Froebelian educators. Froebelians established fee-paying kindergartens for young children in Britain in the late nineteenth century.[2] Educationalist Gavin Bolton has recognized that their use of action songs and rhymes in these institutions was a significant early instance of 'dramatic activity'.[3] In the early twentieth century, an increasing number of Froebelians were taking up positions in infant and elementary schools in the state system[4] and were keen to ally the name of their founder with emerging approaches to progressive education.[5] The use of drama was one way in which their practice developed and spread in state schools.

This chapter explores this legacy and considers how debates about precisely what sort of drama activities were most appropriate reflected key questions for educators in this period and indeed today. These questions concern the relationship between freedom (child-directed learning) and guidance (teacher input). This was something that Froebel himself wrestled with and, according to historian Joachim Liebschner, found 'especially difficult'.[6] In today's English Foundation Stage curriculum, applicable to children from birth to five in both schools and other early years settings, practitioners are expressly required to deliver a 'mix of adult-led and child-initiated activity'.[7] The statutory document states that the optimum combination of these types of activity will vary from child to child and practitioners themselves must judge what is appropriate. However, governmental demands for a demonstrable increase in academic achievements even for very young children are currently tending to encourage more formal instruction.[8]

In respect of teaching (through) drama, the question could be formulated in these terms: Is it more beneficial for children to improvise their own dramatic productions or should they be guided, at least for some of the time, by the use of scripted material prepared by adults? Improvised role-play and children's own creations have dominated British drama lessons since the Second World War.[9] In the first half of the twentieth century, however, many Froebelian educators interested in this new, progressive aspect of education used scripted material as a significant part of their pedagogy. The use of plays for older children joined seamlessly onto the use of kindergarten rhymes for the very young. This is evidenced by the fact that *Child Life*, the journal of the Froebel Society's British branch from 1891 to 1939, contained numerous advertisements for, reviews of and articles about plays written for children to perform. In total, 119 published works, covering 624 individual plays, are mentioned in one of these contexts. Analysing this material in conjunction with the plays themselves, which were frequently written by teachers and prefaced with detailed commentaries, yields a multifaceted perspective on the topic. What emerges is that both playwrights and educators were frequently alive to the potential criticism that using adult-created material could undermine drama's progressive credentials. They, therefore, sought ways to demonstrate their commitment to child-centred education by aiming to inspire children's independence and creativity, both within the confines of the staged performances and within their wider lives.

Concerns about scripted material

The fact that the use of Froebel's action rhymes and songs required adults to exercise a high degree of control over children was a subject of discussion among British Froebelians in the nineteenth century. An English version of *Mutter and Kose-Lieder*, edited by Mrs E. Berry and Mme Michaelis, was published in Britain during the 1880s and proved popular: the first part of this volume went through three editions within a year.[10] The book consisted of music and rhymes together with precise suggestions of what kind of accompanying dramatic action would be appropriate. Sometimes an element of choice was incorporated, such as in *Side by Side,* 'where each child chooses the plant he represents'.[11] Nonetheless, the overall impression is of prescription, despite Ada (Mrs Edward) Berry's assertion that the mistress 'may at her pleasure give the children an opportunity of making changes and additions'.[12] Emily Shirreff, a passionate advocate for both women's higher education and Froebelian principles,[13] wrote the introduction to the second part of the book and alluded to criticism made of the games that 'the free activity of the children is fettered'.[14] She was unapologetic about this: 'The leadership of the teacher in Kindergarten games is altogether according to the children's natural wishes' and the submission of the individual will for the collective good is a 'valuable moral discipline'.

Not all educators in the late nineteenth century and early twentieth century found this quite so easy to accept. Froebel had high-minded ambitions for what his pedagogy would achieve: 'an intuition of the complex relationship between our inner and outer lives' leading to an understanding of the 'harmonious interconnection' between all things.[15] According to the Cambridge academic H. Courthorpe Bowen, writing in 1893, the child's 'own actions and creations' were indispensable for forging this link between inner and outer.[16] For some Froebelians, the games as they were commonly played in

British kindergartens, were therefore not fulfilling this purpose. E. R. Murray, later to be vice principal of the Maria Grey training college in London and author of key Froebelian tracts,[17] claimed, at a conference in 1901, that the games were frequently 'the dullest drudgery', with children required to perform them in the same way time and time again,[18] whereas they should be promoting the 'cultivation of originality and freedom of expression'.[19] The solution was that the 'children should be directing the game'. In practice, however, this meant that a child 'captain' took control, thus limiting the freedom of the others. In fact, like Shirreff, Murray insisted that a benefit of the games was that they taught 'obedience to the law',[20] that they should not, therefore, be changed 'too often' and, if they allowed for only a few principal parts with the other children limited to embodying vegetation or geographical features, that was the way of the world and also a lesson worth learning.

Dramatic activities for older children were seen by Froebelian educators at the turn of the century as a natural progression from the action rhymes and songs. Grace Lockwood argued in 1899: 'We don't wish our *little* ones to *act* but it seems to me that acting (dramatic representation) should lead on naturally from the games.'[21] However, just as with the kindergarten rhymes, the question of how scripted such activities should be was important. Early twentieth century drama pioneers Harriet Finlay-Johnson and Henry Caldwell Cook both believed that children should create their own plays as this was an effective way for children of all ages to learn across the curriculum.[22] Finlay-Johnson wrote: 'The play must be the child's own. However crude the action or dialogue … it would fitly express the stage of development arrived at by the child's mind and would, therefore, be valuable to *him* as a vehicle of expression and assimilation.'[23] Even though the subject matter Cook was interested in was the work of Shakespeare, it was nonetheless his intention that the children should improvise and then formalize their own versions of the works rather than perform the scripts as an adult company would.

A belief in the value of the children's own creations, developed with perhaps a delicate guiding hand, was evident in the writings of Froebelians throughout the 1891–1939 period. In a 1927 article in *Child Life*, Nora Ensor described the development of dramatic play from a simple 'show me' of a four-year-old to children of nine or ten writing and producing their own plays.[24] A handbook for teachers published in 1931 and edited by the Froebelian educator and well-known children's writer Enid Blyton claimed that the child loves to imitate and this should be built on by the teacher whose role it is to help 'weave his actions into little stories and plays with his companions'.[25] As the child becomes older, his 'plays' are based more and more firmly on the stories and pictures which he encounters. By the age of six, these become more formalized, with 'episodes and scenes' and 'expression in literary language'.[26]

This begs the question of how compatible the published playscripts were with Froebelian and progressive educational ideals. The reviews of these scripts, particularly in the earlier decades of the journal, often contained a whiff of disdain for their use, even when praising the products as essentially suitable. For example, a review of *Little Plays for Little People*, published in January 1911, stated: 'Simple dramas are always welcome and these are well-planned and prettily illustrated … yet one wonders whether children's own impromptu representations of the fairy tales are not of more value and interest to themselves.'[27] In an issue later that year, a review dismissed a collection of dramatized nursery rhymes with the comment, 'We leave nothing for imagination if we dramatize for children.'[28] In a review of *Three Mother Story Plays* in 1926, the reviewer commented, 'The little players had best be left to adapt stories for themselves.'[29]

It is possible, however, to detect a hint of dissonance between the high-minded ideals of the influential minority which was willing and able to promulgate its theories in public and the actual practice of other teachers. Nora Ensor, in the article quoted above, expressed her concern about the use of drama productions for 'educational stunts' for the glory of the teacher and the school.[30] The use of performance events to showcase and promote the work of an institution was a long-standing Froebelian tradition, as Westberg, writing in this volume, has demonstrated with reference to Swedish practice in the early twentieth century.[31] Ensor, however, believed that the annual Christmas concert should be discouraged. She illustrated this with the story of 'Mona', praised by her audience for being a 'perfectly sweet little Cowslip', whose educational development would have been much more effectively fostered had she simply been encouraged to play at being a fairy in her own way.[32] There is an interesting parallel here with a *Child Life* article from 1910 about the performance of kindergarten games at school festivals and open days. H. Brown-Smith summarized a Froebel Society discussion in which the participants agreed that 'the tendency to regard games as a performance should be checked'.[33]

Growing acceptance

In the late 1920s and in the 1930s, the use of drama teaching of all kinds was rising in prestige and popularity in state schools for children of all ages. As Ensor said in her 1927 article, the use of drama activities would 'not fail to mark the teacher as satisfactorily up-to-date'.[34] Drama as a method of learning across all areas of the curriculum gained approval in reports by the Board of Education's Consultative Committee in 1926, 1931 and 1933 (the Hadow Reports). The 1926 report, *The Education of the Adolescent*, suggested that 'some dramatic work associated with good literature may well be attempted, as is already done in some schools'.[35] The 1931 report, *The Primary School*, praised the use of drama because it was 'good fun', promoted 'power of expression in movement', 'perception and feeling', and also 'good voice production and seemly speech'.[36] The 1933 report, *Infant and Nursery Schools*, declared that a 'basic interest of children for which the school should provide an opening is the love of acting'.[37] The Board of Education's *Handbook of Suggestions for Teachers* also provides evidence for official enthusiasm around this period. This volume, first published under that title in 1927, was 'completely remodelled' in 1937 to incorporate the Hadow findings.[38] The 1927 edition is positive about children from the age of six onwards creating their own dramatizations of stories in the context of English teaching and in order to bring subjects such as history to life.[39] However, the section on dramatic work is more detailed and extensive in the 1937 edition, which notes that 'recent years' have seen 'a notable growth of interest in dramatic activity in schools'.[40]

There were a number of drivers for this increased interest. Bolton has identified that one of these was a focus on 'speech training' or elocution.[41] This is evident in the 1931 Hadow comment about 'seemly speech'. The *Handbook of Suggestions* also places emphasis on the point that 'drama is a most effective method for improving the clarity and fluency of children's speech'.[42] Contributors to *Child Life* in the 1930s also refer to the importance of elocution. L. G. Studman, for example, wrote that 'we want them [children] to speak clearly, so we use dramatic work as a motive to induce them to do so'.[43]

Bolton also identifies the increasing status of the science of child psychology, both among educationalists and the public more generally, as an important influence on drama's increasing prestige.[44] This growing interest is indicated in an editorial in *Child Life* in June 1936, which claimed that the 'ordinary reader of the daily papers' had now become aware of the work of Freud and Jung.[45] Child psychology rose in prominence through the work of Susan Isaacs, a revisionist Froebelian[46] who became Head of the Department of Child Development at the London Institute of Education in 1933.[47] Isaacs defended children's 'free dramatic play' as an arena in which they could 'work out their inner conflicts in an external field, thus lessening the pressure of the conflict and diminishing guilt and anxiety'.[48] Some educators subsequently espoused the view that other dramatic activities could also promote self-expression and creativity and could, therefore, have a positive psychological benefit. In an article promoting dramatic work for young children, Rosalind Vallance claimed that 'let's pretend' was 'a safety-valve' through which otherwise dangerous passions could be released.[49] In 1938, Brooke Gwynne (also a lecturer at the London Institute of Education) noted that previous generations had felt that acting was a 'dangerous art', but this had now changed.[50] In this school of thought, temporarily taking on the role of a negative character could be purging rather than corrupting. Such views were not held universally. A reviewer of a 1938 collection, *Ring up the Curtain*, complained that the actors were given 'full rein for anti-social conduct'.[51] One character (who ultimately gets her comeuppance) is required to mistreat her golliwog and call it a 'horrid black thing'.[52] The reviewer comments, 'If Mary chooses to throw herself into this with understanding and interest, there is trouble ahead for everyone.'[53]

This increased approval of dramatic activities in schools brought with it a greater (but not universal) acceptance of the use of published playscripts as part of this process. Many comments in reviews of playscripts in the pages of *Child Life* from the late 1920s and 1930s were positive and in some cases quite glowing. The 1928 reviewer of *One Act Plays of To-day* said the series had been 'deservedly successful' and expressed gratitude to those responsible.[54] An article in the same year presented a list of recommendations of suitable plays and described John Hampden's *Nine Modern Plays* and *Two Modern Plays for Juniors* as 'delightful … every play is a gem'.[55] In 1935, *Child Life* issued a 'special drama' number, which included a review article entitled *The Choice of Plays for Young Children*, which suggested criteria for selecting such plays ('simple' 'natural' 'cheerful') and recommended a large number, with an appendix of others suggested by teachers who had 'tried them out'.[56] The use of scripted plays was compatible with the 1937 *Handbook of Suggestions for Teachers*, which also offered advice about the choice of plays for use with children from seven to eleven in the junior school ('not too obviously written down to children,' and 'free from the vices of artificiality')[57] and encouraged the 'keen English teacher' to an occasional attempt at 'dramatic production on a large scale'.[58]

How scripted plays fostered creativity

The views and responses of the playwrights themselves are a key part of the story of the use of scripted drama. It is clear from paratexts (textual information outside the main body of the work, such as publishers' notes or a preface) that these writers were often practising educators who had direct experience of putting on their work with children. As using dramatic activities in lessons was still considered cutting-edge educational practice in the late 1930s, these were necessarily progressive teachers. Quite a few of them can be identified as Froebelian. Enid Blyton, despite her aforementioned espousal of children's own play-making, was also a prolific playwright, and her *Six Enid Blyton Plays: School edition* was (unfavourably) reviewed in *Child Life* in December 1935.[59] Linda Chesterman dedicated her 1937 volume to 'the children of Grove House School (Froebel Ed. Ins) who helped me make this book'.[60] The work of these educators was dismissed by Henry Caldwell Cook as 'playlets ... written by inexperienced school mistresses' (also described as 'dear ladies') which 'have no spark of literary value nor any dramatic power whatever'.[61] Bolton offers a similarly uncharitable assessment in a brief aside about 'inferior texts for children' which emerged in the mid-twentieth century.[62] Nonetheless, these playwrights attempted to engage and inspire children's own creativity in a number of ways and thus, both through text and paratext, made a significant contribution to the debate about freedom and guidance.

Sometimes the playwrights explicitly reflected on the creative process and the role of scripted plays within it. Playwrights, or editors of volumes of plays, argued that they were not violating but rather building on children's natural play impulses. Laurence F. Kelly, who wrote the foreword for a book of puppet plays, argued that they 'lure[d] the child onward to do better the kind of thing, to play the sort of game which the child himself has always done and played anyhow'.[63] Some make the point that the use of prepared plays was supposed to inspire, not replace, children's own dramatic creations: Tryce M. Baumgartner argued: 'The best thing for them is to make their own plays, but they need leading in this.'[64] Maude L. Darvell and Grace M. Tuffley also stated explicitly that their plays should not be used as a substitute for freer dramatic work but were suitable for use on 'various occasions', perhaps meaning school concerts rather than everyday classroom work.[65]

Many playwrights offered advice about how the children should be taught to perform the plays. A theme to emerge was that children should be allowed to interpret the work freely, making the text their own. Linda Chesterman explained that she had avoided 'elaborate directions' because the teacher and children should 'construct and *produce their own play* from the material presented'.[66] Reed Moorhouse addressed children directly on the subject of interpreting mime: 'I will not tell you *how* to do them. I wish you to make things up for yourselves. It is surprising what children *can* do.'[67] Others had a perhaps rather romantic view of children's creative spirit and what it might bring to the play: John Hampden, who compiled many volumes of plays for school use, suggested that it was appropriate for children's imagination to be given free rein in a play entitled *Elfin Hall*: 'They know more of elfland than any adult producer can remember.'[68]

In different ways, playwrights found opportunities within their scripts to leave space for varying interpretations. In her play, *Pierrot and Pierrette,* Baumgartner built in occasions where characters needed to perform a dance or a song without specifying further details. Of course, it was possible that such textual gaps would be filled by the teacher/producer rather than the child, but Baumgartner was clear in her introduction that 'self-expression' was the aim. A formal dance might need instruction but 'other movements and gestures should be discovered by the players'.[69] Similarly, Ruth Clarke stated that in performances of her dramatic dances, it would 'be well to leave the choice of actions to the children'.[70] It is interesting, however, that sometimes playwrights could choose to stimulate creative responses precisely by being extremely prescriptive. An example of this is the striking *Snowwhite* (sic) by A. I. King. King saw the play as facilitating 'an outlet for emotion' (recalling the psychological justification for drama that became prevalent in the 1930s) and tried to achieve this by providing the dwarfs with distinctive and complex characters. The fourth dwarf, for example, was a 'lover of beauty, wistful, can be bitter; his moods change'.[71] Bringing that to life would have been quite a challenge for the child actor.

Other playwrights were interested in more radical approaches, shying away from the traditional play in favour of forms of drama that maximized child engagement and participation. An example is the shadow play, championed by Hugh Chesterton, where a narrator read the story and actors appeared in silhouette behind a curtain. No specific instructions were provided for them.[72] Similarly, E. A. Jelf wrote a book of plays in which children interpreted stories through dance.[73] Although he was more prescriptive than Chesterton about the movements required, his starting point, as he explained in *Child Life,* was that children had a natural ability to tell story through movement. Their 'high spirits and abandon', leading to additions and deviations, would, therefore, enhance the play.[74] Such sentiments echo Froebelian and other progressive views on the importance of the child's own contribution to his/her learning.

Scripted plays as a resource for the creative life

Another way in which scripted plays could encourage children's creativity was by providing them with resources for their imagination. This was something which the plays had in common with storytelling in all its many forms. All the same, it is important to acknowledge this aspect of what the playwrights were trying to achieve. Moreover, their contribution was potentially extremely powerful. No other medium controlled children's movement and speech in so direct a fashion. Playwrights tried to use this capacity to model and promote an imaginative life.

One aspect of such a life was the world of magic, particularly that of fairies. Of the 624 plays referred to in *Child Life,* 53 were original fairy stories, and many more were derived from traditional tales in which magic and magical creatures played some part. Fairies had been overwhelmingly popular in the Victorian era[75] and by the 1930s, some playwrights began to comment negatively on their dominance and insist that they were moving away from such 'well-worn tracks'.[76] However, this theme by no means disappeared. John Bourne, who edited a 1934 volume of plays, wrote about the unfortunate prevalence of 'goody-goody fairies' thirty years previously, and yet his own contribution to his collection was nothing more radical than a tale of elves in fairyland who paint the daffodils red before apologizing and being mildly admonished.[77] These plays frequently showed recognizably modern children interacting with the world of fairies in a way that was life-enhancing. The ability to see fairies was a special privilege often denied to adults: 'Grown-up heads are full of other things' like, according to a character in a play by Maude S. Forsey, 'cigars and pipes and paying the butcher.'[78] The implication is clear: enjoy this while you can.

The animation of toys is another magical trope which is central to a number of plays. A theme to emerge is that children should care properly for their toys. Mary, from *Trouble in Toyland,* for example, complains about her shabby playthings but when the Queen of Toyland threatens to turn her into a 'looby-loo with one eye, one ear and no hair', she asks her mother to mend them and promises never to hurt them again.[79] Patty, from Rose Fyleman's *The Fairy and the Doll*, is similarly careless, but her doll rejects an opportunity to escape out of stout loyalty and a conviction that, deep down, she is truly loved after all.[80] The anthropomorphism necessarily implied that toys were entitled to dignity and respect. This amounted to a celebration and encouragement of children's right to imaginative play which was in line with Froebel's core values.

Play is also celebrated in the promotion of children's games and cultural artefacts such as nursery rhymes. This is central to many of the playscripts, particularly those connected to the kindergarten rhymes and action songs. In some cases, in plays for younger children, the rhyme or game itself, perhaps in a slightly extended version, is the whole of the play: indeed the border between rhyme and play is porous. Plays for older children were built on this tradition by developing a backstory for a familiar rhyme or song. Violet M. Methley's *Lavender's Blue*, for example, showed King Azure and Queen Emerald arguing over the colour of the plant, thus offering an explanation for the repeated line 'lavender's blue, dilly dilly, lavender's green' in the traditional folksong.[81] Such an approach was designed to encourage engagement and appreciation, perhaps at an age when children might begin to lose interest in simple rhymes. In a similar vein, another popular topic for plays for junior (seven- to eleven-year-old) children was the interweaving of nursery rhymes, often to humorous effect. Many concerned modern children being magically whisked to nursery rhyme land and meeting a host of familiar characters.[82] This playful intertextuality took inspiration from Lewis Carroll's 1865 *Alice's Adventures in Wonderland*.[83] The plays, however, offered children a uniquely immersive experience in the nursery rhyme world, where they could interact with the characters in an almost literal way. This was a heritage to be enjoyed and played with.

Some of the scripts modelled children's own free play. One example was Mary Farrah's 1917 *The Doll's Election,* in which three girls play with their dolls, boasting to each other about how 'forward' the dolls are in their development and how clothes suit their 'complexion splendidly'. Despite a generally positive presentation of women's suffrage, play is seen here as a preparation for a rather limited, gendered adulthood.[84]

Margaret Ashworth's representation of play scenarios was also heavily gendered, with boys and girls having stereotypical interests.[85] Nonetheless, the scenarios presented are rich and complex. In *Ready for Daisy,* for example, we see negotiations about roles, a common and developmentally important feature of imaginative play.[86] The children's concern with their toys' feelings is treated with a respectful seriousness, which mirrors children's own seriousness in their play.[87] Ashworth's work reflects and encourages children's creative worlds and their expression of them.

Conclusion

The growth of dramatic activity in British schools in the early twentieth century provides a powerful example of the increasing prevalence of child-centred, progressive educational methods. Its embrace by Froebelian educators in particular is indicative of their willingness to graft new methodologies onto their core values. As evidenced by the quantity of references in *Child Life,* scripted plays were used alongside freer, child-directed approaches, provoking the question of how much adult guidance was appropriate. This chapter has demonstrated that there was a range of views amongst progressive educators, with some condemning the use of scripts as unnecessarily restrictive. However, many of the playwrights demonstrated through their work that they valued children's creativity. The resources they produced had the potential, in the hands of sensitive educators, to lead to individual responses and thus ultimately to foster independence. As teachers respond today to the pressure for more adult-directed approaches, those who continue to value children's own contribution to their learning can take some heart from this. There may be a variety of ways to inspire creativity and ultimately set children free if this long-term aim is held firmly in view.

Notes

1 H. Caldwell Cook, *The Play Way: An Essay in Educational Methods* (London: William Heineman, 1917), 1.

2 Jane Read, 'Bringing Froebel into London's Infant Schools: The Reforming Practice of two Head Teachers, Elizabeth Shaw and Frances Roe from the 1890s to the 1930s', *History of Education* 42, no. 6 (2013): 745–64.

3 Gavin Bolton, *Acting in Classroom Drama: A Critical Analysis* (Stoke-on-Trent: Trentham Books, 1998), 7.

4 Read, 'Bringing Froebel into London's Infant Schools', 2013.

5 Kristen D. Nawrotzki, 'Froebel is Dead; Long Live Froebel! The National Froebel Foundation and English Education', *History of Education* 35, no. 2 (2006): 209–23.

6 Joachim Liebschner, *A Child's Work. Freedom and Play in Froebel's Educational Theory and Practice* (Cambridge: Lutterworth Press, 1992), 55.

7 Department of Education [England], 'Statutory Framework for the Early Years Foundation Stage', 2014, Available online: http://www.foundationyears.org.uk/files/2014/07/EYFS_framework_from_1_September_2014__with_clarification_note.pdf (accessed 23 August 2015).

8   Guy Robert-Holmes, 'High Stakes Assessment, Teachers and Children', in *Exploring Education and Children: From Current Certainties to New Visions,* ed. Dominic Wyse, Rosemary Davis, Phil Jones and Sue Rogers (London: Routledge 2015), 72–82.

9   David Hornbrook, *Education and the Dramatic Art,* 2nd edn (London: Routledge, 1998).

10 Mrs E. Berry and Mme Michaelis (eds), *Kindergarten Songs and Games* (London: W. Shepherd, 1883).

11 Ibid., 10.

12 Ibid., no page number.

13 Emily Shirreff, *Kindergarten: Principles of Froebel's System and their Bearing on the Education of Women. Also remarks on the Higher Education of Women* (London: W. Swan Sonnenschein, 1882).

14 Berry and Michaelis (eds), *Kindergarten Songs and Games,* 1883.

15 Jane Read, 'Free Play with Froebel: Use and Abuse of Progressive Pedagogy in London's Infant Schools 1870- c.1904', *Paedagogica Historica* 42, no. 3 (2006): 306.

16 H. Courthorpe Bowen, *Froebel and Education by Self-Activity* (London: Heinemann, 1893), 7.

17 E. R. Murray and Henrietta Brown Smith, *The Child under Eight* (London: E. Arnold, 1919).

18 E. R. Murray, 'On Kindergarten Games' in 'Kindergarten Games: A Criticism of Froebelian Paedagogy', *Conference Supplement to Child Life* 3, no. 11 (1901): 169.

19 Ibid., 175.

20 Ibid., 176.

21 Grace Lockwood, 'Games in the Kindergarten and Transition Class', *Child Life* 1, no. 2 (1899): 99. (Emphasis in the original).

22 Cook, *The Play Way,* 1917.

23 Harriet Finlay-Johnson, *The Dramatic Method of Teaching* (London: James Nisbet, 1912), 19.

24 Nora Ensor, 'The Development of Dramatic Expression', *Child Life* XXIX, no. 39 (1927): 77 9.

25 Enid Blyton (ed.), *Modern Teaching in the Infant School, Vol 3: Handwork, Games and Music* (London: George Newnes Ltd, 1931), 179.

26 Enid Blyton (ed.), *Modern Teaching in the Infant School, Vol 1: Reading, Writing and Arithmetic* (London: George Newnes Ltd, 1931), 27.

27 Review of *Little Plays for Little People*, M. L. Noyes and Blanche H. Ray, *Child Life* X111, no. 61 (1911): 30.

28 Review of *Easy Games for Little Players: A Collection of Dramatized Nursery Rhymes,* Margaret Boughton, *Child Life* XIII, no. 68 (1911): 254.

29 Review of *Three Mother Story Plays*, Evelyn Townsend, *Child Life* XXVIII, no. 136 (1926): 28.

30 Ensor, 'The Development of Dramatic Expression', 1927, 76.

31 See the chapter by Johannes Westberg in this volume.

32 Ensor, 'The Development of Dramatic Expression', 1927, 77.

33 H. Brown-Smith, 'The Use and Abuse of School Festivals and Games', *Child Life* X11, no. 6 (1910): 243.

34 Ensor, 'The Development of Dramatic Expression', 1927, 76.

35 Board of Education, Consultative Committee, *The Education of the Adolescent* (London: HMSO, 1926), 191.

36 Board of Education, Consultative Committee, *The Primary School* (London: HMSO, 1931), 104, 95.

37 Board of Education, Consultative Committee, *Infant and Nursery Schools* (London: HMSO: 1933), 129.
38 Peter Gordon, 'The Handbook of Suggestions for Teachers: Its Origin and Evaluation', *Journal of Educational Administration and History* 17, no. 1 (1985): 41–8.
39 Board of Education, *Handbook of Suggestions for Teachers* (London: HMSO, 1927).
40 Board of Education, *Handbook of Suggestions for Teachers* (London: HMSO, 1937), 375.
41 Gavin Bolton, 'Changes in Thinking about Drama in Education', *Theory Into Practice* XXIV, no. 3 (1985): 151–7.
42 Board of Education, *Handbook of Suggestions for Teachers*, 1937, 375.
43 L. G. Studman, 'Dramatic Work', *Child Life*, XXXIII, no. 150 (1930): 8.
44 Bolton, *Acting in Classroom Drama*, 1998.
45 Editorial, *Child Life* 2, no. 6 (1936): 81.
46 Patricia Giardiello, *Pioneers in Early Childhood Education* (London: Routledge, 2014).
47 Philip Graham, *Susan Isaacs: A Life Freeing the Minds of Children* (London: Karnac Books, 2009).
48 Susan Isaacs, *Intellectual Growth in Young Children* (London: Routledge and Kegan Paul, 1930), 102.
49 Rosalind Vallance, 'Psychological Values in Dramatic Work for Young Children', *Child Life*, New Series 12 (1935): 181.
50 Review of Lecture, 'Dramatic Work in School – 1', Miss Brooke Gwynne, *Child Life* IV, no. 2 (1938): 288.
51 Review of *Ring up the Curtain, Books 1, 2, and 3*, ed. D. G. Gardner, *Child Life* IV, no. 3 (1938): 45.
52 D. G. Gardner, 'Trouble in Toyland', in *Ring up the Curtain, Book 1*, ed. D. G. Gardner, (London: McDougall Educational Co., 1937), 38.
53 Review of *Ring up the Curtain, Books 1, 2, and 3*, *Child Life* (1938), 45.
54 Review of *One Act Plays of To-day*, ed. J. W. Marriott, *Child life* XXX, no. 144 (1928): 108.
55 'Books for School Plays', *Child Life* XXX, no. 145 (1928): 140.
56 Ella Adkins, 'The Choice of Plays for Young Children', *Child Life*, New Series 12 (1935): 189.
57 Board of Education, *Handbook of Suggestions for Teachers*, 1937, 375.
58 Ibid., 376.
59 Review of *Six Enid Blyton Plays*, Enid Blyton, *Child Life*, New Series 12 (1935): 187.
60 Linda Chesterman, *Music for the Infant School: Part 2: Six Little Plays and Ten Dances* (London: George Harrap, 1937), title page.
61 Cook, *The Play Way*, 188.
62 Bolton, 'Changes in Thinking about Drama in Education', 153.
63 Laurence F. Kelly, 'Foreword', in *Puppetry and Puppet Plays for Infants, Juniors and Seniors*, ed. Arthur B. Allen (London: Allman and Sons, 1937), 8.
64 Tryce M. Baumgartner, *Animula and Other Plays for Children* (London: S. Allen Warner, 1920), 4.
65 Maude L. Darvell and Grace M. Tuffley, *Plays in Rhyme for Little Ones* (London: Evans Brothers, 1925), 4.
66 Chesterman, *Music for the Infant School: Part 2*, 1937, 7. (Emphasis in the original).
67 Reed Moorhouse (ed.), *With Pipe and Tabor* (London: E. P. Dutton, 1928), 152. (Emphasis in the original).
68 John Hampden (ed.), *Six Modern Plays and Two Old Plays for Little People* (London: Thomas Nelson and Sons, 1931), 184.

69 Baumgartner, *Animula and Other Plays for Children*, 4.

70 Ruth Clarke, *Dances for the Four-to-Seven Year Olds* (London: J. Curwen and Sons, 1927), v.

71 A. I. King, 'Snowwhite', in *New Plays for Boys and Girls*, ed. A. I. King (London: Evans Brothers, 1936), 9–10.

72 Hugh Chesterton, 'A Shadow Play: Jack and the Beanstalk', in *The Third Book of School Plays: Plays for the Younger Ones*, ed. Unknown (London: Evans Brothers, 1928), 19–20.

73 E. A. Jelf, *Jill's Magic Island and Other Stories* (London: Thomas Nelson and Sons, 1934).

74 Ernest Arthur Jelf, 'Writing Plays for Children', *Child Life*, XXXIV, no. 153 (1931): 17.

75 Jan Susina, 'Dealing with Victorian Fairies', *Children's Literature* 28 (2000): 230–7.

76 Margaret Ashworth, *Six Plays for Little Ones* (Oxford: Oxford University Press, 1937), 3.

77 John Bourne (ed.), *New Plays for Boys and Girls* (London: Lovat Dickson, 1934), 7.

78 Maude S. Forsey, *The Chinese Lanterns: A Christmas Playlet for Children* (London: Frederick Warne, 1937), 15.

79 Gardner, *Trouble in Toyland*, 46.

80 Rose Fyleman, 'The Fairy and the Doll', in *Eight Little Plays for Children*, ed. Rose Fyleman (London: Methuen, 1926), 35–8.

81 Violet M. Methley, 'Lavender's Blue', in *The Mulberry Bush and Other Plays*, ed. Violet M. Methley (London: Collins' Clear-type Press, 1927), 39–48.

82 Rose Fyleman, 'Mother Goose's Party: A Play for Small Children', in *Seven Little Plays for Children*, ed. Rose Fyleman (London: Methuen, 1928), 74–94; Enid Blyton, 'A Visit to Nursery Rhyme Land', in *Six Enid Blyton Plays – School edition*, ed. Enid Blyton (London: Methuen: 1936), 83–110.

83 Lewis Carroll, *Alice's Adventures in Wonderland* (London: MacMillan, 1865).

84 Mary Farrah, *The Doll's election: A Play for Children* (London: Curwen and Sons, 1917), 3.

85 Margaret Ashworth, 'Ready for Daisy', in *Six Plays for Little Ones*, ed. Margaret Ashworth (London: Oxford University Press: 1937), 35–44.

86 Anthony D. Pellegrini, *The Role of Play in Human Development* (Oxford: Oxford University Press, 2009).

87 John Wall, *Ethics in the Light of Childhood* (Washington: Georgetown University Press, 2010).

Figure 9.1 Elsa Walters, *Activity and Experience in the Junior School*, London: National Froebel Foundation, 1949.

9

Freeing the Child: Froebelians and the Transformation of Learning through Play, Self-Activity and Project Work in English Junior School Classrooms, 1917–52

Jane Read

Friedrich Froebel is best known for his visionary concept of the kindergarten, which spread rapidly beyond its origins in 1840 in rural Prussia.[1] In the United Kingdom, the Froebel Society (FS) for the Promotion of the Kindergarten System was formed in 1874 and included lectures, publications and training for Froebelian teachers, known as kindergartners, amongst its primary aims.[2] Yet in his text, *The Education of Man* (1826), Froebel set out an extensive pedagogy for older children on the basis of his practice at his school at Keilhau, but this was overshadowed by his later invention. From the second decade of the twentieth century, the UK FS increasingly focused on the education of children from seven to eleven and, in 1917, changed its name to the Froebel Society and Junior Schools Association; thus, the study for this chapter begins in that year. It ends in 1952, when celebrations were held to mark the centenary of Froebel's death and the diamond jubilee of the Froebel Educational Institute (FEI), London. In that year, Eglantyne Mary Jebb, principal of FEI, claimed that 'Froebel-trained teachers have made a most important contribution to better teaching in Junior schools'.[3]

FEI became the foremost Froebelian training college in the United Kingdom after its foundation in 1892. Although the majority of its graduates worked in middle-class, fee-paying schools and kindergartens, others began to gain employment in state nursery, infant and junior schools where the majority of children received their education. In line with official prescriptions, teaching in state schools in the nineteenth century was disciplinarian, with children required to sit still in overcrowded classrooms and learn by memorizing; Froebel's conception of active learning, drawing on children's interests expressed through creative play, had no place. From the 1890s, Froebel-trained teachers sought to implement his practice in state infant schools for children aged five to seven by introducing play with Froebel's gifts and occupations alongside teaching of the 3Rs of reading, writing and arithmetic.[4] Given the impact of their work in infant schools, this study interrogates Jebb's 1952 claim and investigates whether Froebel-trained teachers were successful in freeing up practice in state junior schools, for children aged seven to eleven, where pressure for formal learning of the 'tool' subjects remained strong.

Drawing on archives and published accounts, the chapter explores the methods Froebelian teachers employed as they sought to implement a play-based curriculum in junior schools in London and the language used to conceptualize change. By attempting to build on the work of their colleagues in infant schools, these teachers sought to achieve the key Froebelian principle of a holistic education which obviated divisions between the stages of education. Nevertheless, the process of pedagogical innovation was not uncontested; Froebelian principles of active learning based on children's own interests in enabling environments were at the heart of their efforts, but their endeavours were slow to take root, often mirroring issues which inhibited progress in infant schools. The Board of Education (BoE) controlled practice in schools, and teachers were concerned about the ability of freer methods to achieve favourable inspection reports and to ensure pupils' success in the exams which governed their progression to the senior schools.[5] Constraints of space, architecture and class size were also significant factors which endured right through to 1952 and beyond.[6]

Investigating teachers' responses to these challenges, the chapter positions developments in junior schools within the wider context of twentieth-century educational discourse. It examines how the FS and the National Froebel Union (NFU) supported teachers entering a new arena for practice and considers policy articulations from the BoE, to establish whether freer practice was likely to be supported or opposed. It also surveys the terminology of new practices to assess how far Froebelian pedagogy underpinned educational discourse during the period. The chapter supports Jebb's claim that progress in transforming teaching methods and classrooms had taken root, perhaps reflecting changing social attitudes to the education of working-class children and, more importantly, the contribution of Froebelian teachers and writers. The chapter concludes by reflecting on what was distinctively 'Froebelian' in these developments, bearing in mind that 'progressivism'[7] and 'influence'[8] are slippery concepts, a concern expressed by Kevin Brehony with regard to claims made for Froebelian pedagogy in particular.[9]

Froebel's views on the education of the child at school

Froebel's holistic conception of education encompassed the span of human life from birth to adulthood. Described as '*Lebenseinigung*', or 'life unity', Froebel's theory drew on the work of German philosopher Karl Christian Krause; Joachim Liebschner interpreted it as 'the living and working together of people in unity, harmony and respect for each other'.[10] In *The Education of Man*, Froebel applied this philosophy of interconnectedness and harmony to the child's progression from home to school and the nature of the learning process, dealing successively with different stages of education. Much of the book deals with children from age seven and draws on his experiences at his school at Keilhau. Although Froebel writes of instruction, this is complementary to encouraging children to observe their local environment, to make connections between themselves and what they observe, and to express themselves through activities of all kinds, including block play, drawing, painting, modelling, singing and stories, exploratory excursions and gardening.[11]

Froebel's perception of the need for children to be active in their learning was taken forward in England in private kindergartens for children aged three to six. Some also offered education for older children, an example being the school for children from age seven run by Bertha and Johannes Ronge in conjunction with their kindergarten in Tavistock Place, London, from 1855 (the frontpiece image of Chapter 2). However, these early efforts were insignificant in terms of their impact on the state schools established from 1870 under the Elementary Education Act; it was not until the revisionist thrust, driven by US educators in the Child Study movement and John Dewey in particular, that the seeds of change began to take root.

The Froebel Society's turn to junior school teaching

For the first forty years of its existence, the FS was concerned principally with promoting kindergartens for children aged three to six. The society began with eighty-six members, overwhelmingly middle-class women, and by October 1875 had formed an examinations committee to draw up a syllabus for a Froebel Society Certificate. The first examinations were held in 1876 and in that year the society established procedures for inspection and registration of kindergartens. The state school system was different, with compulsory education in elementary schools, from age five in infant schools, progression to the junior school at age seven, and in senior schools to age fourteen, from 1918, and to fifteen after the 1944 Education Act.

The FS's focus of interest began to change in the second decade of the twentieth century. The Child Study movement emerged in the United States in the 1890s and provided new psychological insights into child development applicable to all age groups; these began to permeate educational discourse in the United Kingdom. FS Council member, Elsie Riach Murray, a key British Froebelian who engaged with these new ideas, reported in 1916 to the council on a meeting held the previous year with the BoE concerning junior schools. The society responded by forming a committee to draw up a list of good schools and to identify areas where schools were needed.[12] The following year it adopted a new name, the Froebel Society and Junior Schools Association, and from this point there was increasing realignment of British Froebelians' focus on the kindergarten to encompass children in junior schools.

The FS journal, *Child Life*, and its successor from 1940, the *National Froebel Foundation Bulletin*, reflect this developing focus: in 1917, an advertisement described the journal as 'for the furtherance of Primary education in this country'.[13] When the society published its jubilee pamphlet, *Then and Now*, in 1925, looking back over its fifty-year history, council member Evelyn Kenwrick, in charge of Froebel teaching at Maria Grey College and head of its Demonstration School, contributed a chapter on the junior school. Kenwrick argued that 'one of Froebel's greatest contributions is his insistence on the possibilities of using the play spirit in the children's education, and transforming it into work in the junior school through socializing influences'.[14]

Two years later, in 1927, *Child Life* requested reports of experiments carried out with children of eight to eleven. During the 1930s, it published articles on the junior school and by 1935 it advertised itself as a journal for teachers of five- to eleven-year-olds.

Although it continued to publish articles for kindergarten teachers, this represents a shift in focus. The junior school was the topic chosen for the society's summer school in 1936, held for teachers in state and private schools; in that year, *Child Life* published three issues on the junior school. Articles published in 1937 on 'Experiments in the Junior School', reflected progressive education terminology at that time; Margaret Ironside, headmistress of Hampden Gurney, a state sector Church of England school in London, discussed implementing free activity; others focused on projects, including puppetry and guilds.[15] Similar articles appeared up to 1952, with a series of articles in the 1940s on the role of subject specialists in what was now termed 'the free activity junior school'. Publication in these journals provided a conduit for the dissemination of new practices; in the case of summer school reports, the content of lectures was able to reach a wider national audience.

The language of active learning

Students in training and teachers were guided in their conceptions of good practice by published literature; a survey of articles in the FS journals and surviving texts used by FEI students in the college archives demonstrate that they increasingly articulated a pedagogy of active, purposeful learning through projects grounded in children's interests. The Froebelian principle of active learning underpinned Dewey's educational vision; grounded in democratic principles, Dewey proposed learning through individual and group work on the basis of project-led teaching which took the community as a foundation for education and reflected children's interests.[16] Projects might draw on language, number-work, geography and history, with varied results, for example, handwork, musical or dramatic performances or puppet shows. Dewey's ideas were introduced to Britain through editions of his essays, including by British Froebelian Joseph John Findlay and by his US disciple William Heard Kilpatrick[17]; gradually, British Froebelians began themselves to contribute to the growing body of literature on projects.[18]

In 1913, the FS published a reprint of *The Dewey School*, originally issued in 1900 by the University of Chicago in the *Elementary School Record*.[19] It included reports of experimental work carried out by staff of the Kindergarten Department, under Dewey's direction, in Chicago's University Elementary School with four- to six-year-olds; this introduced kindergarten teachers and those working in infant schools to a programme for a year's work.[20] The revised edition, published by the society in 1929, reported on the work of all children in the school, not just the youngest children, on the grounds that 'purposeful centres of interest, under the name of "projects," are being introduced into the most progressive schools'.[21] Also in 1929, Murray's presidential address to the FS focused on projects and, with lectures by other Froebelians at the summer school on projects, was subsequently published in *Child Life*.[22] Just as Froebelians such as Frances Roe were seeking to convince infants teachers that free activity supported learning of the three 'R's of reading, writing and arithmetic,[23] so too did those Froebelians working in junior schools reassure teachers that project work addressed the whole curriculum, albeit alongside more formal teaching of the three 'R's. Janet Payne and Florence Webb argued at the 1929 summer school that project work led children to engage more fully with these core subjects,[24] while accounts by participants explained their developing understanding of what it meant to use children's interests as the basis for projects, rather than imposing those of the teacher.[25]

Kevin Brehony argued that the contribution of the child study theorists, including Dewey, to English education, has not gone uncontested,[26] yet, Dewey's reinterpretation of Froebel provided lifeblood to a pedagogy that had become ossified and increasingly irrelevant. Responding to the new ideas and insights emerging from child study in particular, Froebelians re-imagined their practice and articulated a revisionist interpretation of Froebel which made his pedagogy fit for purpose in the new, scientifically oriented twentieth-century world.[27] Elsie Murray and Henrietta Brown Smith were early and prominent contextualizers of Froebel within the new discourse[28]; later in the period, Thomas Raymont, a long-standing member of Froebel organizations with wide experience as examiner and inspector of Froebel training courses, set out the problems facing those trying to introduce Froebelian pedagogy in state junior schools.[29]

During the 1930s, *Child Life* published reviews of the burgeoning Froebelian literature for teachers on implementing projects in classrooms, along the lines set out by Dewey and his interpreters. Two examples are books by Hilda Gull and Joyce Kenwrick.[30] Gull had a wide-ranging career in education, as lecturer at Cheltenham Ladies College and at Bingley Training College, as Inspectress of Schools for Liverpool Education Committee and for Practical Subjects for the NFU, which set examinations for the Froebel training colleges. Gull established a two-year Froebel certificate course in Liverpool for teachers in state elementary schools, which encompassed education from nursery to school-leaving age. The course provided a conduit for new methods, including project work, to be introduced in Liverpool's junior and infant schools. In her 1932 book, Gull differentiated between the Froebelian practice of correlation[31] and projects, arguing that the former was based on the teacher's initiative; although children might enjoy the activities, 'they did not undertake them to achieve a purpose which was essentially their own'.[32] Here lay the difference to the project, which arose 'out of [children's] own felt need and purpose'. Gull's book was enthusiastically reviewed in *Child Life*: 'The book is just what teachers have been asking to have. It is practical, it has knowledge of the teacher's needs and difficulties'.[33] Gull lectured on projects at the 1933 Froebel Society Summer School, stressing how 'reading, writing and number, far in advance of anything that a teacher would have dared to put in a syllabus for children of that age',[34] had arisen naturally in the carrying out of a project.

Joyce Kenwrick, lecturer at Edge Hill Training College, Liverpool, explained how her understanding of implementing projects in junior schools was underpinned by her reading of Dewey; 'interest' and 'centres of interest'[35] recur in her text as key terms articulating the new Froebelian language expressing unity and child-led practice. In a foreword to Kenwrick's book, Brown Smith pointed out that projects did not necessarily lead to handwork but to 'a play, pageant, exhibition, collection, a book, a magazine, and sometimes merely a desire for knowledge'[36]; she stressed that Kenwrick's book was not intended to induce imitation by its readers: each project had a unique source, a 'chanciness', which arose from particular circumstances. Brown Smith's warning was apposite; Kenwrick described projects carried out in her school, tempting teachers to simply use it as a template for their own practice. Literature published later in the 1930s provided short guides for teachers on topics discussed by Gull and Kenwrick, including books on dustmen, firemen and postmen, reflecting also Dewey's view of the community as a foundation for learning.

Experiments, activity, interest and purpose

Innovatory practice was commonly described as experimental in the theoretical and practical literature published in the period up to 1952. Teachers wrote of their work as 'experiments',[37] a term also prominent in literature by Froebelian infant school teachers,[38] reflecting the focus on the scientific approach to education, instigated in particular by the Child Study movement and adopted by Maria Montessori to describe her pedagogy. Other terminology echoed Froebel's language, with activity, interest, exploration and experience as recurrent motifs; an education with these principles at the centre provided children with purpose and encouraged their engagement in the learning process.[39] A series of articles initiated by Froebelian writer Nancy Catty in 1949 on subject teaching in 'free activity' schools addressed the requirement for an in-depth study of core subjects utilizing project-based methods.[40]

Textbooks for Froebelian and state school teachers discussed new methods, as in John Adams' popular textbook, *Modern Developments in Educational Practice*, first published in 1922 and issued in a revised edition in 1928, which included a chapter on projects.[41] Dewey's argument for connection between school and community was expressed by G. Cons and Catherine Fletcher, lecturers at Goldsmiths Training College, London, as 'actuality'; their experiment centred on 'activity' and focused on social education and citizenship fostered through a range of experiences.[42] Some authors specifically cited Froebel in discussions of teaching for children over age six. Frank Smith and A. S. Harrison, writing in 1937, suggested that 'Froebel's concept of "self activity" has steadily pervaded schools for older children, and its influence is now seen in all stages of the educational process. Froebel, in fact, produced a revolution of thought ... by the release of the child's activity in school'.[43] All of this bode well for transformation of practice in the junior school.

Froebelian training for the state junior school 1917–52

Training in Froebelian colleges was governed by NFU regulations and students took compulsory and optional written examinations for their qualifications; students chose to specialize in teaching children under or over eight years of age. Increasingly, exam papers across the range of qualifications offered by the NFU reflected the new discourse of activity, projects and interest.

The NFU Trainer's Diploma, taken by those seeking to teach in training colleges, with special reference to the work of infant and junior schools, increasingly included reference to state junior schools, signifying a changing focus for Froebelian career paths. In 1925, the Principles of Education (exam) paper asked students to write on the function of the junior school in the modern state, providing opportunity for discussion, for example, on developing notions of democratic citizenship in young children, or on preparing children to think independently and creatively, rather than merely reiterating facts taught by rote. The NFU Teachers' Certificate compulsory paper, organization and method, sought to elicit students' knowledge and understanding of methods for teaching school subjects. A question from 1937 reflects the Froebelian adoption of Deweyan pedagogy: 'Give an account of a piece of work which you have observed or undertaken with a group of children which might be called a "project," and show for what reasons it might be so described.'[44] In 1938, the topic-based nature of the questions, drawing on children's interests, is much in evidence, for example, asking how teachers might use the cinema or wireless in children's education. Other questions drew on the potential for topic work to include subjects such as geography: 'Your school is situated *either* in the centre of a town *or* in a village. What use would you make of this environment when directing the interests of your children? State the age of the class you have in mind.'[45] The use of the term 'directing' in this question suggests that, despite acknowledging the benefits of child-initiated projects, some Froebelians could not quite dissociate themselves from teacher-led attitudes. The difficulties of large classes and fixed desks, which Froebelian infant school teachers identified as barriers to introducing activity learning, applied equally to junior schools.

Teachers who trained outside the Froebel colleges and university graduates who wished to teach along Froebelian lines sat the NFU's special course. A question set in 1937 asked students to discuss activity-based teaching of the junior school curriculum rather than subjects,[46] demonstrating that this was an important conduit for conveying pedagogy of 'activity' and 'experience' to those on the periphery of the Froebel movement.

Board of Education and local education authority policy

Literature and training provided Froebelian teachers and students with the theoretical rationale and methodology for change in junior school teaching, but Board of Education (BoE) policy would be crucial for its implementation. Apart from in London, teachers were required to conform to the policy dictates of the BoE enforced by His/Her Majesty's Inspectors [HMI]. Significantly, by the late 1920s, BoE policy documents articulated a less formal conception of junior school education than formerly; in the BoE's 1929 survey, *The New Prospect in Education*,[47] the state junior school was envisaged as preparing children for the senior school, but developing its own special methods and acquiring its own separate status. When the survey was published, the BoE was already collecting evidence for its consultative committee report on the Primary School under the chairmanship of Henry Hadow.[48]

The FS submitted evidence to the committee setting out the distinctively Froebelian principle of continuity between the stages of education, together with comments on teacher training and the aims of the junior school. The junior school was conceptualized as 'the time for becoming acquainted with the wonder and variety of the world; for ranging and discovering; for following where interest led; not for a narrowing down of knowledge to within the given range of an examination syllabus, nor for concentration on a specified group of facts'.[49] Suggestions were given for project work and the teaching of 'the tools of learning' – the three 'R's. The society argued against the requirement to follow a fixed timetable, arguing that it should be the responsibility of the head teacher to ensure that important subjects were not omitted.

The Report of the Consultative Committee on the Primary School, 1931 was couched in language reflecting Froebelian principles, providing a validation of its pedagogical approach: 'Primary education would gain greatly in realism and power of inspiration if an attempt were more generally made to think of the curriculum less in terms of departments of knowledge to be taught, and more of activities to be fostered and interests to be broadened.'[50] Froebelian principles were evident in terms used to describe the curriculum, for example: 'harmonious interplay' and 'unity',[51] while the school was described as 'not the antithesis of life, but ... its complement and commentary'.[52] This report from the consultative committee represented an official affirmation of what Froebelians held dear.

Schools in London were under the jurisdiction of the London County Council and, as with HMI reports elsewhere, reports from its team of inspectors also articulated the discourse of activity learning. The junior department at Coverdale School in West London, a school used by FEI for teaching practice, was described in 1949 as 'progressive, contented and purposeful',[53] while in 1948, the junior department at the 'Marlborough' was said to be successfully implementing activity methods; some eighteen years earlier, Frances Roe and her colleague E. R. Boyce had introduced Froebelian free-activity methods into the school's infant department.[54] Along with the literature and training discussed here, central government and local education policy from the period reinforced the rhetoric of change which guided practice in schools.

Evidence for Froebelian practice in London junior schools

Evidence from London state junior schools suggests that children increasingly experienced a Froebelian education, grounded in Deweyan project work with a focus on community involvement and social learning which freed them from their fixed desks and enabled them to transform their classrooms as they learnt through 'projects'. Literature from the period discusses varied teaching, with both individual and group work; at Kender Street School in Deptford, south east London, Head Teacher Lilian Pierotti introduced individual methods in 1930, an innovation praised by the school's inspectors.[55] Pierotti tutored for the FS, contributed to *Child Life* and later served as principal of the Froebelian Bedford Training College. Kender Street had been remodelled as Junior Mixed and Infant School in 1928 and became a demonstration school for Goldsmiths Training College in 1935. Cons and Fletcher described their introduction of 'actuality' in the school's Junior Department as an 'educational experiment' intended to foster children's understanding and appreciation of work which supported their community. Children paid visits to learn about local services, with talks in the school from workers including dustmen, firemen and postmen. A conference held in connection with the experiment suggested an underpinning Froebelian ethos: 'The desire was ... to touch the imagination of the children and ... to bring them into close touch with reality.'[56] Pierotti gathered praise in the school's 1947 inspection report for dividing the school day into two periods, for 'undirected activities' and practice in the three 'R's. Inspectors commented on the volume of visitors, up to 800 per term, from the United Kingdom and overseas, including local education authority inspectors and officials and training college principals, an achievement of significance for the dissemination of the school's experimental practice. Echoing the argument of Froebelian infant head teachers, the report noted that standards in the three 'R's 'have certainly not suffered by the substitution of free activity for the formal traditional methods'.[57]

Evidence from other schools demonstrates how activity, interest and purpose underpinned projects drawing on the local environment. The road safety project carried out in 1937 at Avonmore School, Kensington, involved activity inside and in the school playground.[58] Increasing traffic posed a hazard in London, so the project had a clear meaning for the children. It also represents a practical example linking to the exam question, cited earlier, which asked students how they would use the environment of the school. At the Jews Free School in Spitalfields, the boys engaged in an extensive project on trains, building a model railway and station, with the name Bell Lane, location of the school.[59]

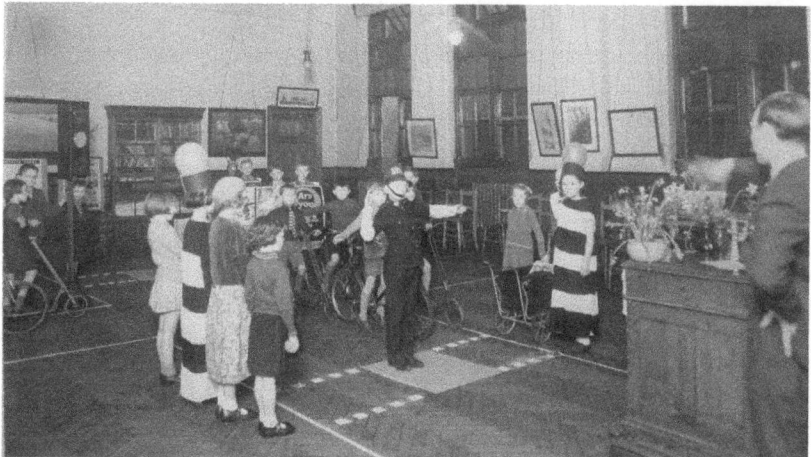

Figure 9.2 Avonmore School, Kensington, 1937. Road safety project. London Metropolitan Archives.

Froebelian pedagogy in the junior school in 1952: Grounds for optimism

Despite Jebb's 1952 claim of a Froebelian victory, progress in achieving change had been slow. The continuing hold that formal methods maintained in subjects such as reading can be seen in photographs from 1938 of Cubbitt Town school, Tower Hamlets[60]; arguably this reflected teachers' reluctance to relinquish them, given the fact that the junior school had to ensure that pupils were prepared for the examinations that gave access to the senior school. Nevertheless, some schools were introducing freer methods for the three 'R's: at Sebbon Street, Canonbury, girls were depicted reading individually but in larger informal groups in 1935.[61] Writing in that year of the consultative committee's report, P. Chart, lecturer at Saffron Walden Training College, had expressed optimism:

> If we visit Junior Schools today, different as each one will be from the others in many respects, we have, perhaps, some sense of disappointment. The 'clear objective' of the Junior School, as envisaged in the Primary School Report, has yet to be expressed in the curriculum and organisation of our Junior Schools. Nevertheless, since the report was published, the way has been prepared for the new school to emerge.[62]

Yet, two years later, Edith Warr argued that while the nursery and infant school had benefited from the work of Froebel, and also of Montessori,[63] the junior school had been left behind, a mere transitional stage between the infant period and adolescence. Susan Isaacs, Froebelian head of Malting House School in Cambridge, supported Warr's view, arguing that the junior school was 'more urgently in need of new life than any other'.[64]

These arguments continued to be made in the post-war period: the need to prepare children for the scholarship examination remained a driving force, but photographs from London schools and contemporary literature illustrate practice was a blend of active, project-based learning alongside desk work. Writers increasingly expressed optimism that change had become embedded in educational thinking.[65]

In assessing the compatibility of Froebelianism with new approaches to teaching which had permeated education in England from the beginning of the century, three elements of change appear to be most significant: first, there was increased understanding of the need for a unified pedagogical underpinning for three- to eleven-year-olds. Froebelians argued for connection between the stages of education and, increasingly, this was reflected in official discourse and in practice, as the freer activity of the infant school began to penetrate junior classrooms, albeit with time still allotted to the tool subjects. Secondly, there was increased awareness of activity and children's interests as driving education; the dominant discourse in the literature of the period reflected the core Froebelian principle of learning by doing. This was articulated by avowed Froebelians and by those outside the Froebel movement. Although school accommodation hampered efforts to reform teaching and learning, teachers increasingly understood that children were more engaged in the educational process when it directly reflected their interests, and the tool subjects were learnt more readily when they had a purpose. For Froebelian teachers in particular, this was achieved most effectively through projects chosen by children. Finally, attention to the democratic conception of the child as citizen, learning about their place in their local community and their responsibilities within it and developing respect for key workers who served its needs are very much a reflection of Froebel's intentions in the *Mother Songs*. Thus, Jebb was right: Froebel teachers *had* made a significant contribution to the children's learning in junior schools by 1952; essential tenets of Froebelian pedagogy had become embedded in conceptions of teaching seven- to eleven-year-olds.

At the root of this narrative of change is the contested balance between freedom and guidance in the educational process, a debate that continues today and is unlikely to be resolved one way or the other, but to always traverse the pendulum. Over the past twenty-five years, the pendulum has been swinging away from the freer methods, which characterized infant and junior school practice in England for much of the twentieth century, and represented the Froebelian impact on state school teaching. Instead, early education is more concerned with preparation for school: instilling the three 'R's and testing children's cognitive development at an ever earlier age. There is a danger that the Froebelian perception of the crucial role of purpose in learning will be lost, and children will, once again, be subjected to rote teaching, albeit in modified form, while teachers dictate the educational process to meet the hegemonic neoliberal agenda.

Abbreviations

BoE   Board of Education.
FEI   Froebel Educational Institute.
FS   Froebel Society.
HMI   His/Her Majesty's Inspectors.
LMA   London Metropolitan Archives.
NFU   National Froebel Union.

Notes

1 Roberta Wollons (ed.) *Kindergartens and Cultures: The Global Diffusion of an Idea* (New Haven, CT: Yale University Press, 2000).
2 Froebel Society. *Report*. June 1875 (London: Edward Stanford, 1875).
3 Eglantyne Mary Jebb, *Survey of the Growth of the Froebel Educational Institute over 60 Years* (London: Incorporated Froebel Educational Institute 1952), 9.
4 Jane Read, 'Bringing Froebel into London's Infant Schools: The Reforming Practice of Two Head Teachers, Elizabeth Shaw and Frances Roe, from the 1890s to the 1930s', *History of Education* 42, no. 6 (2013): 745–6.
5 Edith Warr, *The New Era in the Junior School* (London: Methuen, 1937); Board of Education, *Educational Reconstruction* (London: BoE, 1943); Thomas Raymont, *Seven to Eleven: Some Problems of the Junior School* (London: Longmans, Green, 1946); Mary Atkinson, *Junior School Community* (London: Longmans, Green, 1949).

6   M. V. Daniel, *Activity in the Primary* School (Oxford: Blackwell, 1947); Atkinson, *Junior School Community*; H. Philips and F. J. C. McInnes, *Exploration in the Junior School* (London: University of London Press, 1950).

7   James M. Lynch, 'What is the Activity School?' *Elementary School Journal* 36, no. 5 (1936): 344–8.

8   Quentin Skinner, 'Meaning and Understanding in the History of Ideas', *Visions of Politics: Volume 1: Regarding Method,* rev edn (Cambridge: Cambridge University Press, 2002), 57–89.

9   Kevin J Brehony, 'The Froebel Movement and State Schooling 1880-1914: A Study in Educational Ideology'. PhD thesis (Milton Keynes: Open University, 1987).

10 Joachim Liebschner, *A Child's Work. Freedom and Play in Froebel's Educational Theory and Practice* (Cambridge: Lutterworth Press, 1992), 27.

11 Friedrich Froebel, *The Education of Man*, trans. W. N. Hailmann (New York, NY: Appleton, [1826] 1887).

12 Froebel Society, *Minutes X* (Froebel Society, 6 March 1916).

13 *Child Life* (1917): 3.

14 Froebel Society, *Then and Now* (London: Froebel Society, 1929), 30.

15 G. M. Ironside, 'Experiments in the Junior School. 1. Free Activity' *Child Life,* New Series 3, no. 3 (1937): 36–8; Lilian Pierotti, 'Experiments in the Junior School. II. Puppetry' *Child Life,* New Series 3, no. 4 (1937): 56–9.

16 John Dewey, *The School and Society* (Chicago: University of Chicago, 1889). For more on J. J. Findlay and Froebelianism, see also Kerry Bethell's chapter in this volume.

17 John Dewey, *The School and the Child*, ed. John Joseph Findlay (London: Blackie, 1906); William Heard Kilpatrick, 'The Project Method', *Teachers College Record* 19, no. 4 (1918): 319–5; see also Charles A. McMurry, *Teaching by Projects: A Basis for Purposeful Study* (New York: Macmillan, 1921); E. A. Hotchkiss *The Project Method in Classroom Work* (Boston: Ginn, 1924); *Curriculum Making in an Elementary School*, Columbia University. Teachers College (New York: Ginn, 1927).

18 Hilda Gull, *Projects in the Education of Young Children* (London and Edinburgh: McDougall: 1932); Joyce Kenwrick, *Junior School Projects* (London: University of London Press: 1935).

19 Froebel Society, *The Dewey School*, 2nd edn, ed. Janet E Payne (London: Froebel Society, 1929), iii.

20 For more on this work at the University of Chicago, see Chapter 7 by Larry Prochner and Anna Kirova in this volume.

21 Froebel Society, *The Dewey School*, iii.

22 Elsie Riach Murray, 'Presidential Address', *Child Life* XXXII, no. 146 (1929): 9–17; Janet E. Payne, 'The "Project" Method and the Three Rs', *Child Life* XXXII, no. 147 (1929): 47–9; Florence E Webb, 'The Project Method and the Three Rs in an Elementary School', *Child Life* XXXII, no. 147 (1929): 50–1.

23 Read, 'Bringing Froebel'; F. Roe, 'From Formal Teaching to Natural Learning', in *Modern Education of Young Children*, ed. Nancy Catty (London: Methuen, 1933): 1–16.

24 Payne 'The "Project" Method'; Webb 'The Project Method'.

25 'The Summer School, by partakers', *Child Life* XXXII, no. 148 (1929): 77–80; An onlooker, 'Projects at the Summer School', *Child Life* XXXII, no. 148 (1929): 80–2.

26 Kevin J Brehony, 'An "Undeniable" and "Disastrous" Influence? Dewey and English education (1895-1939)', *Oxford Review of Education* 23, no. 4 (1997): 427–45;

Kevin J. Brehony, 'Transforming Theories of Childhood and Early Childhood Education: Child Study and the Empirical Assault on Froebelian Rationalism', *Paedagogica Historica: International Journal of the History of Education* 45, nos. 4 and 5 (2009): 585–604.

27 Kevin J Brehony, 'English Revisionist Froebelians and the Schooling of the Urban Poor', in *Practical Visionaries: Women, Education and Social Progress 1790-1930*, ed. M. H. Hilton and P. Hirsch (London: Longman, 2000): 183–99.

28 Elsie Riach Murray, *Froebel as a Pioneer in Modern Psychology* (London: George Philip, 1914); Henrietta Brown-Smith (ed.), *Education By Life*, 7th edn (London: George Philip, 1928).

29 Thomas Raymont, *Seven to Eleven* (London: Longmans, 1946).

30 Gull, *Projects*; Kenwrick, *Junior School Projects*.

31 Mabel Bloomer, *A Year in the Infant School: A Fully Correlated Scheme of Work* (London: Gresham, 1910).

32 Gull, *Projects*, 32–5.

33 Anon, 'Book news', *Child Life* XXXV, no. 156 (1932): 26.

34 Anon, 'The Twentieth Summer School', *Child Life* no. 161 (1933): 80–1.

35 Kenwrick, *Junior School Projects*.

36 Ibid., ix.

37 Ironside, 'Experiments'; Pierotti, 'Experiments II'; Pierotti, 'Experiments IV. Puppets and How to Make Them', *Child Life*, New Series 3, no. 7 (1937): 106–8; Barbara Priestman, 'Experiments in the Junior School III. Guilds', *Child Life*, New Series 3, no. 5 (1937): 74–5; Warr, *New Era*.

38 E. R. Boyce, *Play in the Infants' School: An Account of an Educational Experiment at the Raleigh Infants' School, Stepney* (London: Methuen, 1938); Read, 'Bringing Froebel'.

39 J. F. Duff, 'Education Through Activity and Experience', *Child Life*, New Series, no. 10 (1935): 136–9, 144; Daniel, *Activity*; W. Kenneth Richmond, *Purpose in the Junior School* (London: Redman, 1949); Elsa H. Walters, *Activity and Experience in the Junior School* (London: National Froebel Foundation, 1949); Philips and McInnes, *Exploration*.

40 Nancy Catty, 'The Place of Subject Teaching in "Free Activity" Schools', *National Froebel Foundation Bulletin*, no. 59 (1949): 1–3.

41 John Adams, *Modern Developments in Educational Practice*, 2nd edn (London: University of London Press, 1928).

42 G. Cons and Catherine Fletcher, *Actuality in Schools* (London: Methuen, 1938); Anon, 'Actuality in Education', *Child Life* 4, no. 7 (1938): 111.

43 Frank Smith and A. S. Harrison, *Principles of Class Teaching* (London: Macmillan, 1937), 27.

44 NFU, *Reports on Examinations* (London: NFU, 1937), 60.

45 NFU, *Reports* (London: NFU, 1938), 61.

46 NFU, *Reports* (London: NFU, 1937), 64.

47 Board of Education, *The New Prospect in Education* (London: BoE, 1929).

48 Board of Education, *Report of the Consultative Committee on the Primary School* (London: BoE, 1931).

49 Board of Education, Consultative Committee, *Summary of Evidence given on Behalf of the Froebel Society and Junior Schools Association* (National Archive). ED10/148. S12(28).

50 Board of Education, *Report*, xix.

51 Ibid., xvii
52 Ibid., xvi.
53 LMA. EO/PS/12/C101/2.
54 Read, 'Bringing Froebel'.
55 LMA. EO/PS/12/K4/52.
56 Anon, 'Actuality in Education', *Child Life* 4, no. 7 (1938): 111.
57 LMA. EO/PS/12/K4/53.
58 LMA. B4924.
59 LMA. E175.
60 LMA, E66.
61 LMA, B1148.
62 P. Chart, 'The Curriculum in the Junior School', *Child Life*, New Series, no. 1 (1935): 5–7.
63 Warr, *New Era*, 1.
64 Susan Isaacs, in Warr, *New Era*, v.
65 Atkinson, *Junior School Community*; Daniel, *Activity*; Atkinson, *Junior School Community*; Philips and McInnes, *Exploration*.

Part Three

Radical by Tradition: Long-Term Perspectives on Kindergarten Education

10

'Come, let us Live with our Children': *Undōkai*, the Children's Play Festival at a Froebelian Kindergarten in Japan, 1889–2015

Yukiyo Nishida and Fusa Abe

Undōkai translates to 'sports day festival' or 'athletic festival' in Japanese, and functions as a display of athletic elements and an opportunity for outdoor play. It was developed in the mid-to-late nineteenth century as a result of social, cultural, religious and educational factors and it has become an most important school event from kindergarten to secondary education. Specifically, *undōkai* in early childhood education is regarded as a unique style of outdoor play which includes play, games, singing, dancing and athletic activities. Despite its sometimes teacher-centred orientation, the *undōkai* of today is similar to the 'play-festival' (*Spielfest*) devised by Friedrich Froebel for use with young children. There have been debates in recent decades about whether *undōkai* is good for young children. This chapter examines the development of one such child-centred *undōkai* as a children's play festival at a Froebelian kindergarten in Japan. The questions addressed include: What are the Froebelian educators' motivations for developing *undōkai*? What does the child-centred *undōkai* look like? And, finally, what was the process for creating the child-centred *undōkai*? The answers to these questions are drawn from early education contexts across time and cultures.

Friedrich Froebel and his 'Play-Festival, *Spielfest*'

Froebel's contribution to early childhood education was the recognition of the value of play, including songs, movements, natural play, self-activity (the so-called 'gifts' and 'occupations') and art work, all of which offer support for children's creative, imaginative, linguistic, mathematical, moral, musical, physical, scientific, social, spiritual and symbolic development.[1] According to Froebel: 'Play is the purest, most spiritual activity of man at this stage, and at the same time, typical of life as whole – of the inner hidden natural life in many and all things. It gives, therefore, joy, freedom, contentment, inner and outer rest, peace, with the world. It holds the source of all that is good.'[2]

Froebel's philosophy of education was based on Christian theology and an image of God. As Froebel wrote, 'It is all about unity; everything is based on unity, strives towards and comes back to unity.'[3] In Froebel's concept, unity meant God, to whom all living things are related. To Froebel, the true method of education thus consisted of considering the mind of the child as a whole in which all the parts work together to produce harmonious unity.[4] In his kindergarten, he wished children to experience the 'unity of life' through various play activities which gave sense, purpose and meaning to children's learning.

Froebel's holistic and play-based curriculum was, and still is, a very important element of early childhood education. The promotion of the child-centred approach to learning by using the gifts and occupations encourages children to engage in unity with nature. 'Come, let us live with our children!' was Froebel's well-known motto:

> The fundamental and living thought of humanity, 'Come, let us live with our children', becomes, when manifested in action, *an institution* for fostering family life and for the cultivation of the life of the nation, and of mankind, through fostering the impulse to activity, investigation, and culture in man, in the child as a member of the family, of the nation, and of humanity; and *an institution* for self-instruction, self-education, and the self-cultivation of mankind, as well as for all-sided and therefore for individual cultivation of the same through play, creative self-activity, and spontaneous self-instruction; first of all, for families and schools for the nurture of little children.[5]

The methodology of Froebel's educational materials, movement plays, games and activities for outdoor play for young children, such as the circle plays, running play, racing games, swinging movement plays, walking games and play with the ball, were introduced in some of Froebel's essays translated and published in 1895 (and later) as *Pedagogics of the Kindergarten*.[6] Froebel embraced the idea and concept of physical movement, space and time of play for young children.

In addition, Froebel acknowledged the importance of festivals, such as birthdays, holy days, family festivals, youth and community festivals. Froebel organized various festivals of play to celebrate the 'unity of life', including the play festival.[7] He organized the first one in the old Altenstein Castle's park in the summer of 1850. Baroness Bertha von Marenholtz-Bülow later reminisced:

> On the 4th of August, at two o'clock in the afternoon, more than three hundred children in five different columns, four abreast, came from the little city of Salzung, and the surrounding villages, Liebenstein, Marienthal, Schweina, and Steinbach. The teachers and kindergarteners at their side, decked with garlands, came singing into the great square, the Altenstein plateau, which had been chosen for the playground. At the entrance, upheld by oak-wreaths, was placed a large crown of flowers, in the midst of which had been chosen for the playground. At the entrance, upheld by oak-wreaths, was placed a large crown of flowers, in the midst of which were to be read the words of Schiller.[8]

Froebel intended the play festival to be pleasurable. Children circled round, with parents and local people looking on and participating in the activities. Young women, trained by Froebel as kindergarten teachers, also enjoyed games, songs and dances with the children, and the event continued for several hours.[9]

The festival expressed of Froebel's educational vision, as the children shared the sense of unity and interconnectedness through various movement plays.[10] Froebel wrote, 'The child-festival of today has given one aspect of the paradise of childhood.'[11] At the end of the day, children were assembled with their parents and Wilhelm Middendorff, a supporter of Froebel's kindergarten, spoke to parents by using Froebel's motto, 'Come, let us live with our children, that all things may be better here on earth,' and expounded on its meaning.[12]

Such a play festival accommodated children's natural development and can be considered a forerunner of later athletic festivals held at schools around the world.[13] Similar types of play festivals have long been part of the educational landscape in Japan, where they are known as *undōkai*. Organized at the school level, *undōkai* brings children, teachers, families and communities together for outdoor events including games and dances. While Japanese *undōkai* did not develop from Froebel's concept and principles of play and his philosophy of the unity of life, recent initiatives have shown that they can be made compatible in a way that is fruitful and meaningful for all participants.

Undōkai and kindergarten

Undōkai has a long history in Japanese school culture as an annual event held outdoors in spring or autumn. *Undōkai* involves athletic and competitive components, along with recreational, entertainment and demonstration elements. It is an event based on Japan's group-oriented nature, culture and traditions. *Undōkai* was developed both as an important school event and as a festival for the community.[14]

There are several views on the origin of *undōkai*. Historians agree that it was an idea brought from Europe; however, there is no precise record of who brought it to Japan, when, or from where. It has been suggested, for example, that the concept of *undōkai* was introduced by French steel engineers while they were working at the Yokosuka Steel Foundry around 1868, the time Japan opened its doors to the Western world in what is known as the Meiji Restoration.[15] Others argue that *undōkai* was imported from Britain, with the first British-modelled *undōkai* held at the Imperial Japanese Naval College in Tokyo in 1874.[16] That event was organized by a British Royal Navy Officer, Sir Archibald Lucius Douglas (1842–1913), who served as an advisor for the Imperial Japanese Navy College.[17] Recreational events, including games and contests such as the three-legged race, spoon race, long jump and pole vault, were presented at the festival.[18] By the end of the 1880s, *undōkai* had spread around Japan and became a thoroughly Japanized event. Although it initially included Western athletic events, eventually *undōkai* became fundamentally a local event with athletic, recreational and entertainment elements.[19] This transformation came not least from the Meiji government's control of local festivals and expectations in this period. The government saw the use of symbolism in festivals, rituals, culture and recreation as an important means of enhancing people's sense of belonging and solidarity with their family, their locality and the nation of Japan.[20]

The development of *undōkai* at Japanese schools was an initiative of Arimori Mori (1847–89), the founder of Japan's modern educational system. When Mori served as Japan's Minister of Education (1885–9), he pushed forward the modernization of the nation through its schools. Japan's educational transition and transformation into a modern education system was characterized by a desire to learn from the West. Mori promoted physical education through *undōkai* as part of the new imperial regime committed to building modern education in Japan and stressed group characteristics to improve young people's physical and mental development.[21] Mori's move of athletic festivals from the Naval College to universities and other colleges, and then to high schools, secondary schools and primary schools, cemented the nation's ability to define 'the legitimate body and the legitimate use of the body' through physical education.[22] According to historian Wolfram Manzenreiter, 'Marching formations and mass calisthenics demonstrated the result of a disciplinary education that put the body into service of the collective.'[23]

During the Russo-Japanese War (1904–5) and the First and Second World Wars, *undōkai* was no longer used for sporting events. Physical education and *undōkai* were adapted for nationalistic purposes and militarization and promoted by the Ministry of Education through the education system. They were also used for imperial training of marching, competition and coordinated group gymnastics in order to reinforce military character and collective identity, thereby unifying the nation with the emperor at its centre.[24] Military-style gymnastics intended to promote loyalty and patriotism became the norm in Japanese education.[25]

Through its promotion by the Ministry of Education, *undōkai* became one of the important school events at all levels of education, including kindergarten. The history of *undōkai* at kindergarten began with the initiation of *undōkai* at primary schools. When the Fundamental Code of Education was proclaimed nationwide in 1872, the elementary school system was established, and there was compulsory schooling for children aged six and older. Although kindergarten education was introduced as *Youchi Shogaku* (preschool education for children under six), it was not included in the official school system in Japan. Nevertheless, kindergartens were generally attached to primary schools, and their curricula – and *undōkai* – were also influenced by those of the primary schools.[26]

Early *undōkai* at kindergarten in Japan possibly took the form of an excursion with outdoor play.[27] The first recorded excursion type of outdoor event was held at *Kaichi Gattuko Fuzoku Matsumoto Yochien* (Kindergarten attached to Kaichi Primary School) in Matsumoto in April 1886. The children went to a mountain, woods and local shrines. They enjoyed various outdoor play activities, such as war play, and play tag, and at the end of the excursion, children enjoyed Japanese sweets, food or fruits given to them by teachers.[28]

The athletic version of *undōkai* in kindergarten started with the Elementary School Order of 1887, which introduced physical education to the curriculum as one of the core subjects. In the early twentieth century, *undōkai* in kindergarten was transformed from an excursion into an athletic event for parents and the local community. The transformation can be traced to the kindergarten attached to Tokyo Women's Normal School (now Ochanomizu University kindergarten). In 1903, the Tokyo Women's Normal School Kindergarten, which served upper-class families, held *undōkai* as a parents' day. It served as entertainment as well as an opportunity for parents to observe kindergarten education and to showcase the school's kindergarten to wider audiences.[29] The children played, danced, sang and engaged in athletic activities along with their parents. This style of *undōkai* became the basis for the 'entertainment and show' style which dominated kindergarten *undōkai* for most of the twentieth century and into the twenty-first.[30]

Undōkai is now an annual event in Japanese kindergartens, with five interrelated goals, connected to the aims of kindergarten education set by the Ministry of Education in Japan: to help children appreciate exercise with other children and foster their interest in sports, to foster group behaviour, to instil in children an appreciation for cooperative play, to promote children's health and well-being and to foster cooperative spirits and responsible attitudes.[31] *Undōkai* usually begins with children marching into the playground. Then, the ceremony starts with the principal's speech, songs are sung to uplift the children's competitive spirits and children liven up the *undōkai* by singing and dancing. The kindergarten is divided into two teams and traditional games such as *tamaire* (throwing a ball into a basket), tug-of-war, three-legged races and a relay typically feature on the *undōkai* programme. The events are entertaining and are intended to challenge the skill of the group, rather than show off individual skill. *Undōkai* requires regulated group behaviour and fosters responsibility and a sense of belonging.

Critical issues for *undōkai* at kindergartens are the time spent on preparation and the degree of teacher direction. Teachers lead the children in daily practice of ceremonies, dances, songs and speeches for months leading up to the *undōkai* event. The songs to be sung at the festival are practised every morning to lift the children's spirits.[32] *Undōkai* at kindergartens are a structured and teacher-controlled event. Specific objectives and orders are given to the children to ensure a recognizable event with a competitive and group-oriented atmosphere. Teachers control or supervise group behaviour, and set rules for games, play and dance like in military training. Although in the past ten years Japan's Ministry of Education and its curriculum policy have claimed to encourage the 'individual characteristics of each child', all of its curriculum discourages the development of individuality and a sense of individual contribution, underscoring instead the benefits of belonging to a group. Various studies, including Kamisuki's, address questions such as: 'Do children really enjoy *undōkai*?'; 'Do we really need *undōkai* at kindergartens?' and more importantly, 'Who is *undōkai* for, anyway?'[33] Researchers, educators and even kindergarten teachers have criticized *undōkai* as a teacher-centred, rather than child-centred, event.

A Froebelian kindergarten in Japan, past, present and future

In this section, we examine the development of *undōkai* at a Froebelian kindergarten in Japan and highlight the Froebelian history of the Glory Kindergarten. During the second half of the nineteenth century, Froebel's kindergarten idea was brought by German and other enthusiasts – the so-called Froebelians – from Germany to other European countries and to the United States and elsewhere, ultimately arriving in Japan in the early 1870s.[34] In Japan as in other contexts, Froebel's theory and methods were translated and transformed to fit with local culture, ideas, values and politics.[35]

In many cases, the spread of Froebel's ideas was undertaken by teachers trained by him or by enthusiasts committed to his philosophy. In Japan, kindergarten education was introduced first by Meiji government officials seeking to create and expand the national education system after the 1868 Meiji Restoration and second by missionary kindergartners. To achieve its goals, the government brought literature on kindergarten education from Europe and the United States. These books were translated into Japanese and used for dissemination of the idea of kindergarten education and the development of Japanese kindergartens. When the first kindergarten was developed in 1876, it was not part of the official schooling system. The Meiji government developed kindergartens for several reasons, the most important being to show the West how Japan formed a modern state in a short period. The Meiji government considered that kindergarten could be a symbol of the rise of the nation-state. The development of Froebel's philosophy of education, however, was not a central issue.[36]

Froebel's own works, such as *The Education of Man* (1826) and *Mother-Play and Nursery Songs* (1844), were excluded from the Ministry of Education's list of required literature for the development of kindergarten education. That was because the ministry sought to exclude the Christian ideas which shaped Froebel's educational principles.[37] Because state Shintoism in Japan could not accommodate Christianity, the religious core of Froebel's philosophy of kindergarten education was omitted in the transfer of the kindergarten education in Japan.[38] Kindergarten movements in Japan were developed by American and European Christian missionary women in the 1880s after the Meiji government lifted the ban on Christianity in 1873.[39] The transfer of new technology and ideas from the Western countries was welcomed, as was made clear by the government slogan 'Import Western technology and ideas.'[40] Although the government needed to accept Christianity in the process of the importation of ideas from the West, it started to take anti-Christian action by the end of the 1880s.[41]

Japan's first official kindergarten was opened in 1876 by the Meiji government with the Ministry of Education. It was attached to the aforementioned Tokyo Women's Normal School and soon became a model school in Japan. Its work attracted interest and by the 1890s large numbers of kindergartens were established on the basis of Froebel teaching methods by using the gifts and occupations.[42] In this first phase of kindergarten in Japan, government kindergartens were oriented towards the goals of government; as a result, there was no freedom of play, there was only dictation work with the Froebel materials. Many educators criticized Froebel's pedagogy before they understood it.[43] On the other hand, missionary Froebelians stressed Froebel's philosophy of education along with Christian identity.[44] The diffusion of a philosophy of education closer to the one held by Froebel was carried out by Christian missionary women from the United States. One of the prominent missionary kindergartens was the Glory Kindergarten, established by Annie Lyon Howe in Kobe in 1889.[45] Howe introduced 'genuine' Froebelian educational and philosophical principles to Japan, and she had a great impact on the development of kindergartens in Japan through her kindergarten and teacher training school and her own Froebelian enthusiasm about early childhood education.

Howe was an American missionary assigned to work in Japan by the American Board of Commissioners for Foreign Missions of the Congregational Church in 1887.[46] She was trained as a Froebelian kindergarten teacher by Alice Putnam (1841–1919) at the Chicago Froebel Association Training School in the United States. In 1889, Howe established the Glory Kindergarten (*Shoei Yochien* in Japanese) and teacher training school (now Shoei Junior College) where she implemented the educational philosophy and practices of Friedrich Froebel. Glory's curriculum included play, games and finger plays, gardening and the care of animals, language, stories and, importantly, the use of gifts and occupations. In keeping with her efforts to make all lessons and symbols multidimensional, Howe stressed music, art and nature study for their scientific, geometric and artistic value. The curriculum was intended to awaken and nurture the mind, soul, body and heart of the child and, at the same time, harmonize the child's relationship with God, humankind and nature in the unity of life.[47] Howe was a Froebelian in the sense that she subscribed not only to the pedagogical aspects of his teachings but also to their spiritual underpinnings. Froebel highlighted the beauty of nature and the unity of life as important elements of kindergarten pedagogy, which were reflected in Howe's creation of a garden at the Glory Kindergarten in 1892. This was probably the first kindergarten garden in all of Japan.[48] As Howe explained:

> We have a beautiful garden with violets, roses, nasturtiums, mignonette, azaleas, carnations, pansies, chrysanthemums and hydrangeas. We plant seeds and gather flowers to take home. We gather leaves and flowers for colour studies until almost any of us can tell red, orange, yellow, green, and purple without any trouble. ... In our playground we have lovely wisteria arbors. One of these is a solid ceiling of purple each spring; that is, the purple flowers hang down inside of the trellis which is on the top of the poles-the leaves covering the top.[49]

Howe also organized the translation of *The Education of Man* and *Mother-Play and Nursery Songs* into Japanese.[50] She believed that those books presented Froebel's fundamental principles about the kindergarten education and system.[51] Howe described her effort to translate Froebel's publications into Japanese: 'I have proved over and over again that Froebel's principles are as true in Japan as they are in Germany and America, and since the best kindergarten work is based upon that book, that book must be Japanned without delay.'[52] In particular, the illustrations accompanying *Mother-Play and Nursery Songs* showed many beautiful and suggestive touches of daily life and culture in Japan and preserved the Froebelian spirit wonderfully well. Howe carefully organized a translation that helped Japanese people understand Froebel's educational principles and the importance of kindergarten education. She also stressed that the education of young children was an important stage of human growth and defined

Figure 10.1 The Garden in the Glory Kindergarten (ca. 1900). Shoei Junior College Archive, Kobe, Japan.

educational appropriateness as what was necessary to an individual child's development, disposition and interests. Fostering the individuality of a child was valued.

Howe emphasized individual freedom of learning and experiencing through various plays.[53] She provided for the dissemination of Froebel's theory and implanted an enthusiasm for child-centred education in Japan. The year after the Glory Kindergarten was established, the Imperial Rescript on Education was issued by the Ministry of Education in 1890. The inculcation of loyalty and an official version of morality became central to the methods of the Japanese school system. There were ceremonial assemblies required by the Ministry of Education based on the Imperial Rescript on Education. Displaying the Imperial Portrait and raising the national flag were required by the Ministry of Education and these were carried out exactly and gravely to make an impression on children in Japan. While nationalism and state initiatives became strong, Froebelian kindergartens, including the Glory Kindergarten, had a comprehensive view of the difficulty of the implementation of Froebel's theory for children in the social and political landscape.[54]

During Howe's forty years in Japan, her kindergarten was impacted by local and national pressures, education policy, the balance of political control and culture and history. However, Howe never wavered in her belief in child-centred education and a wish for each child to become a perfect representation of that divine inner law through his own personal choice; education must show him the ways and means of attaining the goal.[55] She pursued what is universal in Froebelian pedagogy which was her child-centred approach and Froebel's motto, 'Come, let us live with our children!'

Figure 10.2 The Glory Kindergarten – Outdoor play (ca. 1900–10). Shoei Junior College Archive, Kobe, Japan.

Howe encouraged teachers to nurture goodness in a child and to discourage any destructive qualities.[56] In 1919, she wrote a message to future Japanese Froebelians, which was included in the 1921 *Report* of the Glory Kindergarten and teacher training school, entitled *Possibilities of Childhood*:

> Can you have a clear vision of the possibilities wrapped up in the eager little souls who come into your kindergarten day by day? Can you have a clear vision of their longing to be led into lives of beautiful achievement? If so, a great hope, purified of selfish desire, purified of ambition will come into your soul to help the children of Japan realize their possibilities. With the vision of hope, you will have the courage, the steadfastness, the patience to work and wait until children of Japan are cared for as they should be and that means much![57]

Although the name, concept and system of kindergarten in Japan remains even today, Froebel's method of education and the Froebelian pedagogy of child-centred education was not deeply rooted except in the Glory Kindergarten. This situation remains the case today.

Undōkai, children's play festival at the Glory Kindergarten

The child-centred approach promoted by Howe and subsequent Froebelian teachers in Japan conflicts with the emphasis on the group and on collective achievement in the way that *undōkai* is commonly offered in Japanese kindergartens. Rather than continuing the *undōkai* along those lines, or simply eschewing the *undōkai* as incompatible, over the last ten years the leaders of the Glory Kindergarten have sought to create a new form of *undōkai* along Froebelian principles. What follows is an examination of how they did so and an assessment of the extent to which this new form can satisfy both Froebelians and those who defend the *undōkai* in its traditional form.

Despite the Glory Kindergarten's Froebelian orientation, its *undōkai* was in the traditional non-Froebelian Japanese vein. Over the last ten years, however, it has re-organized and transformed its *undōkai* into a child-centred *undōkai* children's festival created by the children themselves, renaming the event in the process to be called *Kodomo no Asobi Matsuri* which means Children's Play Festival in Japanese. Glory's Froebelians wished to organize a *Spielfest* as Froebel did for children. Since the 2008 revision of the *Course of Study for Kindergarten*, the Ministry of Education guideline,[58] They shifted their approach towards children and tried to include children's voice and perspectives. This strategy was different from the traditional question and answer communications where teachers knew the answers of questions they asked children. Glory Froebelians started to listen to children and asked questions that took children further in their thinking and explored their ideas, which allowed children to find ways, express their thoughts, reflect on and then articulate the new thinking and ideas.

In addition, Glory Froebelians set the theme, '*Nobinobi Jyujitsu Hoiku*', which means encouraging a child to learn freely, flexibly and actively, and to experience a sense of fulfilment in acting by him- or herself. At the Glory Kindergarten, the implementation of '*Nobinobi Jyujitsu Hoiku*' provides long, uninterrupted periods of ninety minutes for spontaneous free outdoor play every morning, a practice in accordance with Annie Howe's motto 'Let children play for their own purposes.'[59] During the '*Nobinobi Jyujitsu Hoiku*' outdoor play time, teachers observe the children's play at different times, locations and dates. An observation template with child development checklists is prepared by the teachers to evaluate and scaffold each child's individual development and experience. This includes all areas of the children's learning experience: physical, social, emotional and cognitive development and interests; their needs; and their dispositions. Glory Froebelians also observe the children's interaction with adults and their peers. Their practices of observing children at play accords with Froebel's assertion that play is necessary for the development of the *whole* child, enlisting all of his or her imaginative powers and physical movements, and exploring his or her interests.

Programming and planning for *undōkai* at the Glory Kindergarten is based on detailed observation by teachers of individual children, beginning two months before the event. Their observations seek to integrate every dimension of the children's daily experiences, encompassing daily routines, the physical environment, relationships and interaction. The teachers prepare reflective journals for each year group. This journal provides a record of the development and learning of each child as well as of the whole group of children to help the teacher reflect on and design activities that support the children's planning for *undōkai*. Observation notes are shared among teachers, and they discuss how they could be extended to scaffold the individual child's development. Reflective journals and the children's individual portfolios are reviewed in weekly staff meetings, to share the children's learning and support and follow-up on any action taken by teachers.

In September, a month before *undōkai*, the teachers at the Glory Kindergarten prepare play facilities and playground equipment for the children and encourage the children's spontaneous free play. While some children play the same as before, other children show interest in playing with the new equipment, such as skipping ropes, stilts, unicycles, hula-hoops, big balls and ball-toss games. Eventually, the children start to say, 'Let's play *undōkai!*' It is a sign of the commencement of the children's play festival, '*Kodomo no Asobi Matsuri*'. Outdoor play at kindergarten becomes a means of experimentation in advance of the scheduled events of children's play festival. Children are encouraged to talk about *undōkai* and the teachers become facilitators of the discussions.

Thus, unlike the traditional teacher-planned *undōkai*, the programme of the Glory Kindergarten's *undōkai* is planned and arranged by the children. They organize the opening ceremony, sing songs they write themselves and choreograph a dance (although the children ask the teacher for suggestions on the latter). The decorations are also designed and organized by the children. The combination of individual and group events is organized according to the children's interests and decisions. The children set the rules for each game and event and discuss what to do in each situation. They also tidy up, act as judges and emcees, organize the opening and closing ceremonies and make speeches. The teachers never give any instructions; instead they respect the children's independence by stepping back while children are discussing their plans, allowing them to learn from their own discoveries and draw their own conclusions.

All of the resulting *undōkai* events include the children's voices. For example, one type of *undōkai* event is called a 'challenge'. These might include activities such as riding a unicycle, leaping over the vaulting horse, performing on the balance beam, hula-hoop, takeuma (stilts), rope jumping and using the horizontal bar. The successful completion of the challenge task is not essential; the most important thing is for children to follow their wishes and to challenge themselves. In the Glory Kindergarten – unlike in mainstream Japanese kindergartens – *undōkai* is made a part of children's daily play activities and value is placed on fostering the spontaneity of children's play and ideas.

The role of teachers is important in this context. Teachers always consider how an adult can support and sustain meaningful play for children. They prepare the environment and materials to meet the needs and interests of children. For *undōkai*, they try to acknowledge when they can step in and help. They are supportive, offering warmth, security, stability and acceptance to each child. Teachers try to listen to the children and make suggestions. The teachers create a learning environment with the intention of ensuring that the children participate in the activities, on the basis of an understanding and anticipation of the individual actions of each child. This approach towards the children's play festival has made it more childcentred than the traditional *undōkai*, but Glory Froebelians feel that they still have a long way to go to reach their goal of a truly child-centred children's play festival. Even after long-term experiences of teaching children in Japan, Annie Howe thought that there was always something new to learn about children.[60] Teachers at the Glory Kindergarten agree and challenge to teach children according to Froebel's motto, 'Come, let us live with our children.' In this

Figure 10.3 Children's Play Festival at the Glory Kindergarten, 2015, Kobe, Japan.

way, Howe's spirit remains in the Glory Kindergarten and at the Shoei Junior College in Kobe, Japan. In 2014, both these institutions marked their 125th anniversaries. As of 2015, the college had graduated 4,787 Froebelian educators.[61] These graduates have been leaders in early childhood education in Japan.

Conclusion

This chapter has described how teacher-centred events such as *undōkai* can be transformed as child-centred activities. The key, as Hiroshi Ashida writes, is a change in the view of the nature of the relationship between the children and teacher.[62] Insisting that the children should be enthusiastically involved in the festival, Ashida called for a better match between their purpose and their execution as a child-centred event.[63] The Glory Kindergarten Froebelians will no doubt be redoubling their efforts in this regard as they plan for the tenth annual children's play festival in 2016. Their journey, as Froebelians, will continue to pursue Froebel's ideals of a 'real' child festival.

Notes

1   S. K. Kochhar, *Methods and Techniques of Teaching* (New Delhi: Sterling Publishers, 1977), 258.
2   Friedrich Froebel, *The Education of Man*, trans. W. N. Hailmann (New York and London: D. Appleton Century, [1826] 1887), 55.

3   Irene M. Lilley, *Friedrich Froebel: A Selection from His Writings* (Cambridge: Cambridge University Press, 1967), 35.

4   J. C. Aggarwal, *Theory and Principles of Education* (New Delhi: Vikas Publishing House, 2002), 144.

5   Friedrich Froebel, *Friedrich Froebel's Pedagogics of the Kindergarten,* trans. Josephine Jarvis (New York: D. Appleton and Company, [1861] 1895), 6.

6   Froebel, *Pedagogics of the Kindergarten.*

7   Joachim Liebschner, *A Child's Work: Freedom and Play in Froebel's Educational Theory and Practice* (Cambridge, UK: Lutterworth Press, 1992), 54.

8   Bertha von Marenholtz-Bülow and Mary Tyler Peabody Mann, *How Kindergarten Came to America: Friedrich Froebel's Radical Vision of Early Childhood Education,* trans. Mrs. Horace Mann (New York: New Press, [1895] 2007), 89.

9   Ibid., 89–90.

10   Ibid., 89; Yumiko Taoka, 'Anthropological Meaning of F. Fröbel's "Festival" [*Fest, Feier*]: In Relation to the "Intuition of Life Unity" [*Ahnung*],' *Departmental Bulletin Paper, Ryukoku University* 474/475 (2010): 2.

11   Cited in von Marenholtz-Bülow and Mann, *How Kindergarten Came to America,* 97.

12   Ibid., 97.

13   Hiroshi Ashida, 'Is the Athletic Festival Undokai Child-Centered? History and Discussion on Athletic Festivals at Japanese Kindergartens', *International Journal of Early Childhood Education* 8, no. 2 (2002): 200.

14   Yuzo Kishino, *Saishin Supo-Tsu Daijiten [The Newest Greater Encyclopedia of Sport]* (Tokyo: Taishukan, 1987]; Jacqueline G. Haslett, 'The Uniqueness of Undokai in Japan: Bringing Community/Family Together through Dance and Sport Like Activities', *Bulletin of Research Institute of Physical Education Chukyo University* 4 (1990): 58.

15   Haslett, 'The Uniqueness of Undokai in Japan', 59.

16   Toshiya Yoshimi, *Undokai to Kindai Nihon [Undokai and Modern Japan],* vol. 6 (Seikyusha, 1999).

17   Ashida, 'Is the Athletic Festival Undokai Child-Centered?'

18   Ibid., 194.

19   Yuzo Kishino, 'Nihon No Undokai No Yurai to Tokushoku [The History and Character of Undokai in Japan],' *Taikuka Kyoiku (Journal of Physical Education)* 12, no. 9 (1964): 2–5.

20   Hideo Sato, 'Undokai', in *Saishin supo-tsu daijiten [The Sports Encyclopedia]* (Tokyo: Taishukanshoten, 1987): 94–7.

21   Bruce M. Burnett and Masato Wada, 'The Ebb and Flow of Japanese Educational Reform'. Australian Association for Research in Education, International Educational Research Conference, Fremantle (2007), 2–3. Available online: http://eprints.qut.edu.au/15748/1/15748.pdf (accessed 15 May 2015).

22   Pierre Bourdieu, 'Sport and Social Class', in *Rethinking Popular Culture: Contemporary Perspectives in Cultural Studies,* ed. Chandra Mukerji and Michael Schudson (Berkeley, CA: University of California Press, 1991), 826.

23   Wolfram Manzenreiter, *Sport and Body Politics in Japan: Routledge Research in Sport, Culture and Society Series* 26 (London: Routledge, 2014), 53.

24   Kishino, 'Nihon No Undokai No Yurai to Tokushoku' [The History and Character of Undokai in Japan].

25   J. Horne, 'Understanding Sport and Body Culture in Japan', *Body and Society* 6 (2000): 79.

26 Eiko Kashiwara, 'Yochien Ni Okeru Undokai Ni Kansuru Ichikosatsu Part 4 Sono Rekishihenseiwotooshite a Study of Undokai in Kindergartens: An Historical Perspective', *Japan Society of Research on Early Childhood Care and Education* 44 (1991): 22–3; Masayuki Shibazaki, 'Naze Yochien De Undokai Wo Surunoka' [Why Do We Need Undokai in Kindergartens?], *Yoji no Kyouiku* [*Early Childhood Education*] 92, no. 10 (1993): 10–18.

27 Masako Kamisuki, 'Naze Yochien De Undokai Wo Surunoka' [Why Do We Need Undokai in Kindergartens?], *Yoji no Kyouiku* [*Early Childhood Education*] 92, no. 10 (1993); Masako Kamisuki, 'Yochien Ni Undokai Wa Iranai' (We Do Not Need Undokai in Kindergarten Education); Masayuki Shibazaki, 'Naze Yochien De Undokai Wo Surunoka' [Why We Do Undokai in Kindergartens].

28 Ibid.

29 Eiko Kashiwara, 'Yochien Ni Okeru Undokai Ni Kansuru Ichikosatsu Part 4'.

30 Ibid., 13.

31 Culture Ministry of Education, Sports Science and Technology Japan (MEXT), 'Course of Study for Kindergarten', Culture Ministry of Education, Sports Science and Technology Japan (MEXT) (Tokyo, Japan, 2008); Ashida, 'Is the Athletic Festival Undokai Child-Centred?'

32 Ibid., 205–6.

33 Kamisuki, 'Naze Yochien De Undokai O Surunoka'; Haslett, 'The Uniqueness of Undokain in Japan'; Kashiwara, 'Yochien Ni Okeru Undokai Ni Kansuru Ichikosatsu Part 4'.

34 Roberta Wollons (ed.), *Kindergartens and Cultures: The Global Diffusion of an Idea* (New Haven, CT: Yale University Press, 2000).

35 Yoko Shirakawa, 'Culture and the Japanese Kindergarten Curriculum: A:l View', *Early Child Development and Care* 123, no. 1 (1996): 183–92; Yukitane Tanaka and Kiyo Sato, 'The Contribution and Influence of Friedrich Froebel's Ideology: The US and Japan', *Hyogo University of Teacher Education Journal* 13, no. 1 (1993): 115–28.

36 Kathleen Uno, 'Civil Society, State, and Institutions for Young Children in Modern Japan: The Initial Years', *History of Education Quarterly* 49, no. 2 (2009): 170–81; Yukiyo Nishida, 'A Chrysanthemum in the Garden: A Christian Kindergarten in the Empire of Japan', *Paedagogica Historica: International Journal of the History of Education* 51, no. 3 (2015): 280–97.

37 Shirakawa, 'Culture and the Japanese Kindergarten Curriculum: A Historical View'.

38 Nishida, 'A Chrysanthemum in the Garden'.

39 Ibid., 283; Roberta Wollons, '*Kindergartens and Cultures: The Global Diffusion of an Idea*, ed. Roberta Wollons (New Haven, CT: Yale University Press, 2000), 9–12; John Macaloon, *Muscular Christianity and the Colonial and Post-Colonial World* (London: Routledge, 2008), 19.

40 John Whitney Hall, *Japan: From Prehistory to Modern Times* (Tokyo: C. E. Tuttle Co, 1971).

41 Nishida, 'A Chrysanthemum in the Garden'.

42 Tanaka and Sato, 'The Contribution and Influence of Friedrich Froebel's Ideology: The US and Japan'.

43 Makoto Tumori, Kubo Ito and Honda Kazuko, *Yochien No Rekishi [The History of Kindergarten]* (Tokyo: Kouseisha Koseikaku , 1959).

44 Nishida, 'A Chrysanthemum in the Garden'; Tsumori, Ito and Honda, *Yochien No Rekishi [The History of Kindergarten]*.

45 Katsuo Takano, *E Eru Hau Jyoshi to Shouei No Ayumi [Miss A. L. Howe and the History of Glory Kindergarten and Training School]* (Kobe, Japan: Shoei Junior College, 1973).
46 Mitsuyo Nishigaki, '*A. L. Hau No Shogai: Nihonno Youji Kyouikuni, Fureberu Seishin Wo Donyushita Fujin Senkyoushi Ani L. Hauno Hataraki to Shiso*' [The Life of A. L Howe: The Development of Froebelian Theory in Japan] (Kobe, Japan: Kobe Local Newspaper Press, 2007).
47 Nishigaki, '*A. L. Hau No Shogai*'.
48 Annie L. Howe, *Shiawase Naru Kanougoto [The Happy Possibilities]* (Kobe: The Glory Kindergarten, 1917); Takano, *E Eru Hau Jyoshi to Shouei No Ayumi*.
49 Ellen F. Beebe, 'The Glory Kindergarten,' in *Woman's Board of Missions of the Interior* (Chicago 1919), 1–4. This was a quotation from an interview with Howe, 3.
50 Anne L. Howe organized the translated and published *Hito not Kyoiku [The Education of Man]* in 1901 and *Haha no yugi oyobi ikuji uta [Mother-Play and Nursery Song]* in 1896. Both books were published by Shoei Junior College (Glory Teacher Training School Press).
51 Howe, *Shiawase Naru Kanougoto [The Happy Possibilities Possibilities]*.
52 Nina C. Vandewalker, *The Kindergarten in American Education* (New York: Macmillan, 1908), 100.
53 Takano, *E Eru Hau Jyoshi to Shouei No Ayumi*.
54 The Kindergarten Union of Japan, 'Thirteenth Annual Report of the Kindergarten Union of Japan', in *Annual Report of the Japanese Kindergarten Union* 83 [1919–22] reprinted edition, Vol. 4 (Tokyo: Nihon Raiburari, 1985), 83. The JKU report was reprinted and republished by Nihon Raiburari in 1985.
55 Takano, *E Eru Hau Jyoshi to Shouei No Ayumi*; Friedrich Froebel and William Nicholas Hailmann, *The Education of Man, Translated and Annotated by W. N. Hailmann* (New York; London: D. Appleton & Co., 1912), 2.
56 Howe, *Shiawas Naru Kanogoto [The Happy Possibilities]*.
57 Annie. L. Howe (ed.), 'Glory Kindergarten 1922', in *Report of Glory Kindergarten and Training School* (Kobe Japan: Shoei Hobo Denshu Sho [Glory Teacher Training School] 1922), 8.
58 Culture Ministry of Education, Sports Science and Technology Japan (MEXT), 'Course of Study for Kindergarten', Culture Ministry of Education, Sports Science and Technology Japan (MEXT) (Tokyo, 2008).
59 Howe, *Shiawas Naru Kanogoto [The Happy Possibilities]*.
60 Annie L. Howe, *KIBO [The Hope]* (Kobe, Shoei Junior College, 1920), 14–18.
61 The record is from Shoei Junior college.
62 Ashida, 'Is the Athletic Festival Undokai Child-centred?', 207.
63 Ibid., 208.

Figure 11.1 Dunedin kindergarten children with Froebel's First Gift, 16 July 1902, *Otago Witness.*

Figure 11.2 Scottish highland dancing at Rachel Reynolds Kindergarten, c. 1920. Dunedin Kindergarten Association, MS-1149/006, Hocken Collections – Uare Taoka o Hākena, University of Otago.

Figure 11.3 Reid Park Kindergarten swinging poi at the Māori and Pacific Polyfestival, 2013. Dunedin Kindergartens – *Mana Manaaki Puawai O Otepoti.*

11

Relocation, Continuity and Change: Dunedin Kindergartens, Aotearoa New Zealand, 1890s–2010s

Helen May

Dunedin Kindergartens – Mana Manaaki Puawai O Otepoti (DK) is the oldest kindergarten association in Aotearoa New Zealand (NZ) and in 2014 celebrated its 125th Jubilee.[1] In Dunedin, an Edinburgh of the South founded by Scottish settlers in 1848, kindergartens have been a place of play and learning, and sometimes refuge, for hundreds of thousands of Dunedin children. Currently, with twenty-three kindergartens, DK is part of a national kindergarten movement. Kindergartens are the largest organization providing early childhood education (ECE) in Aotearoa NZ, mainly serving children aged two to four with children starting school on their fifth birthday. Kindergarten is embedded into the cultural landscape. Judith Duncan, kindergarten teacher and scholar, claims, 'Kindergarten arguably is as "New Zealand" as "kiwi fruit" "pavlova" and "buzzy bee".'[2] Kindergartens were once the flagship for part-day preschool education and being a 'kiwi kindy kid' was a rite of passage, but now they are but one of many government-funded ECE options. Currently, 62 per cent of children attending ECE are enrolled in a range of 'education and care' options for children from birth to five years.[3] In order to match these offerings, some kindergartens have extended their opening hours and age range, but kindergartener professionals wonder whether this amounts to the diminishing of their distinctive heritage in the diverse ECE landscape. This chapter draws on archival images and documents collated for DK's jubilee and presents vignette insights into the kindergarten journey from Bad Blankenburg in the 1840s, across oceans, continents, cultures and centuries, to the furthest outpost of kindergarten colonial endeavour. The photos overleaf (Figures 11.1, 11.2, 11.3) are exemplars of this relocation, evidence of shifts in the language and understandings of children's learning, the cultural artefacts of kindergarten, as well as the political and social landscape of ECE in Dunedin specifically and Aotearoa NZ as a whole. Yet amidst the relocation and adaptation, some enduring Froebelian metaphors of kindergarten pedagogy and practice are evident. Four broad pedagogical metaphors are explored within the colonial kindergarten setting of the Dunedin, specifically, and Aotearoa NZ broadly, past and present; originally expounded by Friedrich Froebel in the practices demonstrated at his Bad Blankenburg kindergarten, and similarly resonating with the ideals of a settler society:

1. Constructing a new world
2. Planting the seeds of the new child
3. Handling the tools of technology
4. Expressing cultural identity.

It is necessary first to outline the colonial context of Aotearoa NZ.

A new world venture

The islands of Aotearoa, named by Māori peoples as the 'land of the long white cloud', were the last frontier for exploration and settlement by Europe's Old World. NZ was on 'the edges of the empire' and regarded as 'Mother England's ... most desirable of progeny'.[4] The New World of the Antipodes was not only about the geography of new lands that Europeans wrongly presumed were empty, but was also imbued with dreams of opportunity and leaving the ills of the Old World (in Britain). The timing of planned colonial settlement of NZ, after the 1840 Treaty of Waitangi, coincided with the emergence of the kindergarten in the Old World. This makes for an interesting case study of the transformation of ideas and institutions across continents and cultural contexts.

NZ's kindergarten story was significantly a *pākehā* (not Māori) settler story until the 1960s when Māori children became a presence in ECE institutions.[5] The idea of the German kindergarten arrived during the 1870s via England and the United States with its Froebelian pedagogy significantly intact. The political context, however, had changed: kindergarten was one of many nineteenth-century institutions accompanying what James Belich titled *The Settler Revolution and the Rise of the Anglo-World*.[6] In 1828, the British Secretary for the Colonies reported, 'Wherever our Empire is acknowledged we have carried thither our language, our laws and our institutions.'[7] Settlers brought a utopian brand of imperialism hoping that the 'healthy New Zealand environment' would 'improve the British race'.[8] By an accident of politics and timing, the kindergarten became an Anglo institution to be 'carried thither'. New ideals of kindergarten childhood sat well in this mix of colonial-utopian endeavour for a 'Better Britain'.[9]

There are parallel elements of utopian endeavour in the Froebel kindergarten that emerged during 'new times' in Germany in the 1840s. Froebel was concerned too that the existing form of education of young children was repressive and wrote, 'The infant school ... only trains the memory, neglecting or insufficiently attending to the creative and expressive needs.'[10] The kindergarten's transportation and transformation beyond Germany began with the 1851 *Kindergarten Verbot* imposed by the Prussian Government after the failure of the 1848–9 revolution. The liberal ideology of opportunity and social reform that sparked the 'Anglo-World settler revolution' similarly imbued the educational ideology of the kindergarten.

The Dunedin Free Kindergarten Association (DFKA) was established in 1889 by settler citizens well connected within church, media, education and political circles.[11] While the pedagogy was Froebelian, the blueprint of operations was imported from the Golden Gate Kindergarten Association, which ran free kindergartens for poor children in San Francisco, California. The free kindergarten had been demonstrated in England and Scotland, and more fully realized in the United States.[12] Its roots were in the German *Volkskindergarten* already seeded before the *Verbot*. The *Volkskindergarten* for working-class children was promoted through the advocacy of Froebel's patron and promoter, Baroness Bertha von Marenholtz-Bülow, who claimed, 'Until the mothers of the lower classes are a better educated race, the education of their children must be in the care of the educated class.'[13] From the 1880s this blueprint was replicated in NZ's four settlement cities of Dunedin, Christchurch, Wellington and Auckland. By the 1880s, a fragile institutional and economic infrastructure re-created many Old World ills and it was evident that a South Seas utopia would be hard to realize. This made the kindergarten seem even more worthwhile, combining settler 'do-it-yourself' endeavour and the Froebelian promise of a 'new child'.

Constructing a new world: Kindergarten block builder

Froebel is most remembered for the kindergarten *Spielgaben*, known in English as 'gifts', a progression of geometric blocks of increasing complexity. The gifts were playthings for self-activity designed to develop the child's senses. Each gift led children to explore what Froebel called the Forms of Life through block building, the Forms of Beauty through creative pattern making and the Forms of Knowledge for understanding mathematics. These gifts were more than playthings, but materials with which children could reveal their individual gifts of creativity, interests and understandings.[14] In elaborating Froebel's teachings, von Marenholtz-Bülow wrote: 'A child's instinct of activity, if properly directed from the beginning, soon shows a marked tendency to artistic production. The plastic instinct is plainly visible in the tendency of a child to form and model. The brick-box meets this tendency as far as architecture is concerned.'[15] Froebel's block-building child is a useful metaphor not only to characterize the 'new child' of the new settler society, but also the building of infrastructure: the homes, schools, roads or bridges that became the essential task by the peoples of new colony.

Settler arrivals to the Otago Peninsula harbour from 1848 were intent on building the proposed town of Dunedin. Within months, the first church and school were operational. By the 1850s, a functioning wooden town had been built. In 1861, gold was discovered in the hinterland and the wealth created a small Victorian city with ornate stone architecture. By the time the DFKA opened its first kindergarten in 1889, the gold was depleted and an economic depression had stalled progress. Behind the architectural facades were wooden slums overcrowded with a populace whose dreams had not been realized.

The kindergarten was one of a range of child-saving initiatives intended to transform the play of slum children in other places, including cities in the United States and the

United Kingdom. Karl Froebel, the brother of Friedrich, described the situation in Edinburgh, Scotland where after 1851 he lived as a refugee: 'Dirty children screaming instead of singing, rolling in the mud or dust instead of dancing; ... playing with fragments of bottles and dishes and dirty pieces of wood, and disgusting bones, instead of bricks, coloured tablets, sticks and peas.'[16] In Edinburgh's colonial namesake, the location of the first kindergarten was known as the 'Devil's Half Acre' and described as 'an overcrowded warren where whole families lived in a single room and for whom the adjacent alley was both bathroom and living room. Here too were opium dens, drinking parlours and houses of prostitution.'[17]

DFKA's first annual report emphasized the purpose of its kindergarten: 'To guard the children of Dunedin from thriftlessness, disease, pauperism, and crime was the desire of those who first spoke of planning a kindergarten in this city.'[18] At a meeting with the colony's Premier, Rt Hon Richard Seddon in 1903, DFKA president Rachel Reynolds described how kindergarten children

> were trained in ways of industry and cleanliness which developed into habits which would remain with them for life. It was rescue work. The children were of the poorest order – Chinese, Assyrians, and so on – and the work being done was saving the colony thousands of pounds. Many of these children if left to develop in their own surroundings, would eventually be criminals, and the kindergartens were saving them by taking them at a pliant stage and putting them on the right track.[19]

Froebel's child builders in the 'Devil's Half-Acre', it was claimed, could make a useful contribution as future citizens of the new colony.

Block building became an essential educational activity in the real life of all kindergartens. It was not only in Dunedin that in the 1900s Froebel's table-top blocks moved onto the floor and sometimes mixed with Montessori's building tower and sized wooden rods.[20] At various experimental kindergartens and nursery schools in the United States, large wooden blocks were introduced to encourage cooperative social play and the exercise of large muscles. These changes were reflective of wider revisions of Froebelian pedagogy in the early twentieth century.[21] DFKA photos of the period show children posed alongside a large block boat and a house for dolls.[22] In the late 1930s, NZ kindergartens introduced multiple unit blocks, still standard today, after visitors to the Harriet Johnson Nursery School in New York measured and copied Caroline Pratt's blocks.[23] From the 1970s, coloured plastic blocks and Lego became available. By then, Dunedin's child builders had for a long time been extending their building skills through carpentry, as well as constructions with large junk boxes, pipes, planks and tyres.

It is also useful to consider the metaphor of the kindergarten block builder as a parallel endeavour to the actual building of kindergartens as new environments for fostering the senses and abilities of the new child. DFKA initially housed its kindergartens in temporary halls. Not until 1914, through the patronage of Rachel Reynolds, was there a purpose-built kindergarten. Two further kindergartens, the Richard Hudson and Kelsey Yarella kindergartens, were built in the 1920s and designed in the Arts and Crafts style by the colonial architect Henry Mandeno; both kindergartens are still functional today. The *Otago Witness* (9 November 1926) reported upon the opening of the Richard Hudson Kindergarten that DFKA founding member Mark Cohen was 'hopeful that in the near future the benefits of the movement in infantile education would spread throughout the city and the suburbs so that more of these institutions could be erected [applause]'. Another founder, Lavinia Kelsey, told the audience: 'It was in the interests of their young children that children should have the best schools, the best teachers, and the best educational facilities to fit them for the battle of life, mentally, physically and morally [applause].' The Hudson family patrons expressed their 'earnest wish that all young children who passed through the school should enjoy a happy childhood and become successful, loyal and worthy citizens of New Zealand … [applause].' The director of education for NZ, Mr J. Caughley, proclaimed that the name ' "Kindergarten" was very suggestive – it was a garden of children. Their children were their best flowers [applause].'[24]

Make–do accommodation arrangements, nevertheless, remained a feature until the 1950s when the government's post-war policy encouraged all children, not just the inner city poor, to attend a kindergarten prior to starting school. Expansion was rapid. In 1944, there were only 2301 children attending the forty-nine free kindergartens nationwide. Between 1946 and 1955, eighty-one kindergartens were opened.[25] Building a school and a kindergarten became synonymous with the building blocks of the good life. A nationwide building programme for kindergartens accompanied suburban expansion, and the resulting modernist buildings are the main infrastructure of kindergartens today nationwide.

By the 2000s, the kindergarten building stock needed refurbishment. DK (the renamed DFKA) again embarked on a building programme, not in new suburbs, because the city had shrunk in population, but rather to refurbish or rebuild according to modern building and earthquake codes. Dunedin's kindergarten children in this period are sometimes pictured with their hard hats, safety cones, carpentry tools and diggers playing 'alongside' these building sites, engaged in the rebuilds, as are their parents, who work with teachers and DK to ensure that their kindergarten incorporates community interests rather than replicate the earlier nationwide plans.[26] These new builds are more diverse in their architecture and better equipped in their services than earlier models, but continue to be easily identifiable as iconic kiwi kindergartens. To celebrate the 125th jubilee, DK rebuilt the flagship Helen Deem Kindergarten that also houses the association offices. That Prime Minister Rt Hon John Key unveiled the kindergarten's *koru* [unfolding native fern] statue and cut the jubilee cake was symbolic of the political recognition of kindergarten's child builders and their buildings in the landscape of Dunedin and Aotearoa NZ.

Planting the seeds of the new child: Gardens and gardeners

In 1840, Froebel renamed his Play and Activity Institute, established at Bad Blankenburg, a '*Kindergarten*'. This signified both a 'garden for children' where they could interact with nature, but also a 'garden of children' that could develop freely under the guidance of the 'gardeners of children', the teachers. The kindergarten thus became a literal activity of productive work and an enduring Froebelian metaphor.

The children had individual garden plots alongside communal garden plots. The garden was a place where children learnt through first-hand experience using real tools amid the actual seasons and soils of nature. Froebel believed in a divine unity and harmony between living things; child gardens were a real-life expression of this.

The plant-like metaphor of childhood was not new. Two centuries earlier, Comenius wrote about the malleability of childhood in *The School of Infancy* (1631):

> It is the nature of everything that comes into being, that while tender it is easily bent and formed. ... A young plant can be planted, transformed, pruned and bent this way or that. When it becomes a tree these processes are impossible. ... It is in this first school that we must plant in a man the seeds of all the knowledge with which we wish him to be equipped in his journey through life.[27]

Froebel might have been reading Comenius when, in *The Education of Man* (1825), he wrote, 'The plays of childhood are the germinal leaves of all later life, for the whole man is developed and shown in these.'[28]

The DFKA founders expressed similar sentiments even though the borrowed mission hall of the first Dunedin kindergarten had no garden space. Kelsey recalled the day in 1889 when the DFKA 'planted the first kindergarten in Dunedin'. The metaphor resonates in Kelsey's description of young children nurtured and tended who, like wilting plants, flourish and grow in a 'kindergarten'[29]:

> Those of us who were present that day and watched the dullness and apathy of these children were astonished in visiting the school four months later at the wonderful change. There were the same children all clad in a uniform 'pinny' and yet how different. Their legs, hands, voices, brains, sympathies all were active in their appointed season. There seemed to be no abnormal growth but a quiet harmony of development.[30]

In 1912 teachers at the new Rachel Reynolds Kindergarten planned their first outdoor garden. By this time, much of the landscape of Aotearoa NZ had been transferred (or confiscated) from Māori ownership to *pākehā* buyers who became intrepid New World gardeners transforming native bush into productive farms. Gardening was in the genes of many settlers, who had once been tenant farmers and labourers in rural Britain, but with families now aspiring to own a garden plot or a farm.

Kindergarten children and teachers continued to garden throughout the twentieth century, although it was not a major activity, but recently DK has been proactive in fostering an ethic of caring for the environment which has placed renewed focus on children's interactions with the natural world. This is part of a wider political movement considering education for ecological sustainability, including its potential for building communities and a sense of belonging.[31] So central has this become to the identity of DK that sustainability features strongly in member kindergartens' web communications. For example:

> Bayfield Kindergarten is nestled in a back section with a large outdoor area bursting with native flora and fauna. Our extensive outdoor play area provides ample opportunity for development of motor skills, social skills, exploration and discovery.

Bayfield prides itself on modelling sustainability through our vegetable gardens, composting and worm farm. We foster a sense of environmental responsibility through our menagerie of animals (budgies, chickens, mice, rabbits and seasonal insects) whose habits, life cycles and care the children learn to respect and nurture.[32]

Richard Hudson Kindergarten participated in a national project, *Titiro Whakamuri, Hoki Whakamua. We can see the future, the present and the past: Caring for self, others and the environment.* One teacher echoed Froebel's words when she told researchers: 'We believe that children are like young and tender plants and that we as teachers, parents, *whānau* [extended family] and caregivers are the loving and caring gardeners who nourish them, and support them so that they can grow into mighty fruitful trees.'[33] The teacher reframed Froebel's garden metaphor in time, place and culture, with the inclusion of the Māori creation story: 'We looked at our philosophy and also reflected on how vital *Papatūānuku* [the earth mother] is to ecological sustainability ... if we look after and respect *Papatūānuku*, she will look after us. ... By learning about *Rakinui/Ranganui* [the father] and *Papatūānuku* we can inspire our children and *whānau* to consider making ecologically sustainable choices.'[34] The ecological and archaeological landscape of Aotearoa with its extinct giant flightless bird, the moa, was similarly embedded by the project's organizers within Froebel's garden metaphor. The project's Māori proverb became:

'*Na te moa I takahi te rātā*'
The rātā [tree] which was trodden on by a moa will never grow straight

Like in the times of Froebel, gardening and sustainability practices in twenty-first-century Aotearoa NZ kindergartens have been harnessed to ideals of social and economic reform. Kindergartner and scholar Jenny Ritchie writes:

Early childhood centres can be viewed as being sites of possibility with regard to transformative education. When educators in these services work closely with *tamariki* [children] and *whānau*, changes such as those required to move our collective consciousness towards ecological sustainability may be reinforced not only in the centre, but also in homes and further into the community.[35]

The outdoor areas of DK have also changed, and now include gardens for seasonal foods that children prepare for snacks or gifts. In amidst the sand, water, climbing, swinging, riding and constructing in the outdoors, native bush and grass plantings, stones and natural materials have replaced earlier artificial surfaces or European deciduous plant imports. DK's logo is an unfolding koru of the kindergarten **k**: Froebel's tender shoot is the native fern, prevalent in Māori carving and art and visible across so much of the landscape of Aotearoa NZ.

Expressing cultural identity: Songs, games and movement

Froebel believed that symbolic activities such as music, songs, movement, games and dance nourished the child's inner imagination and life as well as providing a means to express cultural understandings.[36] Von Marenholtz-Bülow outlined the scope of Froebel's vision:

> Froebel … demands that mothers and governesses should daily nourish the musical instincts of their little ones by singing to them.
>
> In the Kindergarten almost all the games, in particular the gymnastic games, are accompanied by the children's singing. It lies in the child's nature that he should whilst playing express the sensations of joy and pleasure in song.
>
> The gymnastic games offer the elements of the dramatic arts, for they represent, in a poetical dress, scenes and occurrences of all kinds taken from Nature and from Life, and they also include the first exercises in the art of dancing. …
>
> The first means for satisfying the poetic instinct are supplied by the learning of little songs and proverbs and by the stories which accompany many of the occupations.
>
> The entire Kindergarten, however, is poetry for a child.[37]

Froebel's original kindergarten resource was the rustic and romantic *Die Mutter-und Koselieder* – The Mothers' Plays and Nursery Songs.[38] Each song was beautifully illustrated and included a finger play and guidance to mothers. Dunedin kindergarten children once sang English translations of Froebel's 'Mother Songs'; Rachel Reynolds's translated copy sat on a shelf in the Rachel Reynold's Kindergarten, until it was transferred to the DFKA archives in 2013.

The rustic scenes and seasons of the Mother Songs were drawn from real-life happenings of Froebel's Keilhau rural community.[39] The romantic idealism was Germanic, although scenes such as the pigeon's dovecot would have been familiar across Old World pastoral communities. While dovecots were unfamiliar to colonial kindergarten children, the Keruru was renamed as the native pigeon and the 'pigeon house' is still performed in kindergartens today. By the 1900s, the colonial kindergarten was emphasizing its Britishness. This was amidst the backdrop of NZ men heading to fight with their British cousins in South Africa and in the European Great War. There was even debate as to whether the kindergarten should change its name. During these times, Dunedin kindergarten children were photographed flag waving in their kindergarten circle games,[40] saluting the British Union Jack flag and posing at play against its backdrop.[41] Kindergarten children were also photographed dancing Scottish highland reels, although many of the children were from Irish Catholic strongholds in South Dunedin. While the cultural context of kindergarten songs, poems and games became significantly British, the Froebelian circle formations and activities remained standard, replicating kindergarten practices worldwide.[42]

That kindergarten children were in NZ is not often evident in the early photographs. It was not until the latter decades of the twentieth century that this began to change. Loosening ties with the 'homeland' and a widening net of migrants, particularly from the Pacific Islands, contributed to an awareness of a heritage that was not British or European. A flourishing local market in children's literature and music, including books in Māori and Pacifica languages, also rewrote the cultural landscape of childhood. The Treaty of Waikangi Tribunal, established in 1975, began the process, still ongoing, of redressing Māori land claims, and political aspirations of *rangatiratanga* (self-determination) for Māori were embedded in the management of education and political institutions. In 1982, the first *Kohanga Reo* (language nests) for Māori immersion ECE were established by Māori because traditional ECE institutions, such as the kindergarten, had failed to nurture the language and culture of Māori children. Thus began a wider transformation in the cultural landscape of ECE programmes with an increasing visibility of *te reo* (Māori language) and *tikanga* (cultural knowledge). This was endorsed in the ECE curriculum *Te Whāriki* (1996), translated as 'a woven mat for all to stand on', and framed around the Principle of *Whakamana* – Empowerment broadly suggesting child agency.[43] *Te Whāriki* was the first bicultural curriculum embedded in the cultural landscape for both Māori and *pākehā* populations, the latter being inclusive of Pacifica peoples and other recent migrant communities.

Rather than sing the songs of Britain or dance highland reels, DK children nowadays more often swing their *poi*, sing *waiata* and perform *kapahaka* (performing arts). Coincidentally, the flax-woven Māori *poi* has similar properties to Froebel's first gift, a knitted soft ball on a string. Chants, songs and dances from the various Pacifica cultures are also performed. The main cultural events for DK are the annual Māori and Pacific Island Polyfestival and *Puaka Matariki*, which mark the Māori New Year. The rising of the *Matariki* is a cluster of stars that forecast the year ahead and herald the Māori New Year. Traditionally *Puaka Matariki* signalled the new planting season and was a time of family gathering, planning and reflection. For DK children and their *whānau*, *Puaka Matariki* is an occasion of celebration, acknowledging the unique place they live in and giving respect to the land. The kindergarten as a cultural site is revealing of the coincidence of Froebelian traditions and current DK practices that have shifted to incorporate indigenous values.

Handling the tools of technology: Occupations and crafts

Froebel developed a range of 'occupations' for children to give scope for design and experiment. They were provided with materials and tools such as paper, wool, peas, sticks, beads, needles, clay, pencils and scissors, and encouraged to weave, sew, prick, model, draw, cut out, fold and paste. Von Marenholtz-Bülow and other interpreters of Froebel's work diligently detailed up to twenty handcraft occupations for the kindergarten.[44] Froebel saw a logical progression in his kindergarten *Spielgaben*: starting with three-dimensional balls and cubes; then representation and the use of area with flat tablet shapes; then lines with sticks; and finally the point with peas and stones. By the 1880s there were standardized English language manuals setting out the materials, tools and tasks for each occupation. That Dunedin kindergarteners followed these prescriptions is evident from photographs showing children, for example, engaged in paper folding.[45] Workbooks too have survived in which trainee kindergarteners demonstrated their proficiency in all the occupations arts.[46] At the 1889 NZ and South Seas Exhibition in Dunedin, there was a display of kindergarten activities that included stick building, stick plaiting, paper plaiting, inlaid mosaics, clay modelling and drawing.[47] Kindergarten work was illustrative of the colony's industrial and technological progress as a new nation.

Weaving was a popular kindergarten activity. A curious link across oceans was the reference by von Marenholtz-Bülow in the 'Importance of Children's Play' (1872) of the 'plaiting' by 'Neuseeländer'. She was referring to Māori, and had clearly seen examples of their fine flax weaving displayed in German museum collections. Von Marenholtz-Bülow wrote, 'By plaiting, a tissue is produced not unlike those plaited mantles the New Zealander's make of sedge and bast, and by a progressive development the patterns rise to the level of the artistic products of the modern loom.'[48]

Recapitulation theory, the view that children, like indigenous peoples, were on a progression towards higher abilities in an industrial society, had been evident in German kindergarten writing of the nineteenth century. Eleonore Heerwart, for example, likened the stages of development in the occupations to 'those of the barbarous tribes who have afterwards excelled in arts and industries'[49]; thus, kindergarten was presented as a conduit to the higher levels of civilization. The German Froebelians' admiration of *Neuseeland* does not appear to have been noticed by Dunedin kindergarteners, but their children did indeed weave. An 1895 report records that children 'sew in bright colours and silks ... weave gay coloured papers ... their hands growing deft and their mind unconsciously developing as they sing about what they are doing.'[50]

In 1896, the Otago school inspectors recommended that all infant classes in schools be taught by using occupation-based kindergarten methods. They argued that children would learn more easily if the 'process was fun', and directed towards the 'understanding of things in an atmosphere of play'.[51] Weaving was one occupation that could be managed en masse in the infant gallery desks of the period. In a 1902 government publicity photo, Māori children at Waikouaiti School, just outside Dunedin, are weaving European baskets, as detailed in some Froebelian manuals.[52] Promoting the benefits of training in 'hand-eye' coordination, the Manual and Technical Instruction Acts (1900, 1902) introduced handwork activities such as plasticine and clay modelling, cardboard work, cane weaving, woodwork, brushwork and drawing in chalk or charcoal, into all primary schools.[53] Moreover, kindergarten occupations were promoted as a foundation for technical education – albeit a much narrower conception of Froebel's earlier 'plays of childhood'.

By the twentieth century, the fine 'hand-eye' work of some kindergarten occupations was phased out and Froebelian manuals shelved. Nevertheless, Dunedin children continued to cut, paste, weave, sew, draw, fold, prick, glue and draw. New activities with a widening range of technologies, materials and crafts were introduced at the behest of various pedagogical influences. These included those formulated by reformist kindergartners at John Dewey's laboratory kindergarten at the University of Chicago.[54] Kindergarten children explored materials through, for example, carpentry, painting, water, sand, dough, cooking, junk, dressing up clothes and puzzles. Photographed for DK's 125th jubilee book, twenty-first-century children are shown (under supervision) drilling and carving the local limestone, using glue guns and staplers to build junk models, stitching cloth with an electric sewing machine and cutting up food with knives. Evident too is the recent integration of information communication technology into kindergarten life. Kindergarten teachers have put digital cameras into the hands of children who document their learning and interests for their own learning portfolio records. iPads are placed on tabletops with endless 'hand-eye' options for puzzles, games, drawing, music, stories and songs. There is an ever-changing mix of popular heritage occupations and progressive technologies. While the technologies have changed over time, the metaphor of technological progress continues to encourage experiment and innovation in the range of kindergarten materials and activities.

Weaving the kindergarten *whāriki*

The metaphors of Froebelian kindergarten practice have endured through time, adapted to their geographic relocations in place, co-opted later pedagogical trends and become inclusive of other cultural landscapes and contexts. This process has been hastened by the national curriculum, *Te Whāriki* (1996), which introduced new understandings of pedagogy and practice and created a common language across diverse ECE services. The emphasis shifted from the detailing of *Spielgaben* and activities of play to enacting the Principles of *Ngā Hononga* as 'Children learn through reciprocal and responsive relationships with peoples, places and things', and *Kotahitanga* that 'reflects the holistic way children learn and grow'.[55] The curriculum was envisaged as a *whāriki*; the Principle of *Whānau Tangata* as a learning partnership between teachers and *whanau*, including children, who together weave the curriculum. There were many possible patterns for this. Froebelian pedagogy was not abandoned and its metaphors were rewoven into a kindergarten *whāriki*, itself with many possible patterns. Lee Blaikie, a senior teacher with DK, recalled her introduction to the draft *Te Whāriki* in 1993: 'We began to play with it, plan with it and use the language. We put the new words of *Te Whāriki* on the walls of our kindergarten linked by coloured strings to photos of our kindergarten activities'.[56]

Thus, the older metaphors of kindergarten practice have been reframed around the language of *Te Whāriki*. The curriculum is founded on the aspiration for children in Aotearoa NZ 'to grow up as competent and confident learners and communicators, healthy in mind, body, and spirit, secure in their sense of belonging and in the knowledge that they make a valued contribution to the world'.[57] Children are constructed as both powerful and participating, premised on principles of the rights of the child and child agency. Researcher and early childhood advocate Anne Smith describes how '*Te Whāriki* provides a model [where] children are valued as active learners who choose, plan, and challenge. This stimulates a climate of reciprocity, "listening" to children (even if they cannot speak), observing how their feelings, curiosity, interest, and knowledge are engaged in their early childhood environments, and encouraging them to make a contribution to their own learning'.[58] *Te Whāriki* expresses many Froebelian aspirations. Froebel's maxim 'Come let us live for our children' still resonates. *Te Whāriki* articulates understandings of the garden of childhood within Aotearoa NZ, including the role of teachers as the gardeners of the children. *Te Whāriki's* kindergarten 'child gardeners' have agency to weave the patterns of their own *whāriki* of learning and design and build 'garden' in the social, cultural and geographic landscape of Aotearoa NZ.

Abbreviations

ANZ   Archives New Zealand.

DK   Dunedin Kindergartens – *Mana Manaaki Puawai O Otepoti.*

DFKA   Dunedin Free Kindergarten Association.

ECE   early childhood education.

HC   Hocken Collections – Uare Taoka o Hakena – University of Otago.

NZ   New Zealand.

Notes

1 Helen May, *People, Places and Play in the 'Child Gardens' of Dunedin: 125 Years of Kindergarten in Dunedin* (Dunedin: Dunedin Kindergartens, 2014).
2 Kiwi fruit and pavlova cake are New Zealand food icons, and buzzy bee is an iconic children's toy. Judith Duncan, 'Aotearoa New Zealand Kindergarten Parents Reflecting on Kindergarten 2006-2007', *The Open Education Journal* 2 (2009): 1–10.
3 Education Counts, *Annual ECE Census Summary Report 2014* (Wellington: Ministry of Education, 2015).
4 Paul Moon, *The Edges of Empire: New Zealand in the Middle of the Nineteenth Century* (Auckland: David Ling Publishing, 2009), 11.
5 Helen May, *The Discovery of Early Childhood*, 2nd edn (Wellington: New Zealand Council for Educational Research Press, 2013).
6 James Belich, *Replenishing the Earth: The Settler Revolution and the Rise of the Anglo-World 1783-1939* (Oxford: Oxford University Press, 2005).
7 Phillip McCann, 'The Newfoundland School Society 1823-55: Missionary Enterprise or Cultural Imperialism', in *Benefits Bestowed? Education and British Imperialism*, ed. J. A. Mangan (Manchester: Manchester University Press, 1988), 101.
8 John Andrews, *No Other Home than This: A History of European New Zealanders* (Nelson: Craig Potton Publishing, 2009), 64.
9 Belich, *Replenishing the Earth*, 457.
10 Friedrich Froebel, 'Appeal in Favour of the Kindergarten' 1844, in *Extracts from Letters Written by Friedrich Froebel*, trans. and ed. E. R. Murray (London: The Froebel School Society and Junior Schools Association, 1936) 23.
11 Kerry Bethell, ' "Not [Just] for a Name that we Plead": Fashioning the Ideological Origins of Early Kindergarten in Dunedin and Wellington, New Zealand, 1870-1913', PhD thesis, Victoria University of Wellington, 2008.
12 Barbara Beatty, *Preschool Education in America* (New Haven: Yale University Press, 1995); Kristen Nawrotzki, ' "Greatly Changed for the Better": Free Kindergartens as Transatlantic "Reformance," ' *History of Education Quarterly* 49, no. 2 (2009): 182–95; Larry Prochner, 'The History of the Kindergarten as New Education: Examples from the United States and Canada, 1890-1920', in *The Development of Early Childhood Education in Europe and North America. Historical and Comparative Perspectives*, ed. H. Willekens, K. Scheiwe and K. Nawrotzki (Basingstoke: Palgrave Macmillan, 2015), 289–308.
13 Ann Taylor Allen, 'Spiritual Motherhood: German Feminists and the Kindergarten Movement, 1848-1911', *History of Education Quarterly* 22, no. 3 (1982): 327.

14   Joachim Liebschner, *A Child's Work: Freedom and Guidance in Froebel's Educational Theory and Practice* (Cambridge: The Lutterworth Press, 1992).

15   Baroness Bertha von Marenholtz-Bülow, 'The Kindergarten and the Importance of Children's Play', in *The Gifts of the Kindergarten*, ed. Hermann Goldammer, trans. William Wright (Berlin S. W: Charles Habel, [1872]1882), XXV.

16   Cited in Kevin J. Brehony, 'A "Socially Civilising Influence"? Play and the Urban "Degenerate"', *Paedagogica Historica: International Journal of the History of Education* 29 (2003): 87.

17   Dorothy Dempster, 'From Patronage to Parent Participation: The Development of the Dunedin Free Kindergarten Association', Dip Ed thesis, University of Otago, 1986, 6.

18   *1st Annual Report of the DFKA*, 1890.

19   'Free Kindergarten', *Otago Daily Times*, 24 December 1903, 5.

20   May, *Discovery of Early Childhood*.

21   Larry Prochner, '"Their Little Wooden Bricks": A History of the Material Culture of Kindergarten in the United States'. *Paedagogica Historica: International Journal of the History of Education* 47, no.3 (2011): 1–21.

22   Rachel Reynolds Kindergarten, c. 1920, DFKA, MS-1149/006, HC.

23   May, *Discovery of Early Childhood*.

24   'Richard Hudson Memorial, Magnificent gift to the Association,' *OW*, 9 November 1926.

25   Helen May, *Politics in the Playground: The World of Early Childhood in New Zealand*, 2nd ed. (Dunedin: University of Otago Press, 2009).

26   May, *People, Places and Play in the 'Child Gardens' of Dunedin*.

27   Johann Amos Comenius, *The Great Didactic*, trans. W. W. Keatinge (London: Adam and Charles Black, [1957] 1910), 58–9.

28   Friedrich Froebel, *The Education of Man*, 1825, trans. W. N. Hailmann (New York: D. Appleton & Company, 1892), 5.

29   *1st Annual Report of the DFKA*, 1890, 11.

30   *25th Annual Report of the DFKA*, 1914, 12.

31   Jenny Ritchie, 'Fostering Communities for Ecological Sustainability Within Early Childhood Education', *Early Education* 46 (2010): 1–14.

32   Bayfield Kindergarten, http://www.dunedinkindergartens.org.nz/Bayfield (accessed 1 April 2015).

33   J. Ritchie, I. Duhn, C. Rau and J. Craw, *Titiro Whakamuri, Hoki Whakamua. We Can See the Future, the Present and the Past: Caring for Self, Others and the Environment* (Wellington: Teaching Learning and Research Initiative, 2010), 15.

34   Ritchie et. al., *Titiro Whakamuri, Hoki Whakamua*, 25.

35   Ritchie, 'Fostering Communities', 11.

36   Tina Bruce, ed., *Early Childhood Practice: Froebel Today* (London: Sage, 2012).

37   Marenholtz-Bülow, 'The Kindergarten and the Importance of Children's Play', XXV–XXVI.

38   Friedrich Froebel, *Mutter- und Koselieder, Dichtung und Bilder zur edlen Pflege des Kindheitlebens. Ein Familienbuch* [Mother Play and Nursery Songs] (Boston: Lee Shepherd Publishing, [1844] 1878).

39   Liebschner, *A Child's Work*.

40   *OW*, 16 July 1902, 46.

41   Rachel Reynolds Kindergarten, c. 1920, DFKA, MS-1149/006, HC. These images showcased 'Dunedin's Great War 1914-1918' memorial exhibition at Toitū – Otago

Settlers Museum http://www.toituosm.com/whats-on/exhibitions/dunedins-great-war-1914-1918 (accessed 1 April 2015).

42 Rachel Reynolds Kindergarten, c. 1920, DFKA, MS-1149/006, HC.

43 Ministry of Education, *Te Whāriki: He Whāriki Matauranga mo nga Mokopuna o Aotearoa. Early Childhood Curriculum* (Wellington: Learning Media, 1996).

44 Liebschner, *A Child's Work.*

45 High Street Kindergarten, 1906, S10–164g, HC.

46 Florence Brickell's Workbook, 1889, DFKA, AG 287, HC.

47 Bethell, ' "Not [Just] for a Name that we Plead" '.

48 Marenholtz-Bülow, 'The Kindergarten and the Importance of Children's Play', XVIII.

49 Cited in Kevin Brehony, 'The Kindergarten in England 1851-1918,' in *Kindergartens and Cultures: The Global Diffusion on an Idea,* ed. Roberta Wollons (New Haven, CT: Yale University Press, 2000), 74.

50 *6th Annual Report of the DFKA,* 1895, 4.

51 *Appendices to the Journal of the House of Representatives,* 1897, E–1B, 41.

52 Waikouaiti School, Otago, 1902, R144899e, ANZ.

53 Helen May. *'I Am Five and I Go to School': Early Years Schooling 1900-2010* (Dunedin: University of Otago Press, 2011).

54 Prochner, 'The History of the Kindergarten as New Education'; see also Chapter 7 by Larry Prochner in this volume.

55 Ministry of Education, *Te Whāriki,* 14.

56 Lee Blackie, interview, 2013.

57 Ministry of Education, *Te Whāriki,* 9.

58 Anne Smith, 'Relationships with People, Places and Things – Te Whāriki', in *Theories and Approaches to Learning in the Early Years,* ed. L. Miller and L. Pound (London: Sage, 2010), 153.

Selected References

Adams, J. (1928), *Modern Developments in Educational Practice*, 2nd edn, London: University of London Press.

Adelman, C. (2000), 'Over Two Years, What Did Froebel Say to Pestalozzi?' *History of Education*, 29 (2): 103–14.

Ailwood, J. (2003), 'Governing Early Childhood Education through Play', *Contemporary Issues in Early Childhood*, 4 (3): 286–99.

Ashida, H. (2002), 'Is the Athletic Festival Undokai Child-Centered? History and Discussion on Athletic Festivals at Japanese Kindergartens', *International Journal of Early Childhood Education*, 8 (2): 193–220.

Baker, B. (1998), 'Child-Centered Teaching, Redemption, and Educational Identities: A History of the Present', *Educational Theory*, 48 (2): 155–74.

Bakker, N. (2013), 'Cylinders and Séances: Elise van Calcar and the Spirit of Froebel', *History of Education*, 42 (2): 147–65.

Bakker, N., Noordman, J. and Rietveld-van Wingerden, M. (eds) (2006), *Vijf eeuwen opvoeden in Nederland: idee en praktijk 1500-2000*, 137–49, Assen: Van Gorcum.

Beattie, N. (2002), *The Freinet movements of France, Italy, and Germany, 1920-2000: Versions of Educational Progressivism*, Lewiston: E. Mellen Press.

Beatty, B. (1995), *Preschool Education in America: The Culture of Young Children from the Colonial Era to the Present*, New Haven, CT: Yale University Press.

Belich, J. (2005), *Replenishing the Earth: The Settler Revolution and the Rise of the Anglo-World 1783-1939*, Oxford: Oxford University Press.

Berry, E. [Mrs] and Michaelis [Mme] (eds) (1883), *Kindergarten Songs and Games*, London: W. Shepherd.

Bethell, K. (2008), ' "Not [Just] for a Name that we Plead:" Fashioning the Ideological Origins of Early Kindergarten in Dunedin and Wellington, New Zealand, 1870-1913', PhD thesis, Victoria University of Wellington.

Bethell, K. (2010), 'To Venture With Purpose: Miss Mary Richmond's 1907 Educational Travels Abroad', in K. Neumann, U. Sauerbrey and M. Wrinkler (eds), *Fröbelpädagogik im Kontext der Moderne. Bildung, Erziehung und soziales Handeln*, 113–26, Jena: Verlag IKS Garamond.

Bolton, G. (1998), *Acting in Classroom Drama: A Critical Analysis*, Stoke-on-Trent: Trentham Books.

Bourdieu, P. (1991), 'Sport and Social Class', in C. Mukerji and M. Schudson (eds), *Rethinking Popular Culture: Contemporary Perspectives in Cultural Studies*, 357–73, Berkeley, CA: University of California Press.

Bloomer, M. (1910), *A Year in the Infant School: A Fully Correlated Scheme of Work*, London: Gresham.

Blow, S. E. (1899), *Letters to a Mother on the Philosophy of Froebel*, New York: D. Appleton and Co.

Blow, S. E. (1908), *Educational Issues in the Kindergarten*, New York: D. Appleton.

Blyton, E. ed. (1931), *Modern Teaching in the Infant School, Vols. 1-3*, London: George Newnes Ltd.

Bolton, G. (1998), *Acting in Classroom Drama: A Critical Analysis*, Stoke-on-Trent: Trentham Books.

Boyce, E. R. (1938), *Play in the Infants' School: An Account of an Educational Experiment at the Raleigh Infants' School, Stepney*, London: Methuen.

Brehony, K. J. (1987), 'The Froebel Movement and State Schooling 1880–1914: A Study in Educational Ideology', 2 vols. PhD thesis, Milton Keynes: Open University.

Brehony, K. J. (1997), 'An "Undeniable" and "Disastrous" Influence? Dewey and English Education (1895-1939)', *Oxford Review of Education*, 23 (4): 427–45.

Brehony, K. J. (1998), ' "Even Far Distant Japan is "Showing an Interest": The English Froebel Movement's turn to Sloyd', *History of Education*, 27 (3): 279–95.

Brehony, K. J. (2000a), 'The Kindergarten in England 1981-1918', in R. L. Wollons (ed.), *Kindergartens and Cultures: The Global Diffusion of an Idea*, 59–86, New Haven, CT: Yale University Press.

Brehony, K. J. (2000b), 'English Revisionist Froebelians and the Schooling of the Urban Poor', in M. Hilton and P. Hirsch (eds), *Practical Visionaries: Women, Education and Social Progress 1790-1930*, 183–200, Harlow: Pearson Education Ltd.

Brehony, K. J. (2001), *The Origins of Nursery Education: Friedrich Froebel and the English System*, London: Routledge.

Brehony, K. J (2003), 'A "Socially Civilising Influence"? Play and the Urban "Degenerate"', *Paedagogica Historica: International Journal of the History of Education*, 29 (1/2): 87–106.

Brehony, K. J. (2006), *Special Issue*: 'Early Years Education: Some Froebelian Contributions', *History of Education*, 35 (2): 167–295.

Brehony, K. J. (2009), 'Transforming Theories of Childhood and Early Childhood Education: Child Study and the Empirical Assault on Froebelian Rationalism', *Paedagogica Historica: International Journal of the History of Education*, 45 (4/5): 585–604.

Brehony, K. J. (2013), 'Juego, Trabajo y Educación: Situando un Debate Froebeliano' [Play, Work and Education: Situating a Froebelian Debate], *Bordón: Revista de Paedagogica: International Journal of the History of Education*, 65 (1): 55–73.

Brown, M. H. and Freeman, N. K. (2001), ' "We don't Play that Way at Preschool": The Moral and Ethical Dimensions of Controlling Children's Play', in S. Reifel and M. H. Brown (eds), *Early Education and Care, and Reconceptualizing Play*, 259–74, London: Emerald Group.

Bruce, T. ed. (2012), *Early Childhood Practice: Froebel Today*, London: Sage.

Bruce, T. (2016), 'Friedrich Froebel', in T. David, K. Goouch and S. Powell (eds), *The Routledge International Handbook of Philosophies and Theories of Early Childhood Care and Education*, 19–25, London: Routledge.

Caldwell Cook, H. (1917), *The Play Way: An Essay in Educational Methods*, London: William Heineman.

Cohen, S. (1979), 'In the Name of the Prevention of Neurosis: The Search for Psychoanalytic Pedagogy in Europe, 1905-1938', in B. Finkelstein (ed.), *Regulated Children, Liberated Children: Education in Psychoanalytical Perspective*, 184–219, New York, NY: Psychohistory Press.

Comenius, J. A. ([1657]1910), *The Great Didactic*, translated by W. W. Keatinge, London: Adam and Charles Black.

Compayré, G. (1892), *The History of Pedagogy*, translated by W. H. Payne, Boston: D.C. Heath & Co.

Courthorpe Bowen, H. (1893), *Froebel and Education by Self-Activity*, London: Heinemann.

Cremin, L. A. (1961), *The Transformation of the School: Progressivism in American Education 1876-1957*, New York: Vintage Books.

Cuban, L. (1993), *How Teachers Taught: Constancy and Change in American Classrooms, 1890-1990*, New York: Teachers College Press.

Cuffaro, H. (1995), *Experimenting with the World: John Dewey and the Early Childhood Classroom*, New York, NY: Teachers College Press.

Cumming, I. and Cumming, A. (1978), *History of State Education in New Zealand 1840-1975*, Wellington: Pitman Publishing New Zealand Ltd.

Cunningham, H. (2005), *Children and Childhood in Western Society since 1500*, London: Longman.

Daniel, M. V. (1947), *Activity in the Primary* School, Oxford: Blackwell.

Darvell, M. L. and Tuffley, G. M. (1925), *Plays in Rhyme for Little Ones*, London: Evans Brothers.

Dewey, J. (1899), *The School and Society*, Chicago: University of Chicago Press.

Dewey, J. (1906), *The School and the Child*, edited by John Joseph Findlay, London: Blackie.

Dewey, J. ([1916] 1966), *Democracy and Education*, London: Collier Macmillan.

Dewey, J. ([1899] 1996), 'Principles of Mental Development as Illustrated in Early Infancy', in L. A. Hickman (ed.), *The Collected Works of John Dewey, 1882–1953*, Charlottesville, VA: Intelex Corporation. (Electronic edition CD-ROM, InteLex) [first published in *Transactions of the Illinois Society for Child Study* 4 (1899): 65–83].

Dombkowski [Nawrotzki] K. (2002), 'Kindergarten Teacher Training in England and the United States 1850-1918', *History of Education*, 31 (5): 475–89.

Duncan, J. (2009), 'Aotearoa New Zealand Kindergarten Parents Reflecting on Kindergarten 2006-2007', *The Open Education Journal*, 2: 1–10.

Elkind, D. (2015), *Giants in the Nursery: A Biographical History of Developmentally Appropriate Practice*, St. Paul, MN: Redleaf Press.

Engels, F. ([1845]1969), *The Condition of the Working Class in England*, London: Panther.

Fallace, T. (2011), 'Tracing John Dewey's Influence on Progressive Education, 1903–1951: Toward a Received Dewey', *Teachers College Record*, 113 (3): 463–92.

Finlay-Johnson, H. (1912), *The Dramatic Method of Teaching*, London: James Nisbet.

Forest, I. (1927), *Preschool Education: A Historical and Critical Study*, New York: Macmillan.

Froebel, F. ([1844]1878), *Mutter und Koselieder, Dichtung und Bilder zur edlen Pflege des Kindheitlebens. Ein Familienbuch,* [Mother Play and Nursery Songs] Boston: Lee Shepherd.

Froebel, F. ([1826]1887), *The Education of Man*, translated by W. N. Hailmann, New York, NY: D. Appleton.

Froebel, F. (1895), *Mottoes and Commentaries of Friedrich Froebel's Mother Play*, translated by H. R. Eliot and S. E. Blow, New York: D. Appleton and Co.

Froebel, F. ([1861]1897), *Pedagogics of the Kindergarten*, translated by J. Jarvis, London: Edward Arnold.

Froebel, F. (1936) 'Appeal in Favour of the Kindergarten 1844', in E. R. Murray (trans. and ed.), *Extracts from Letters Written by Friedrich Froebel*, London: The Froebel School Society and Junior Schools Association.

Fulmer, G. (1918), *The Use of the Kindergarten Gifts*, Boston: Houghton Mifflin.

Giardiello, P. (2014), *Pioneers in Early Childhood Education*, London: Routledge.

Gordon, P. (1985), 'The Handbook of Suggestions for Teachers: Its Origin and Evaluation', *Journal of Educational Administration and History*, 17 (1): 41–8.

Graham, P. (2009), *Susan Isaacs: A Life Freeing the Minds of Children*, London: Karnac Books.

Gull, H. (1932), *Projects in the Education of Young Children*, London and Edinburgh: McDougall.

Gupta, A. (2015), *Diverse Early Childhood Education Policies and Practices: Voices and Images from Five Countries in Asia*, New York: Routledge.

Gutek, G. L. (2001), *Historical and Philosophical Foundations of Education: A Biographical Introduction*, 3rd edn, Upper Saddle River, NJ: Merrill Prentice Hall.

Habermas, J. (1987), *The Theory of Communicative Action; Lifeworld and System: A Critique of Functionalist Reason*, Cambridge: Polity Press.

Hall, P. (1998), *The Social Construction of Nationalism: Sweden as an Example*, Lund: Lund University Press.

Hart, S. P. (2011), 'Female Leadership and the "Cult of Domesticity": The Contributions of Elizabeth Harrison and Rumah Crouse to the Chicago Kindergarten Movement, 1879–1920', *American Educational History Journal*, 38 (1): 127–44.

Harrison, E. and Woodson, B. (1905), *The Kindergarten Building Gifts: With Hints on Program Making*, 2nd edn, St. Louis, MO: Sigma.

Haslett, J. G. (1990), 'The Uniqueness of Undokai in Japan: Bringing Community/Family Together through Dance and Sport Like Activities', *Bulletin of Research Institute of Physical Education Chukyo University*, 4: 57–66.

Hatje, A.-K. (1999), *Från treklang till triangeldrama: Barntädgården som ett kvinnligt samhällsprojekt under 1880-1940-talen*, Lund: Historiska Media.

Hobsbawm, E. J. (1992), *Nations and Nationalism since 1780: Programme, Myth, Reality*, Cambridge: Cambridge University Press.

Huizinga, J. (1998), *Homo Ludens: A Study of the Play-element in Culture*, London: Routledge.

Hook, S. ([1939]1995), *John Dewey: An Intellectual Portrait*, New York: Prometheus Books.

Horne, J. (2000), 'Understanding Sport and Body Culture in Japan', *Body and Society*, 6 (2): 73–86.

Hotchkiss, E. A. (1924), *The Project Method in Classroom Work*, Boston: Ginn.

Howe, A. L. (1917), *Shiawase Naru Kanougoto [The Happy Possibilities]*, Kobe: The Glory Kindergarten.

Howlett, J. (2013), *Progressive Education: A Critical Introduction*, London: Bloomsbury.

Hughes, J. L. (1910), *Froebel's Education Laws for All Teachers*, New York: D. Appleton.

Huyssen, D. (2014), *Progressive Inequality: Rich and Poor in New York, 1890-1920*, Cambridge, MA: Harvard University Press.

Isaacs, S. (1929), *The Nursery Years*, London: Routledge and Kegan Paul.

Isaacs, S. (1930), *Intellectual Growth in Young Children*, London: Routledge and Kegan Paul.

Jackson, P. W. (1998), 'Child-Centered Education for Pacific-Rim Cultures?' *Early Child Development and Care*, 143: 47–57.

Jackson, P. W. (1999), 'Froebel Education Re-Assessed: British and German Experience, 1850–1940', *Early Childhood Development and Care*, 149: 11–25.

Jackson, P. W. and Lee, S.-W. (1996), 'Froebel and the Hitler Jugend: The Britishing of Froebel', *Early Childhood Development and Care*, 117: 45–65.

Jebb, E. M. (1952), *Survey of the Growth of the Froebel Educational Institute Over 60 Years*, London: Incorporated Froebel Educational Institute.

Jeynes, W. H. (2006), 'Standardized Tests and Froebel's Original Kindergarten Model', *Teachers College Record*, 108 (10): 937–59.

Kamisuki, M. (1993), 'Naze Yochien De Undokai Wo Surunoka' [Why Do We Need Undokai in Kindergartens?], *Yoji no Kyouiku [Early Childhood Education]*, 92 (10): 199–225.

Kashiwara, E. (1991), 'Yochien Ni Okeru Undokai Ni Kansuru Ichikosatsu Part 4 Sono Rekishihenseiwotooshite a Study of Undokai in Kindergartens: An Historical Perspective', *Japan Society of Research on Early Childhood Care and Education*, 44: 22–3.

Katz, L. G. and Chard, S. C. (2013), 'The Project Approach: An Overview', in J. Roopnarine and J. E. Johnson (eds), *Approaches to Early Childhood Education*, 279–95, 6th edn, Boston: Pearson.

Kilpatrick, W. H. (1916), *Froebel's Kindergarten Principles Critically Examined*, New York: Macmillan.

Klein, B. (2010), 'Cultural Loss and Cultural Rescue: Lilli Zickerman, Ottilia Adelborg, and the Promises of the Swedish Homecraft Movement', in H. Joas and B. Klein (eds), *The Benefit of Broad Horizons: Intellectual and Institutional Preconditions for a Global Social Science*, 261–80, Leiden: Brill.

Knoll, M. (2015), 'John Dewey as Administrator: The Inglorious End of the Laboratory School in Chicago', *Journal of Curriculum Studies*, 47 (2): 203–52.

Kochhar, S. K. (1977), *Methods and Techniques of Teaching*, New Delhi: Sterling Publishers.

Krieg, M. H. (1872), *The Child, its Nature and Relations; An Elucidation of Froebel's Principles of Education*, New York: E. Steiger.

Lall, M. (2011), 'Pushing the Child Centered Approach in Myanmar: The Role of Cross National Policy Networks and the Effects on the Classroom', *Critical Studies in Education*, 52 (3): 219–33.

Liebschner, J. (1991), *Foundations of Progressive Education*, London: The Lutterworth Press.

Liebschner, J. (1992), *A Child's Work: Freedom and Play in Froebel's Educational Theory and Practice*, Cambridge: The Lutterworth Press.

Lilley, I. M. (1967), *Friedrich Froebel: A Selection from his Writings*, London: Sage.

Lindberg, M. (1991), *90 års barnomsorg 1874-1964: En utvecklingsstudie*, Norrköping: Institutionen för förskollärarutbildning.

Loewenberg Ball, D. K. and Cohen, D. K. (1999), 'Toward a Practice-Based Theory of Professional Education', in G. Sykes and L. Darling-Hammond (eds), *Teaching as the Learning Profession: Handbook of Policy and Practice*, 3–32, San Francisco: Jossey-Bass.

Louv, R. (2010), *Last Child in the Woods: Saving our Children from Nature-Deficit Disorder*, New York: Atlantic Books.

Mann, H [Mrs] and Peabody, E. (1864), *The Moral Culture of Infancy and Kindergarten Guide*, Boston: Thomas Oliver Hazard Perry Burnam.

Marenholtz-Bülow, B. M. [Baroness] von (1855), *Women's Educational Mission: Being an Explanation of Froebel's System of Infant Gardens*, London: Darton and Co.

Marenholtz-Bülow, B. M. [Baroness] von (1877), *Reminiscences of Froebel*, translated by M. Mann, Boston: Lee and Shepherd Published.

Marenholtz-Bülow, B. M. [Baroness] von ([1872] 1882), 'The Kindergarten and the Importance of Children's Play', in H. Goldammer (ed.), *The Gifts of the Kindergarten*, translated by William Wright, V11–XL, Berlin S. W: Charles Habel.

Marenholtz-Bülow, B. M. [Baroness] von ([1894] 1889), *The Child And Child-Nature*, translated by Alice M. Christie, Syracuse, NY: C.W. Bardeen.

Marenholtz-Bülow, B. M. [Baroness] von and Peabody Mann, M. T. ([1895] 2007], *How Kindergarten Came to America: Friedrich Froebel's Radical Vision of Early Childhood Education*, translated by H. Mann [Mrs], New York: New Press.

Marx, K. ([1867]1990), *Capital: A Critique of Political Economy. Volume 1*, translated by Ben Fowkes, London: Penguin Books in association with New Left Review.

Mayhew, K. C. and Edwards, A. C. (1936), *The Dewey School: The Laboratory School of the University of Chicago 1896-1903*, New York: D. Appleton-Century Company.

McCallum, J. and Sullivan, G. (1990), *Kelburn Normal School 75th Jubilee, 1914-1989*, Wellington: Kelburn Normal School.

McMurry, C. A. (1921), *Teaching by Projects: A Basis for Purposeful Study*, New York, Macmillan.

McCann, P. (1988), 'The Newfoundland School Society 1823-55: Missionary Enterprise or Cultural Imperialism', in J. A. Mangan (ed.), *Benefits Bestowed? Education and British Imperialism*, 93–111, Manchester: Manchester University Press.

May, H. (2005), *School Beginning: A 19th Century Colonial Story*, Wellington: New Zealand Council for Educational Research Press.

May, H. (2009), *Politics in the Playground: The World of Early Childhood in New Zealand*, 2nd edn, Dunedin: University of Otago Press.

May, H. (2011), '*I Am Five and I Go to School*': *The Work and Play of Early Education in New Zealand*, Dunedin: University of Otago Press.

May, H. (2013), *The Discovery of Early Childhood,* 2nd edn, Wellington: New Zealand Council for Educational Research Press.

Ministry of Education (1996), *Te Whāriki: He Whāriki Matauranga mo nga Mokopuna o Aotearoa. Early Childhood Curriculum*, Wellington: Learning Media.

Moon, P. (2009), *The Edges of Empire: New Zealand in the Middle of the Nineteenth Century*, Auckland: David Ling Publishing.

Morgan, H. (2011), *Early Childhood Education: History, Theory and Practice*, Lanham, MD: Rowman and Littlefield.

Morris Matthews, K. (2005), *In Their Own Right: Women and Higher Education in New Zealand Before 1945*, Wellington: New Zealand Council for Educational Research Press.

Murray, E. R. (1914), *Froebel as a Pioneer in Modern Psychology*, London: George Philip.

Murray, E. R. and Brown-Smith, H. (1919), *The Child Under Eight*, London: E. Arnold.

Nawrotzki, K. D. (2005), 'The Anglo-American Kindergarten Movements and Early Education in England and the USA, 1850–1965', PhD. diss., University of Michigan.

Nawrotzki, K. D. (2006), 'Froebel is Dead; Long Live Froebel! The National Froebel Foundation and English Education', *History of Education*, 35 (2): 209–23.

Nawrotzki, K. D. (2009), ' "Greatly Changed for the Better": Free Kindergartens as Transatlantic Reformance', *History of Education Quarterly*, 49 (?): 182–95.

Nawrotzki, K. D. (2014), 'Kevin Brehony (1948-2013)', *History of Education: Journal of the History of Education*, 43 (3): 575–8.

Neville, R. (1970), *Play Power*, St. Albans: Paladin.

Nishida, Y. (2015), 'A Chrysanthemum in the Garden: A Christian Kindergarten in the Empire of Japan', *Paedagogica Historica: International Journal of the History of Education*, 51 (3): 280–97.

Nishigaki, M. (2007), '*A. L. Hau No Shogai: Nihonno Youji Kyouikuni, Fureberu Seishin Wo Donyushita Fujin Senkyoushi Ani L. Hauno Hataraki to Shiso*' [the Life of A. L Howe: the Development of Froebelian Theory in Japan], Kobe, Japan: Kobe Local Newspaper Press.

O'Day, R. (2000), 'Women and Education in Nineteenth-Century England', in J. Bellamy, A. Laurence and G. Perry (eds), *Women, Scholarship and Criticism: Gender and Knowledge c. 1790-1900*, Manchester: Manchester University Press.

OECD (2001), *Starting Strong: Early Childhood Education and Care*, Paris: OECD.

Pacini-Ketchabaw, V. and Taylor, A. (eds) (2015), *Unsettling the Colonial Places and Spaces of Early Childhood Education*, New York: Routledge.

Pellegrini, A. D. (2009), *The Role of Play in Human Development*, Oxford: Oxford University Press.

Pestalozzi, J. H. ([1781]1787), *Leonard & Gertrude: An Attempt to Help Mothers to Teach Their Own Children*, London: Swan Sonnenschein and Co.

Philips, H. and McInnes, F. J. C. (1950), *Exploration in the Junior School*, London: University of London Press.

Pietsch, T. (2013), *Empire of Scholars: Universities, Networks and the British Academic World 1850-1939*, Manchester: Manchester University Press.

Popkewitz, T. S. ed. (2000), *Educational Knowledge: Changing Relationships Between the State, Civil Society and the Educational Community*, Albany, NY: SUNY Press.

Popkewitz, T. S. ed. (2005), *Inventing the Modern Self and John Dewey*, New York: Palgrave Macmillan.

Porter, R. and Teich, M. (eds) (1988), *Romanticism in National Context*, Cambridge, UK, Cambridge University Press.

Pouwelse, W. J. (1993), *Haar verstand dienstbaar aan het hart. Middelbaar onderwijs voor meisjes, debatten, acties en beleid 1860-1917*, Amsterdam: Het Spinhuis.

Prochner, L. (2011), ' "Their Little Wooden Bricks": A History of the Material Culture of Kindergarten in the United States', *Paedagogica Historica: International Journal of the History of Education*, 4 (3): 1–21.

Prochner, L. (2015), 'A History of Kindergarten as New Education: Examples from the United States and Canada, 1890–1920', in H. Willekens, K. Scheiwe and K. Nawrotzki (eds), *The Development of Early Childhood Education in Europe and North America: Historical and Comparative Perspectives*, 289–308, London: Palgrave Macmillan.

Raymont, T. (1946), *Seven to Eleven: Some Problems of the Junior School*, London: Longmans, Green.

Read, J. (2006), 'Free Play with Froebel: Use and Abuse of Progressive Pedagogy in London's Infant Schools 1870- c.1904', *Paedagogica Historica: International Journal of the History of Education*, 42 (3): 299–323.

Read, J. (2013), 'Bringing Froebel into London's Infant Schools: The Reforming Practice of Two Head Teachers, Elizabeth Shaw and Frances Roe from the 1890s to the 1930s', *History of Education*, 42 (6): 745–64.

Reimers, L. (1983), *Alice Tegnérs barnvisor*, Bromma: Edition Reimers.

Ricoeur, P. and Taylor, G. H. (1986), *Lectures on Ideology and Utopia*, New York: Columbia University Press.

Ritchie, J. (2010), 'Fostering Communities for Ecological Sustainability Within Early Childhood Education', *Early Education*, 46: 1–14.

Ritchie, J., Duhn, I., Rau, C. and Craw, J. (2010), *Titiro Whakamuri, Hoki Whakamua. We Can See the Future, the Present and the Past: Caring for Self, Others and the Environment*, Wellington: Teaching Learning and Research Initiative.

Robert-Holmes, G. (2015), 'High Stakes Assessment, Teachers and Children', in D. Wyse, R. Davis, P. Jones and S. Rogers (eds), *Exploring Education and Children: From Current Certainties to New Visions*, 72–82, London: Routledge.

Roe, F. (1933), 'From Formal Teaching to Natural Learning', in N. Catty (ed.), *Modern Education of Young Children*, 1–16, London: Methuen.

Roopnarine, J. L. and Metindogan, A. (2013), 'Early Childhood Education Research in Cross-National Perspective', in B. Spodek and O. N. Saracho (eds), *Handbook of Research on the Education of Young Children*, 2nd edn, 555–72, New York: Routledge.

Rose, E. (1999), *A Mother's Job: The History of Day Care, 1890-1960*, New York: Oxford University Press.

Ross, E. D. (1976), *The Kindergarten Crusade: The Establishment of Preschool Education in the United States*, Athens, OH: Ohio University Press.

Rousseau, J. J. ([1762] 1979), *Emile, or On Education*, translated by with an introduction by A. Bloom, New York: Basic Books.

Schiller, F. von ([1794] 1994), *On the Aesthetic Education of Man in a Series of Letters*, translated by Reginald Snell, Bristol: Thoemmes.

Shapiro, M. S. (1983), *Child's Garden: The Kindergarten Movement from Froebel to Dewey*, University Park, PA: Pennsylvania State University Press.

Shiell, A. (2012), *Fundraising, Flirtation and Fancywork: Charity Bazaars in Nineteenth Century Australia*, Newcastle upon Tyne: Cambridge Scholars Press.

Shirakawa, Y. (1996), 'Culture and the Japanese Kindergarten Curriculum: A Historical View', *Early Child Development and Care*, 123 (1): 183–92.

Shirreff, E. (1882), *Kindergarten: Principles of Froebel's System and their Bearing on the Education of Women. Also remarks on the Higher Education of Women*, London: W. Swan Sonnenschein.

Sikemeier, J. H. (1921), *Elise van Calcar-Schiotling: Haar Leven en Omgeving, Haar Arbeid, Haar Geestesrichting*, Haarlem: Tjeenk Willink and Zn.

Singer, E. (1996), 'Prisoners of The Method: Breaking Open the Child-Centred Pedagogy in Day Care Centres', *Early Years Education*, 3 (2): 28–40.

Skinner, Q. (2002), *Visions of Politics*, rev ed., vol. 1, Cambridge: Cambridge University Press.

Smith, A. (2010), 'Relationships with People, Places and Things – Te Whāriki', in L. Miller and L. Pound (eds), *Theories and Approaches to Learning in the Early Years*, 149–62, London: Sage.

Smith, F. and Harrison, A. S. (1937), *Principles of Class Teaching*, London: Macmillan.

Snider, D. J. (1900a), *The Life of Frederick Froebel: Founder of the Kindergarten*, Chicago, IL: Sigma.

Snider, D. J. (1900b), *The Psychology of Froebel's Play-Gifts*, St. Louis, MO: Sigma.

Sobel, D., Bailie, P. E., Finch, E., Kenny, E. K. and Anne Stires, A. (2016), *Nature Preschools and Forest Kindergartens: The Handbook for Outdoor Learning*, St. Paul, MN: Redleaf Press.

Sommestad, L. (1998), 'Human Reproduction and the Rise of Welfare States: An Economic-demographic Approach to Welfare State Formation in the United States and Sweden', *Scandinavian Economic History Review*, 46 (2): 97–116.

Susina, J. (2000), 'Dealing with Victorian Fairies', *Children's Literature*, 28: 230–7.

Sutton-Smith, B. (2001), *The Ambiguity of Play*, Cambridge, MA: Harvard University Press.

Takano, K. (1973), *E Eru Hau Jyoshi to Shouei No Ayumi* [Miss A. L. Howe and the History of Glory Kindergarten and Training School], Kobe, Japan: Shoei Junior College.

Tanaka, Y. and Sato, K. (1993), 'The Contribution and Influence of Friedrich Froebel's Ideology: The US and Japan,' *Hyogo University of Teacher Education Journal*, 13 (1): 115–28.

Tanner, A. (1904), *The Child: His Thinking, Feeling, and Doing*, Chicago: Rand McNally.

Taoka, Y. (2010), 'Anthropological Meaning of F. Fröbel's "Festival" [*Fest, Feier*]: In Relation to the "Intuition of Life Unity" [*Ahnung*],' *Departmental Bulletin Paper, Ryukoku University*, 474/475 (2010): 595–616.

Taylor, A. (2013), *Reconfiguring the Natures of Childhood*, New York: Routledge.

Taylor, A. Blaise, M. and Giugni, M., ' "Haraway's Bag Lady Story-Telling": Relocating Childhood and Learning within a Post-Human Landscape', *Discourse: Studies in the Cultural Politics of Education*, 34 (1): 48–62.

Taylor Allen, A. (1982), 'Spiritual Motherhood: German Feminists and the Kindergarten Movement, 1848-1911,' *History of Education Quarterly*, 22 (3): 323–35.

Taylor Allen, A. (1988), ' "Let Us Live With Our Children": Kindergarten Movements in Germany and the United States, 1840-1914,' *History of Education Quarterly*, 28 (1): 23–48.

Telders, J. M. (1931) *Fröbel*, Groningen: Noordhoff.

Tennant, M. (2013), 'Fun and Fundraising: The Selling of Charity in New Zealand's Past', *Social History*, 38 (1): 46–65.

Uno, K. (2009), 'Civil Society, State, and Institutions for Young Children in Modern Japan: The Initial Years', *History of Education Quarterly*, 49 (2): 170–81.

Vallberg Roth, A.-C. (2002), *De yngre barnens läroplanshistoria: Från 1800-talets mitt till idag*, Lund: Studentlitteratur.

Van Calcar, E. (1861–2), *Onze ontwikkeling of de magt der eerste indrukken*, 6 vols., Amsterdam: van Gelder.

Van Calcar, E. ([1875] 1905), *Fröbels methode tot harmonische ontwikkeling van lichaam en geest* 7th edn, Den Haag: Ykema.

Van Calcar, E. ([1880] 1912), *Maakt de kinderen gelukkig: Beknopte handleiding om zich in korten tijd Fröbel's opvoedingsleer eigen te maken*, 6th edn, III–VII, Maassluis: N.V. Maassluische Boekhandel.

Van Drenth, A. and de Haan, F. (1999), *The Rise of Caring Power: Elizabeth Fry and Josephine Butler in Britain and the Netherlands*, Amsterdam: Amsterdam University Press.

Wall, J. (2010), *Ethics in the Light of Childhood*, Washington: Georgetown University Press.

Walters, E. H. (1949), *Activity and Experience in the Junior School*, London: National Froebel Foundation.

Warr, E. (1937), *The New Era in the Junior School*, London: Methuen.

Webber, D. (2003), 'Understanding Charity Fundraising Events', *International Journal of Nonprofit and Voluntary Sector Marketing*, 9 (2): 123–4.

Weber, E. (1969), *The Kindergarten: Its Encounter with Educational Thought in America*, New York: Teachers College Press.

Weber, M. and Kalberg, S. (2002), *The Protestant Ethic and the Spirit of Capitalism*, Oxford: Roxbury Publishing.

Westberg, J. (2008), *Förskolepedagogikens framväxt: Pedagogisk förändring och dess förutsättningar, ca 1835-1945*, Uppsala: Acta Universitatis Upsaliensis.

Westberg, J. (2010), 'The Making of Froebelian Heroes: Ellen and Maria Moberg in the History of Swedish Kindergartens', in K. Neumann, U. Sauerbrey and M. Wrinkler (eds), *Fröbelpädagogik im Kontext der Moderne. Bildung, Erziehung und soziales Handeln*, 133–45, Jena: Verlag IKS Garamond.

Westberg, J. (2011a), 'Den svenska importen av Fröbel', in A. Åkerlund (ed.), *Kulturtransfer och kulturpolitik: Sverige och Tyskland under det Tjugonde århundradet*, 17–37, Uppsala: Historiska institutionen, Uppsala.

Westberg, J. (2011b), 'The Funding of Early Care and Education Programmes in Sweden, 1845-1943', *History of Education*, 40 (4): 465–79.

Weston, P. (2002), *The Froebel Educational Institute and the Origins and History of the College*, London: University of Surrey Roehampton.

Whitbread, N. (1972), *The Evolution of the Nursery-infant School: A History of Infant and Nursery Education in Britain, 1800-1970*, London: Routledge and K. Paul.

Wiggin, K. D. (1893), *The Kindergarten*, New York: Harper & Bros.

Wilderspin, S. (1825), *Infant Education; or Remarks on the Importance of Educating the Infant Poor*, London: W. Simpkin and R. Marshall.

Winterer, C. (1992), 'Avoiding a "Hothouse System of Education": Nineteenth Century Early Childhood Education from the Infant Schools to the Kindergartens', *History of Education Quarterly*, 32 (3): 289–314.

Wollons, R. (ed.) (2000), *Kindergarten and Cultures: The Global Diffusion of an Idea*, New Haven, CT: Yale University Press.

Zetterholm, F. (1969), *Barnvisan i Sverige: barnvisans blomstring kring sekelskiftet; bakgrund, genrer och motiv*, Stockholm: Proprius.

Index

Page numbers with (f) refer to photographs.

Lightning Source UK Ltd.
Milton Keynes UK
UKHW020814300620
365784UK00003B/133

9 781350 069930